The First Book of
Harvard Graphics®

The First Book of

Harvard Graphics®

Jack Purdum

HOWARD W. SAMS & COMPANY
Macmillan Computer Publishing

To my wife, Karol

FIRST EDITION
FIRST PRINTING—1990

International Standard Book Number: 0-672-27310-1
Library of Congress Catalog Card Number: 90-62054

Acquisitions Editor: *Scott Arant*
Manuscript Editor: *Gary Masters*
Illustrator: *Tom Emrick*
Cover Artist: *Held & Diedrich Design*
Indexer: *Joelynn Gifford*
Production: *Claudia Bell, Lisa Bucki, Brad Chinn,*
Sally Copenhaver, Travia Davis, Jill Glover, Denny Hager,
Marj Hopper, Tami Hughes, Chuck Hutchinson, Jennifer Matthews,
Cindy L. Phipps, Joe Ramon, Dennis Sheehan, Bruce Steed,
Mary Beth Wakefield, Nora Westlake

Printed in the United States of America

Contents

6   Text and Organizational Charts, *173*

7   Drawing Custom Charts, *211*

vii

8   Templates, Macros, and Other Advanced Features, *245*

A   The Standard ASCII Character Set, *277*

B   Harvard Graphics Symbols, *283*

Index, *293*

Preface

Visual communication has always been one of the most effective means of transmitting ideas and information. Harvard Graphics brings the efficiency of visual communication to the personal computer. This book will show you how to use most of the features in Harvard Graphics through a series of thorough yet easily understood discussions. When you finish this book, you should be able to exploit the power of Harvard Graphics to the fullest extent of your own creativity.

Everyone should read the first three chapters. After you complete them, you will understand how to use the basic features of Harvard Graphics. Then you can skip to whatever chapter you find most interesting.

As always, this book is not the result of my efforts alone. First, I would like to thank Scott Arant, the technical staff at SAMS, and Gary Masters. Without their efforts, this book would have remained an idea instead of a reality. I would also like to thank Dave Cooper, Don Dudine, Carl Landau, Chuck Lieske, and Jim Rheude for their efforts and contributions. And last, but far from least, I need to thank my family for being so understanding about the deadlines that caused missed family opportunities.

Introduction

From the first time humans scratched a drawing in the dirt with a stick, pictures have been used as a means to communicate ideas. Although technology has certainly replaced sticks and dirt, the principle remains unchanged: A visual image is one of the best ways to communicate information.

What Harvard Graphics (which will be referred to as HG from now on) provides is a simple yet effective means to present information visually. Carrying the previous analogy one step further, HG is the modern-day stick and your computer is the dirt. The beauty of this synergistic system is that you still control the stick. You can stay within the limits of the predefined charts provided by HG or you can express yourself freely through its many options. The choice is yours.

The Goals of This Book

This book will show you how to use HG quickly and effectively. The book was written with two types of readers in mind: beginners to HG and intermediate users of the program. If you are a beginner, you might be under pressure to finish a report within a few days. Perhaps the boss just dropped HG on your desk and told you to have the charts for the annual report ready by Tuesday. If you're in this predicament, this book can get you up and running with HG so that you can finish that report on time.

After you have mastered the basics (and some of the pressure is off), this book will show you how to exploit the many advanced features of HG so that you can express your individual creativity. Because HG is so easy to use, you can make dozens of subtle changes in a chart within a matter of minutes. With HG's numerous features, you're bound to find some combination of graphics that presents your information most effectively. And because you don't have to wait (or pay!) for a graphic artist to make each revision, experimentation is easy and even enjoyable.

How This Book is Organized

xii

This book has three main parts. Chapters 1-3 introduce the terminology, menus, and practical details that you must understand to use Harvard Graphics effectively. These chapters lay the foundation for discussions in the rest of the book; please read them before you attempt the exercises in the later chapters. Chapters 4-7 give you valuable hands-on experience designing, creating, and revising professional-quality charts. The rest of the book explains how to use HG's advanced features.

Chapter 1 begins with a list of common terms you will encounter when working with charts in HG. You will also learn how to select and use menu options, how to load a chart from disk, how to save a chart that you have created, and how to print your chart.

Chapter 2 gets you up and running in HG by introducing bar and line charts, which are easy to create and have a wide variety of applications. Creating a bar chart will quickly familiarize you with HG's overall command structure. You should read Chapter 2 in its entirety because it discusses the basic HG menus in detail. By the time you've finished this chapter, you will feel at home with almost every aspect of HG.

Chapter 3 discusses how to import data into HG, that is, how to enter information into HG without having to type it in directly. In Chapter 2 you will enter data into HG yourself because this is a quick and easy way to become familiar with HG. More often, however, the information to be charted already exists in computer-readable form. For example, your data might be have been created by spreadsheets (Lotus 1-2-3, Supercalc, or Excel), databases (FoxPro or dBASE), financial and accounting programs (DacEasy or Quicken), or word processors (Microsoft Word or WordPerfect). If the data you want to chart was produced by one of these (or similar) programs, chances are good that you can import it into HG without having to retype it. Importing data saves time and reduces data entry errors. Because you'll want to import your data from external sources whenever possible, you'll learn this procedure early in this book.

Chapters 4 through 7 explore the remaining basic chart types in detail. These chapters build upon the base of information laid down in the first three chapters. Chapter 8 addresses more advanced topics, such as slide shows, chart templates, and other special features available in HG.

Tips and Cautions

As you read this book, you will notice that some text appears inside boxes. These boxes contain tips or cautions about using HG. Following the tips will give your work a more polished look, and observing the cautions might save you from some aggravation later on.

Quick Steps

Important procedures in HG are presented as a series of steps, called *Quick Steps*. Because Quick Steps are short summaries, you will find them useful whenever you need to review a previously covered topic. Refer to the inside front cover of this book for an alphabetical listing of Quick Steps.

Trademark Acknowledgments

All terms mentioned in this book that are known to be trademarks or service marks are listed below. In addition, terms suspected of being trademarks or service marks have been appropriately capitalized. SAMS cannot attest to the accuracy of this information. Use of a term in this book should not be regarded as affecting the validity of any trademark or service mark.

1-2-3 and Lotus are registered trademarks of Lotus Development Corporation.

DacEasy is a registered trademark of DacEasy, Inc.

dBASE is a registered trademark of Ashton-Tate Corporation.

FoxPro is a registered trademark of Fox Software.

Harvard Graphics, PFS, PFS: GRAPH, and PFS: Professional Write are registered trademarks of Software Publishing Corporation.

Microsoft, Microsoft Excel, and Microsoft Word are registered trademarks of Microsoft Corporation.

Quicken is a registered trademarkof Intuit Software.

Supercalc is a registered trademark of Computer Associates International, Inc.

WordPerfect is a registered trademark of WordPerfect Corporation.

xiv

Getting Started With Harvard Graphics

In This Chapter

1

▶ *Selecting the appropriate chart*
▶ *Making menu selections*
▶ *Editing data*
▶ *Preparing to create a chart*
▶ *Loading, saving, and printing a chart*

This chapter discusses different types of charts and the types of data used to construct them. This information will help you make the best chart selection for your particular circumstances. The chapter also demonstrates how to make menu choices by showing you how to perform the fundamental operations in HG—editing data and creating, loading, saving, and printing a chart.

Before you can construct a chart, you first need to consider the nature of the data you are working with. This will help you organize your charting work and make it easier to use the many features of HG.

Types of Data

Most data falls into one of two categories: 1) *flows*, and 2) *stocks*. Understanding the distinction between these two data types will help you make better chart selections.

Flow Data

A *flow variable* is one that requires a time factor; that is, flow data is a quantity measured over a period of time. If I ask you what your income is and you tell me $100, it is not clear to me what your income is. Do you have a part-time job and make $100 a week? Do you work in an office and make $100 a day? Or are you a consultant who makes $100 per hour? The point is that income cannot be properly stated unless a time factor (for example, per week, per day, per hour, or so on) is included in the statement. In the language of HG, flow data is referred to as a flow variable and the time factor as a *time subscript*.

Stock Data

Stock data is a quantity measured at a point in time. In the language of HG, a *stock variable* does not require a time subscript. For example, if I ask you how much you have in your savings account and you say $100, the amount makes sense without further explanation.

Stocks, Flows, and Chart Selection

Some types of charts are better suited to flow data than to stock data. For example, HG provides a variant of the basic line chart called a Trend chart. The name itself suggests the tracking of data through time, often with the goal of forecasting future movements of the data. Obviously you would use flow data with the Trend chart.

On the other hand, organizational charts and many text charts depict the status of an organization at a specific point in time. You would use stock data for such charts.

2

In the business arena, the data in an income statement are usually flow variables. Both earnings and expenses are summarized *per quarter* or *per year*, which indicates that these are both flow variables. On the other hand, most of the data found in a balance sheet are stock variables. For example, accounts receivable, cash, payable, and inventory are all measured at a point in time and, hence, are stock data.

In the world of variables and their data, stocks are the snapshots and flows are the movies. Stocks capture the data at a moment in time, and flows let us view the data through time. Although you can make a movie out of snapshots, it is far less effective than a true motion picture. Likewise, applying flow data to a chart that is best suited for stock data is likely to result in a graphic that falls short of its full potential.

Table 1-1 will help you make the proper chart selection. It lists the four basic types of charts available in HG along with the corresponding data that you usually use with those charts.

3

Table 1-1. *Chart Types and Associated Data Types*

Chart	Data type
Text	Stock data. Text charts include title (organizational) charts, lists, columns of data, and forms.
Pie	Stock data. Pie charts show how a whole is divided into its parts. A double pie chart could depict flow data because it can show how the whole changes over time.
Bar/Line	Flow data. Bar and line charts usually show the changing of data over time.
Area	Flow data. Area charts are similar to bar charts.
Hi/Low/Close	Flow data. These charts often show stock prices over time.

HG includes several variants for each of the basic chart types listed in Table 1-1. Just remember to consider the nature of your data *before* you plunge into the task of making a chart.

Common Chart Elements

Before you can construct a chart, you need to understand the elements that are common to almost all charts. The terminology used for these elements varies, but we will define them using the same terminology found in the HG software.

Figure 1-1 shows an Income and Expenses chart for the Pfeiffer Company, a hypothetical company we will use in many examples. Each chart element is indicated with a circled number and is explained briefly in the next section. (Detailed information about each element is presented in later chapters.)

4

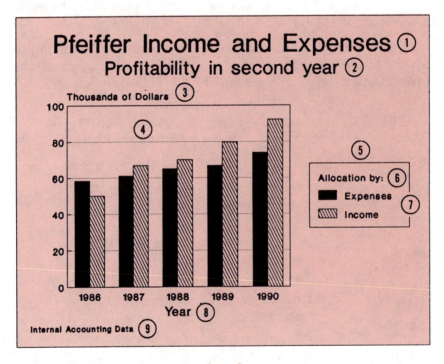

Figure 1-1.   Elements of a chart

1. Title

This is the primary title of the chart. When people look at a chart, their eyes are drawn first to the graphic representation of the chart itself (that is, the bars, lines, and so on). The second element of the chart a viewer sees is the title. Because the information in the chart itself might not be obvious, the title should briefly inform readers as to what they are viewing.

2. Subtitle

The subtitle lets you expand upon the information presented in the title. If the purpose of the chart is to convince or persuade, you can use a subtitle to reinforce the conclusion to be drawn by the viewer.

3. Y Axis Label

The Y axis label tells the viewer what the vertical units on the chart represent. The information in this axis is often numeric data. However, forms, text charts, and organizational charts are exceptions to this. In Figure 1-1 the data is expressed in thousands of dollars along the Y axis. In other charts, the units on the Y axis might represent interest rates, gallons, pounds, or other units of measure.

5

> ▶ **Tip:** Every chart should have labels for both the Y and X axes. Without labels, the viewer has no idea what the units on the chart represent.

4. Grid Lines and Tick Marks

Grid lines help the reader understand the meaning of the data by associating the data in the chart with its corresponding unit of measure. For example, in Figure 1-1, the grid lines help the reader associate the height of the vertical bars with the appropriate dollar value.

Tick marks are similar to grid lines, except that they do not span the entire chart. In Figure 1-1 you can see a tick mark clearly just to the right of the number "20" on the vertical axis. Although grid lines and tick marks are not required elements, they can make a chart more readable.

5. Legend

A legend identifies the symbols, such as bars or lines, used to construct the chart. In Figure 1-1, the legend indicates that the two types of vertical bars represent expenses and income. Always use a legend when you present more than one kind of data in the same chart.

6. Legend Title

A legend title clarifies or provides additional information about the legends used in the chart.

7. Legend Series Labels

6

A legend series label identifies each kind of data presented in the chart. HG consistently refers to each type of data as a *series*. In academic disciplines, the term *data variable* is more common than *data series*.

8. X Axis Label

This label tells the viewer what the horizontal units on the chart represent. In Figure 1-1, the X axis represents time in years.

9. Footnote

A footnote indicates the source of the data used in the chart. Although footnotes are often placed near the bottom of a chart, they are important.

Later chapters explain each of these chart elements in greater detail. You need to become familiar with the basic chart elements for two reasons. First, you will be using these chart elements in virtually all of the charts that you create. Second, HG uses these terms as input prompts in many of the menu options you must use to create your own charts. Understanding what the elements are and how they are used will make it easier for you to create your own charts. Take a few minutes to study each chart element shown in Figure 1-1 before proceeding to the next section.

Making Menu Selections

Let's suppose that you want to reproduce the chart shown in Figure 1-1. The best way to learn how to use HG is to actually run the program as you read this text. We will assume that you have installed HG in accordance with your particular hardware environment and that you are currently in the directory that contains the HG software. To start HG, type **HG** and press Enter. After a moment, you will see the Main Menu of HG as shown in Figure 1-2.

7

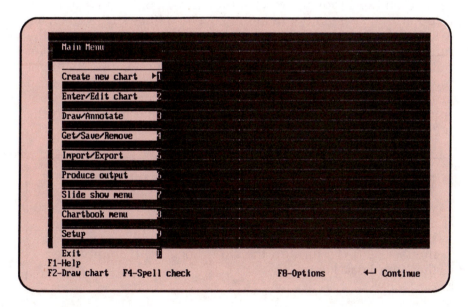

Figure 1-2. The Main Menu of Harvard Graphics

Throughout your sessions, HG will offer you a variety of menu options from which to choose. The menu option you select determines what HG does next. As a general rule, there are three ways to select an option from a menu. The next three sections describe these selection methods.

1. Highlight a Selection and Press Enter

When you start HG, notice that the first option in the Main Menu Create New Chart is shown in a different color than the rest of the menu options. If you are using a monochrome display, the first option will appear in reverse video. In either case, the first menu option is said to be *highlighted*. (You can't see the highlighting in Figure 1-2, but you can tell that Create New Chart is the highlighted menu option by the triangular mark near the end of this menu option and to the left of the number 1.) A highlighted menu option is termed the *current* option; if you then press Enter, it becomes the *active* menu option. Therefore, the first method for selecting a menu option is to highlight the desired option and then press Enter.

You can use the *arrow keys* or a mouse to highlight different menu options. On some keyboards, the arrow keys are located on the 2 (down arrow), 4 (left arrow), 6 (right arrow), and 8 (up arrow) keys on the numeric keypad. Other keyboards have a set of four arrow keys between the right Shift key and the numeric keypad. Pressing the down arrow highlights the menu option below the current option (for example, the highlight moves from menu option 1 to menu option 2). Pressing the up arrow highlights the menu option above the current option. Continue to press either of these keys to move the highlight to the menu option you want to select.

8

> ► **Tip:** If you are using the arrow keys on the numeric keypad, be sure the Num Lock key light is off; otherwise, pressing the arrow keys will produce the number above the arrow (for example, instead of moving the highlight down, pressing the down arrow key will generate the number "2"). To turn off the Num Lock light, simply press the Num Lock key.

2. Highlight a Selection and Press the Left Mouse Button

If you are using a mouse, slide the mouse down to highlight a menu option below the current option. Move the mouse up to highlight a menu option above the current option.

Pressing the left mouse button (also called "clicking") then selects the highlighted menu option. Pressing the right mouse button is the same as pressing the Esc (Escape) key—it cancels the current menu option.

If menu option 1 (Create New Chart) is highlighted, moving the mouse up or pressing the up arrow will not cause the highlight to "loop around" to the bottom option in the Main Menu (Exit). Likewise, if you are at the bottom menu option, moving the mouse down or pressing the down arrow key will not cause highlight to move to the menu option at the top of the menu list.

3. Press the Hot Keys

The third way to select a menu option is to press its *hot key*. A hot key is a number or letter that represents a specific menu option. If you look closely at Figure 1-2, you will see that each menu option has a number located directly to its right, except for the last menu option (Exit) which has the letter *E* to its right.

9

Why does the last menu option have a letter for its hot key rather than a number? As a rule, hot keys require only a single keystroke—note that you don't have to press Enter after you press a hot key. Using numbers to select the last option, which is the tenth in the list, would require *two* keystrokes (a "1" and a "0"); this does not meet the hot key criterion of requiring only one keystroke. Because Exit starts with the letter "E," the authors used *E* as the hot key.

> ▶ In summary, the three ways to select a menu option are: 1) use the arrow keys to highlight a menu option and press Enter, 2) move the mouse to highlight a menu option and press the left mouse button, or 3) press the appropriate hot key.

Moving Around a Menu with Pseudo Hot Keys

HG provides yet another way to move from one option in a menu to another. If you look at Figure 1-2 again, you will note that the first letter of each menu option begins with a capital letter. Further inspection shows, however, that these capital letters are not unique. Create new chart (menu option 1) begins with the letter *C*, but so does Chartbook menu (menu option 8).

Press the *C* key. This immediately highlights the Chartbook menu option. Now press the *C* key again. This highlights the Create new chart again. Now press the *S* key. The Slide show menu option becomes highlighted. Press the *S* key again to highlight the Setup option. Notice, however, that these keys do *not* behave like hot keys because they do not select the menu option. Rather, these *pseudo hot keys* merely cause a menu option to become the current, or highlighted, menu option—they do *not* execute that option.

You can use pseudo hot keys to move rapidly from one place to another within a menu without actually selecting (activating) the new option. Another advantage of pseudo hot keys is that your fingers don't have to leave the letter keys to highlight a new menu option. This is a blessing for people who don't like to fumble for the arrow keys or number keys.

10

> Ⓞ **Caution:** Notice that the second option in the Main Menu, Enter/Edit chart, begins with an E. However, if you press the E key, you will exit the program rather than select the Enter/Edit chart menu option. This is because the letter E is the hot key for exiting the program and hot keys take precedence over pseudo hot keys. Therefore, be sure there is no conflict between hot keys and pseudo hot keys before you use a pseudo hot key to move around within a menu.

Editing Information in HG

Before you can proceed much further, you need to learn how to edit information that you enter into HG when creating a chart. At various times, HG will ask you to enter information into the program. As you type you might notice that you've made a mistake or that you must alter some of the information you entered. Fortunately, any information you type in response to an HG question is collected in a mini-editor that's built into HG.

The HG editor, or data editor, serves two primary purposes: to insert or delete information and to provide a means to reposition the cursor. The HG editor is not a "stand-alone" editor in the sense that you can use it to write letters. Rather, the HG editor's sole purpose is to make your job of data entry in HG as easy as possible.

As you read this section about the HG editor, try to gain experience with as many of the editing features as you can. The list of keys used for editing is short (see Table 1-2), but after you've learned these keys, you can significantly reduce the time you spend editing or modifying your charts.

11

Table 1-2. ***Editing Keys and Their Functions***

Key	Function
Insert/Delete Characters	
Ins	Toggle between Overstrike and Insert modes
⇦	Delete the character to the left (also called Backspace)
Del	Delete the character under the cursor
Ctrl-Ins	Insert a line
Ctrl-Del	Delete a line
Cursor Movement	
↑	Move up one line
↓	Move down one line
←	Move left one character
→	Move right one character
Ctrl-→	Move right one word
Ctrl-←	Move left one word

Continued

Table 1-2. *(continued)*

Key	Function
Cursor Movement Within Fields	
Tab	Move to next field for input
Shift-Tab	Move to previous field
Home	Move to first entry of current group
End	Move to last entry of current group

Insert/Delete

The HG data editor is in *overstrike mode* by default. In this mode, if you use the left arrow key to back up a few letters and then begin typing, you will overwrite the existing characters on the screen.

If you need to insert characters in a line, use the arrow keys to move the cursor to the appropriate position, and press the Ins (Insert) key. This places the data editor in *insert mode*. Notice that the cursor size is larger (a *block cursor*) when you are in insert mode. By looking at the size of the cursor, you will immediately know whether you are in insert or overstrike mode. If you press the Ins key again, the editor toggles to overstrike mode.

To delete a character, place the cursor on the character to be deleted and press the Del (Delete) key. The Del key always deletes the character under the cursor. You can delete a character to the left of the cursor by using the Backspace key. The Backspace key resembles a left-pointing arrow and is usually located on the top right of the keyboard above the Enter key.

To delete a line, position the cursor on the line to be deleted and press the Ctrl (Control) and Del keys at the same time. This erases all the characters on the line with the cursor.

To insert a line, position the cursor where you want to insert the new line. Press the Ctrl and Ins keys at the same time. The lines above the cursor will remain unchanged, but all lines below the cursor will be moved down one line.

> ⊘ **Caution:** Be careful when using the delete-line feature. If an input form has multiple columns, Ctrl-Del may delete the data across several columns. In other forms, Ctrl-Del deletes only the data in the column in which the cursor appears. As a rule, if the cursor is on a line that spans more than one column of data, do not use the Ctrl-Del feature unless you want to delete the data in all columns.

Cursor Movement

The arrow keys do exactly what you expect them to do. The up and down arrows move the cursor up or down one line on the screen. The left and right arrows move the cursor one character to the left or right.

The Tab key moves the cursor to the next input item, or *input field*. Almost always located to the left of the Q key, the Tab key is often depicted by the symbol of opposite-facing arrows. If you press the Shift and Tab keys at the same time, the cursor moves to the previous input field.

13

> ▶ **Tip:** The term *input field* is merely the location at which you enter information into HG. When you create your own charts, almost all of your work consists of filling in the input fields that HG displays on the screen. An *input screen* is simply a screen of one or more input fields.

The Home key moves the cursor to the first item of an input screen. The End key moves the cursor to the last item in an input screen.

Pressing the Ctrl and right-arrow keys at the same time moves the cursor to the next word in the current input field. Pressing the Ctrl and left-arrow keys moves the cursor to the previous word in the current input field. These Control-key combinations, or key sequences, make it easier for you to edit a long series of words, such as chart titles.

Preparing to Create a Chart

Before you can actually begin to create a chart, you first must tell HG about the hardware environment in which it is operating. To do so, select the Setup option from the HG Main Menu.

You only need to go through the Setup process once (unless you change your hardware environment). HG stores all of the Setup information that you enter so that the program does not have to ask you the same questions every time you use it. Select the Setup option (9) to display the Setup menu on the screen; then, select the Defaults option.

Setting up the Defaults

14

Selecting the Defaults option displays the Default Settings screen, as shown in Figure 1-3. Now, let's discuss the input fields in the order that they appear on the screen.

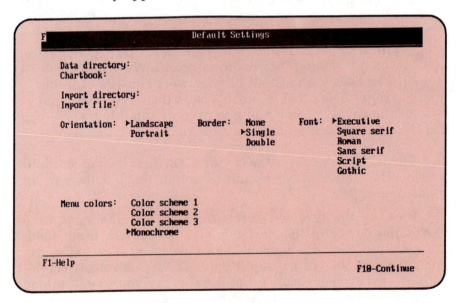

Figure 1-3. The Default Settings screen

Data Directory

The Data directory tells HG where to look for your data files when you run the program. When you use the `Get/Save/Remove` option from the Main Menu, HG searches the specified directory to find the necessary chart files.

Be sure to enter the full path name for the directory you want HG to search. For example, if you are storing the charts for the 1990 annual reports in a subdirectory named REP1990 below the directory HG, you must enter the full path name `C:\HG\REP1990` not merely `REP1990`. If you are using floppy disks, you might want to use drive B for your data files. In this case, you would enter `B:` in this field.

> ▶ **Tip:** You should keep the charts associated with different projects in different subdirectories. If you are using a floppy disk system, consider using one disk for each project's charts. If you ever need to reconstruct the project charts at a later time, this approach to storing chart files will make the job much easier.

15

Chartbook

A chartbook can be thought of as a collection of empty charts. This setting lets you specify a chartbook to be loaded automatically by HG when you run the program. You will learn more about chartbooks in later chapters. For now, leave this field blank.

Import Directory

As we mentioned earlier in this chapter, the raw data to be charted often already exists in some computer-readable form. HG provides a variety of ways to read, or *import*, that data into HG so that you don't have to retype it. If, for example, you are using Lotus 1-2-3 spreadsheet data for your charts, you might want to enter the directory name where the spreadsheet data files are stored.

If you don't plan to use the import feature, you can leave this field blank.

Import File

This field lets you supply a file name for the type of data that you will be importing. For example, if you plan to import a lot of Lotus files, you might want to set this field to *.WKS (for version 1A) or *.WK1 (for later versions), because these file name extensions are common to Lotus data files. If you will be importing ASCII (text) files, you might enter *.ASC.

For now, leave this field blank. You will have a better understanding of what to enter in this input field after you read the detailed information about importing data files in Chapter 3.

Orientation

16

The orientation of a chart determines how it is printed. The *Portrait* mode prints a chart "normally"—from top to bottom. *Landscape* mode prints a chart "sideways." If you are using 8½-by-11-inch paper, the 11-inch side appears at the top of the chart in Landscape mode. In the Portrait mode, the 8½-inch side appears at the top. The default mode is Landscape mode.

Border

When you print a chart, you can choose to have HG outline that chart with a border. The Single option prints a border using a single line, and the Double option prints a double-line border. If you don't want to use a border, select None.

Figure 2-3 in Chapter 2 shows a chart with a single-line border. The single-line border sets the chart off nicely from other material in a report and gives it a crisp, uncluttered look. Select a single-line border for now, and then experiment with the other two options later to see how they affect your charts.

Be aware that if you select a border option, HG does *not* display the border on the screen as you create the chart; the border appears only when you print the chart.

Font

The font option lets you select different fonts for use in your charts. For now, let's stay with the default font (Executive).

Menu Colors

This option determines the colors used by HG when displaying menus on the screen. If you have a color monitor, you should try all three color schemes to decide which you like best. If you don't have a color monitor, you should set this option to Monochrome. Note that this setting doesn't alter the way HG runs.

Exiting the Default Settings Screen

17

If you change your mind about any of the answers you entered in the Default Settings screen, press the Home key to return to the first input field in this screen. You can also press the Shift-Tab combination to move backward through the list. After you have the settings the way you want them, press the F10 key to leave this screen and continue to the next Setup option. (If you are using a mouse, press the right button.)

Setting up Printer 1

The Printer 1 option of the Setup menu tells HG the type of printer you will be using. Selecting this option displays a list of printers that can be used with HG. Use the arrow keys or mouse to highlight your printer selection; then press Enter.

Another menu appears on your screen to let you assign Printer 1 to a specific parallel or serial port. Most printers are parallel printers and most are set up as LPT1. Press Enter to accept this default setting. If you have a serial printer, this menu lets you specify the correct Baud rate, Parity, Data bits, and Stop bits. See your printer documentation for information about these settings. After you make your selections, press Enter; the Setup Menu will reappear on the screen.

Setting up Printer 2

The Printer 2 option works like the first option. Select this option only if you have two printers connected to your system. If you create a lot of charts, you might, for example, use a high-speed printer for draft copies of charts and a second (laser) printer for final copies. In this case, you would specify the laser printer as Printer 2 by selecting the appropriate name from the listing and pressing Enter.

Once again, another menu appears on your screen to let you assign Printer 2 to a parallel or serial port. Most printers are parallel printers, and because this is your second printer, you probably should select LPT2 from the list. If you have a serial printer, this menu lets you specify the correct Baud rate, Parity, Data bits, and Stop bits. See your printer documentation for information about these settings. After you make your selections, press Enter; the Setup Menu will reappear on the screen.

18

> ▶ **Tip:** If your printer is not listed among the Printer 1 choices, you still might be able to use it. Many non-standard printers have "emulation modes" that cause them to behave like one of the standard printers. Check your printer documentation to find out if your printer can emulate one of the printers listed; then, select that printer from the list.
>
> If your printer does not appear in the list and it does not have an emulation mode, you still might be able to use it. It's possible that one of the modes in the list will work with your printer even though your printer manual doesn't say so. Try using some of the popular printer selections (for example, IBM or Epson); chances are good that one of these will work.

Setting up the Plotter and Film Recorder

The Plotter and Film Recorder options are similar to the printer options discussed in the previous sections. Select these options only if you are using either a plotter or film recorder to produce your charts. HG displays a list of the types of these devices that it supports. Select the appropriate devices, and press Enter. At the next menu, supply the appropriate parallel or serial port information; then press Enter to return to the Setup Menu.

Setting up the Screen

The Screen option lets you change the screen mode (CGA, EGA, VGA, and so on) that HG uses in its displays. Because the HG installation program selected the best display option for your current system, you won't need to change these settings unless you upgrade to a higher-resolution display. Press the Esc (Escape) key to return to the Setup Menu.

Selecting the Color Palette

The Color Palette option lets you adjust the color palette used with your charts. For now, ignore this option.

19

You've now supplied HG all the Setup information it need to function correctly; you now can start creating charts. If you press the Esc key twice or the F10 key and then Esc, you will return to the HG Main Menu.

Loading a Chart from Disk

The HG package includes several sample charts with which you can experiment. In this section you will learn how to load a chart from disk and how to return to the HG Main Menu afterward.

Getting a Chart

To load an existing chart from a disk file, first select the Get/Save/Remove option (4) from the HG Main Menu (see Figure 1-2). This displays the new Get/Save/Remove Menu to the right of the Main Menu, as shown in Figure 1-4.

Now, select the Get Chart option (1). This displays the Select Chart screen, which is HG's file selection screen. At the top of

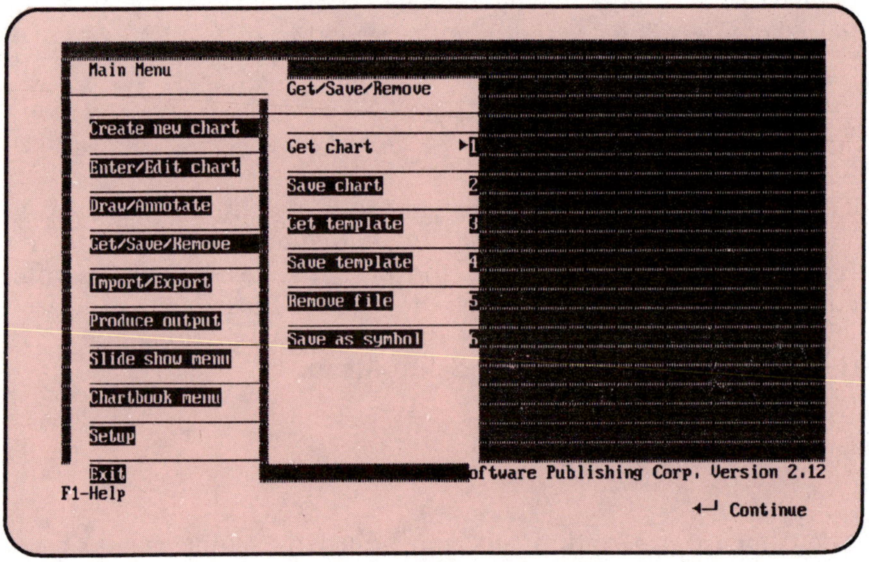

20

Figure 1-4.   The Get/Save/Remove menu

the screen is name of the directory that HG will search for the chart files on disk. This directory is the same path name that you entered when you selected the Setup option earlier. The cursor will be positioned at the Filename field waiting for you to enter the name of the file you want to load.

Selecting a Chart

You can select a file in one of two ways. First, you can simply type the name of the file and press Enter. Note that all HG chart files have the file extension of CHT (for example, SAMPLE.CHT). The second way to select a file is to highlight the file you want to load (by using the arrow keys or moving the mouse), and then press Enter.

HG reads the selected data file and immediately displays the chart on the screen. When you finish viewing the chart, press any key to continue. (The spacebar is a good choice because it's difficult to miss.)

Q **Loading an Existing Chart**

1. Start the HG program or (if it is running) press Esc.	Displays the HG Main Menu.
2. Press 4.	Selects the Get/Save/Remove option.
3. Press 1.	Selects the Get Chart option.
4. Press ↓ to highlight the desired chart file, or type the chart file name.	Specifies the chart file you want to load.
5. Press Enter when you've highlighted the desired chart or typed its name.	Selects the chart file named and displays it on-screen.
6. Press the spacebar to end viewing.	Removes the chart from the screen. □

Returning to the Main Menu

21

Depending on the sample chart you selected, HG will display one of several input screens. Because you don't want to alter the chart now, simply press F10 twice or Esc twice to return to the HG Main Menu. (If you are using a mouse, clicking the right button performs the same actions as pressing the Esc key. Click the right button twice to return to the Main Menu.)

If you want to take a break and end this session with HG, you can either select the Exit option from the Main Menu or press E. If you want to examine other sample charts, simply follow the previous Quick Steps and select another chart file name.

Saving a Chart to Disk

To save a chart to disk, you must first return to the HG Main Menu by pressing the Esc or F10 key twice when you have finished creating the chart. Then, select the Get/Save/Remove option (4) from the Main Menu. When the Get/Save/Remove menu appears on the screen (see Figure 1-4), select the Save Chart option.

You will need to enter three pieces of information before you can save the chart to disk: a directory name, a file name, and a description of the file.

Directory

You must specify the directory where the chart will be saved. When the Save Chart screen first appears, this field is already filled in with the directory name you supplied in the Data Directory field of the Default Settings screen. If the directory name appearing on the screen is correct, press Enter; otherwise, type the correct name and then press Enter.

Chart Will Be Saved As

This prompt asks you to type the file name under which the chart will be stored on disk. Pick a name that hints at the contents of the file. For example, if the chart shows the year-end balance sheet for 1990, you might call the file YEBAL90. HG will automatically supply the CHT file extension (for example, YEBAL90.CHT).

22

Description

By default, HG uses the title of the chart as its description. You will see this description displayed on the Select Chart screen as you go through the process of loading a chart. If you prefer a different description, press Ctrl-Del to remove the default description and type the new one. After you press Enter, HG will save the file on disk. Press Esc to return to the Main Menu.

⊘ **Caution:** Always save a new chart *before* you attempt to print it; otherwise, you risk losing your chart should HG run into trouble during the printing process. Although HG is good at sensing when the printer is not on-line, when it's out of paper, and so on, it cannot contend with all possible problems. Rather than jeopardize your work, save the chart first.

Q **Saving a Chart**

1. Press Esc.   Displays the Main Menu.

2. Press 4.   Selects the Get/Save/Remove
                                       option.

3. Press 2.   Selects the Save Chart
                                       option.

4. Type a chart name and   Specifies the name the
   press Enter. (You do not   chart will be stored under
   need to include the .CHT   on disk.
   extension name.)

5. Type a brief chart   Describes the contents of
   description and press   the chart file. After you
   Enter.   press Enter the chart is
                                      saved on disk.

6. Press Esc.   Returns you to the Main
                                      Menu.   □

23

Printing a Chart

Now that your chart is safely stored on disk, it's time to print it.
Select the Produce Output option (6) from the Main Menu. When the
Produce Output menu appears select the Printer option. (We will
assume for now that you are using a printer rather than a plotter or
other device to print your chart.) After you select the Printer
option, HG displays a Printer Chart Options screen similar to that
shown in Figure 1-5.

Quality

The Quality option determines the print quality of the chart.
Draft quality prints a chart the fastest, but the chart will lack
detail. Use Draft mode when you want a quick approximation of
how the chart will look. *Standard* quality prints the chart slower
than Draft but still fairly fast. Standard mode also shows greater
detail and is often used when a chart is in the final stages of
"fine tuning." *High* quality is used for the final output of the
chart because it produces the most detailed graphics. Dot matrix
printers print very slowly in this mode.

Use the arrow keys to highlight your selection and press Enter; or move the highlight with the mouse and click the left button; or make your selection using the hot keys (D, S, H).

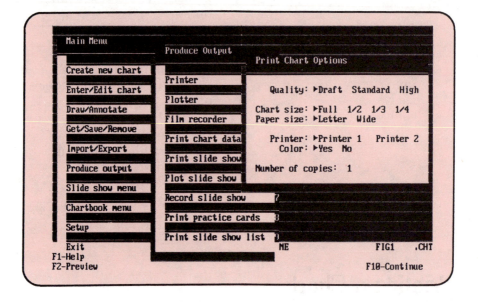

Figure 1-5. The Print Chart Options screen

Chart Size

Chart size refers to the amount of space the chart will occupy on the page. The Full option uses the entire sheet to print the chart, and the other options use the portion of the page specified by the fractions listed. Use the arrow keys, mouse, or press the 1 pseudo hot key to select the desired option and press Enter.

Paper Size

If your printer uses 8 ½-by-11-inch paper, select the Letter option. If you are using a wide-carriage printer and paper, select the Wide option and press Enter.

Printer

This option lets you print on either of your two printers, assuming you have two printers connected to your system. Select the appropriate printer and press Enter. If you only have one printer, select Printer 1 and press Enter.

Color

If you are lucky enough to have a color printer, answer Yes. If not, select No and press Enter.

Number of Copies

If you want to print multiple copies of the chart, simply type the number of copies you want printed. The default is 1 copy.

25

> ▶ **Tip:** If you select the Printer option and all of the Print Chart fields are already set to their proper values, simply press the F10 key to print the chart.

Q Printing a Chart

1. If chart is not already loaded, follow the **Load Chart Quick Steps**.	Loads the chart. (You must load a chart before you can print it.)
2. Press Esc.	Returns you to the Main Menu. You can print a chart from the Main Menu only.
3. Press 6.	Selects the Produce output option.
4. Press 1.	Selects the Printer option.
5. Press H, then Enter.	Selects high quality output.
6. Press 1, then Enter.	Specifies a half-page chart.
7. Press Enter.	Accepts the default paper size (Letter).

8. Press Enter.

Accepts the default printer (1).

9. Press N, then Enter.

Specifies that the printer is not a color printer.

10. Press F10.

Accepts the default number of copies (1), and prints the chart using the settings just specified. ☐

What You Have Learned

You now know about data and chart types, how to use the HG menu system and its keys, how to set up the default values used by HG, and how to load, save, and print a chart. You might want to experiment more with the sample charts provided by HG until you are comfortable with how HG works.

26

Bar and Line Charts

In This Chapter

▶ *Learning how to create bar and line charts*

▶ *Becoming familiar with HG's data input structure*

▶ *Using special chart effects*

Bar and line charts are most often used with flow data. A common use of a bar or line chart is to show company sales over several years. However, you can also use bar charts with stock data to show the comparative distribution of data, such as company sales by office, at a point in time; all of the bars (sales offices) taken together could then show the distribution of company sales by region.

The Create New Chart Menu

Start the HG program by typing HG at the DOS prompt and pressing Enter. Now, select the Create new chart option from the Main Menu. You can select from the menu by pressing the hot key (1), by using the arrow keys to highlight the option and pressing Enter, or by moving the mouse to highlight the option and clicking the left button. This displays the Create New Chart menu (see Figure 2-1), which lists the different types of ready-made charts available to you (plus several other options we will ignore for now). Now select the Bar/Line option by using the mouse, the hot key 3, or the pseudo hot key B.

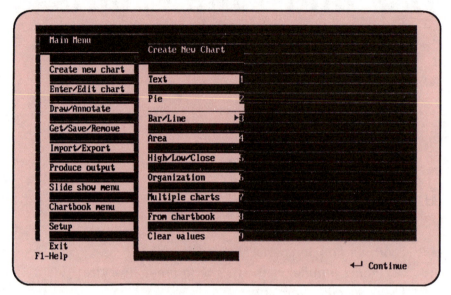

Figure 2-1. Create New Chart menu

The X Data Type Menu

After you select the Bar/Line option, the screen displays the X Data Type Menu, shown in Figure 2-2. Notice that this menu appears to "overlay" a second menu; that is, there seems to be another menu behind the X Data Type Menu. HG is telling you that you must first enter information in the X Data Type Menu screen before you can proceed to the "background" menu.

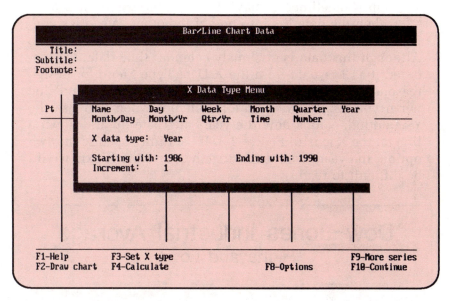

Figure 2-2.   X Data Type Menu

The X Data Types

HG lets you place 11 types of data on the X axis of a chart. The 11 options—such as Name, Day, Week, and so on—appear near the top of the X Data Type Menu. These data types fall into four general categories: name, calendar time, time, and numeric.

Name

The Name option merely signifies that you want the X axis associated with a name. For example, if you want to show the distribution of grades in a class, you would name the grades "A," "B," "C," "D," and "F" on the X axis. Or, if you are charting the sales figures for each person in a sales office, you would name each salesperson on the X axis.

Use the Name option whenever the information on the X axis is *not* measured in numbers or units of time.

▶ **Tip:** Sometimes it pays to use the ꜱᴍᴀʟʟ Name option even when the data fits into one of the other categories. Figure 2-3 shows a bar chart with years on the X axis. Although this data is obviously calendar time data, we specified it as Name data from the X Data Type Menu for design reasons. You can print the X axis labels on a second line when you use the Name option, but not when you use the Year option. Notice how the years alternate up and down a line on the X axis in Figure 2-3. If we didn't specify the Name option, the years would run together, and the X axis would be difficult to read.

30

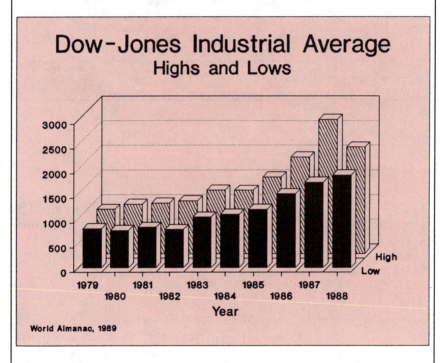

Figure 2-3. Using the Name option to create a more readable chart

To place a label on a second line when using the Name option, type a vertical bar before the label; everything after the vertical bar moves to the second line. For example, if you enter the following label:

June | 1989

HG displays it as:

June
1989

To create the X axis labels shown in Figure 2-3, you would enter the first three entries as follows:

1979
| 1980
1981

The vertical bar preceding the second entry tells HG to display the year "1980" on the second line of the X axis.

31

Calendar Time

Eight of the eleven X axis data types fall into the category of calendar time. If your raw data consists of calendar-type information, you will usually select one of the following menu options: Day, Week, Month, Quarter, Year, Month/Day, Month/Yr, and Qtr Yr. (The previous Tip explains a possible exception.)

▶ **Tip:** With most lists of pre-defined menu options, when you specify the first letter of an option, HG automatically inserts the rest of the word into the input field. That is, pressing the Y key writes the word "Year" into the X data type input field.

Time

The Time option signifies that you want to associate the data with the time of day. When entering the start and end values for time data, you need to specify either AM or PM. For example, if you are charting the number of incoming phone calls throughout the workday, you might enter the starting value as 9:00 AM and the ending value as 5:00 PM.

Numeric

If the X axis contains numeric data, select the Numbers option. You can specify any number, including decimal fractions and numbers expressed in scientific notation (for example, 1.332E10).

Starting With and Ending With

Use the Starting with and Ending with fields to set the starting and ending values for the X axis. In our example in Figure 2-2, the starting and ending years are 1986 and 1990, respectively. HG automatically scales the X axis data to fit within the range of values you enter. These entries are optional. If you've selected the Name option from the X Data Type Menu, leave these entries blank.

32

> ▶ **Tip:** Bar charts appear cluttered when you use too many bars. You should limit bar charts to 15 bars along the X axis. If your chart needs to show more than 15 X-axis data points, you should consider using a different type of chart.

Increment

The last input field on the X Data Type Menu specifies the increment to be used for the X axis. The Increment entry determines the intermediate values between the starting and ending values along the X axis. In our example, the X axis income values represent yearly figures; therefore, we specified an increment value of 1 (year), as shown in Figure 2-2.

If your chart uses a large number of X-axis data points, you might need to adjust the increment value so that the labels on the X axis don't run together.

> ▶ **Tip:** When the time of day is the unit of measure for the X axis, you must specify the increment in minutes, not hours. Therefore, a time increment will always fall within the range of 1 through 60.

After you enter the increment value, the X Data Type Menu disappears and the "background" screen, Bar/Line Chart Data, becomes active.

Bar/Line Chart Data Screen

You use the Bar/Line Chart Data input screen to enter most of the actual data that will appear in your chart. This screen is shown in Figure 2-4. The sections that follow discuss each input field separately.

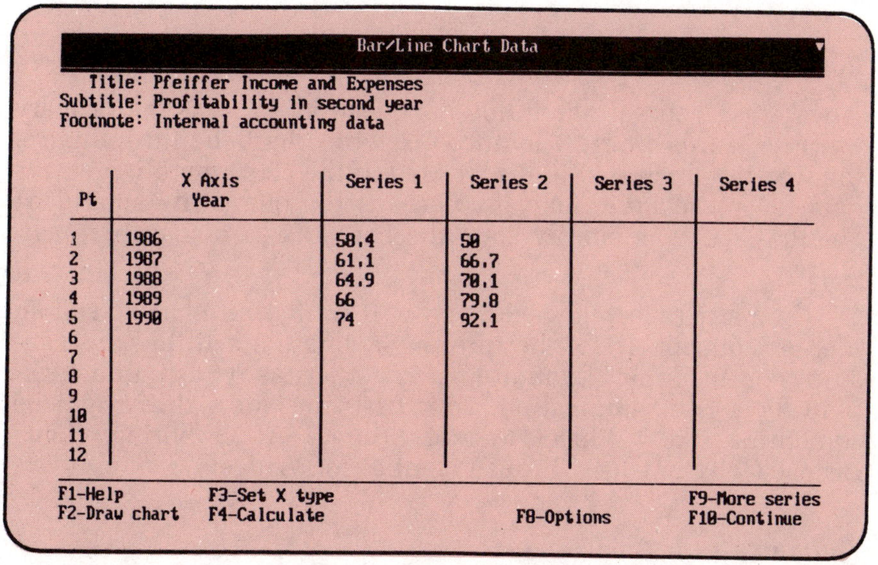

33

```
╔══════════════════════════════════════════════════════════════╗
║                    Bar/Line Chart Data                      ▼ ║
╠══════════════════════════════════════════════════════════════╣
    Title: Pfeiffer Income and Expenses
 Subtitle: Profitability in second year
 Footnote: Internal accounting data

         │ X Axis   │          │          │          │
     Pt  │ Year     │ Series 1 │ Series 2 │ Series 3 │ Series 4
    ─────┼──────────┼──────────┼──────────┼──────────┼─────────
     1   │ 1986     │ 58.4     │ 50       │          │
     2   │ 1987     │ 61.1     │ 66.7     │          │
     3   │ 1988     │ 64.9     │ 70.1     │          │
     4   │ 1989     │ 66       │ 79.8     │          │
     5   │ 1990     │ 74       │ 92.1     │          │
     6   │          │          │          │          │
     7   │          │          │          │          │
     8   │          │          │          │          │
     9   │          │          │          │          │
    10   │          │          │          │          │
    11   │          │          │          │          │
    12   │          │          │          │          │

 F1-Help          F3-Set X type                    F9-More series
 F2-Draw chart    F4-Calculate          F8-Options  F10-Continue
```

Figure 2-4. *Bar/Line Chart Data screen*

Selecting a Chart Title

The title is the first element of the chart the viewers will *read* and the second element they will notice. (Most people notice the graphics of a chart before they focus on the title, labels, or other text accompanying it.) Because the title is the first text the viewer reads, it deserves special attention. When deciding on a chart title, you should carefully consider the content and purpose of your chart, as well as your viewing audience. Let's take a closer look at these special considerations.

Contents

The title of a chart is often dictated by the data presented in the chart. If, for example, the chart shows company sales data, the title should include both the company name and the word "sales." If the chart shows the number of widgets produced at an Ohio plant, both "widgets" and "Ohio" should appear in the title. A good title lets the viewer know immediately what information is being presented in the chart. You shouldn't have a problem choosing a meaningful title if you exercise a little common sense and keep an eye to the data being presented.

Purpose

Always ask yourself the following question: What is the primary purpose of this chart? The purpose of the chart should influence the way in which the title is worded. If the chart merely presents data for subsequent analysis, perhaps the chart title should be "neutral"; that is simply state the contents as discussed previously.

In many cases, however, you will want your chart to sell an idea or concept. If so, the title might include a little salesmanship. For example, if you are using a chart as part of a business plan for a loan application, your first idea for a title might be something like "Widget Market Study." A bit boring, right? Instead, why not use "Profit Potential for Widgets"?

Audience

Your viewing audience should also influence the wording of the chart title. For example, "The Marginal Propensity to Consume" might make sense to an economist, but it doesn't convey much information to anyone else. A good title should stimulate the interest of the audience and make them want to study the chart in detail. In short, the chart should both be informative and interesting to your audience.

After the title helps capture the audience's attention, the information presented in the chart should sustain their interest.

Medium

A chart prepared with HG can be displayed in several different ways: on a computer screen, on the printed page using a printer or plotter, or on film. The medium you use to display the chart will influence its title, especially if the chart is in a slide presentation. If you plan to make a slide with the chart and then show the slide to several hundred people in one room, you should make the title lettering large enough for everyone in the room to read it clearly. Using larger letters, however, requires shorter titles because you have less space for the title.

On the other hand, if you are using the chart in a written report and each person has their own copy, you can use titles with smaller letters. Therefore, the title can be longer. **The maximum length of the title field is 60 characters, including blank spaces**. However, if you select large letters, the practical limit might be as few as 20 letters. (We will show you later in the chapter how to set the title letter size.)

Keeping in mind the considerations of contents, purpose, audience, and medium, enter a *tentative* title for your chart. After all, HG makes it a snap to revise a title later if you (or others) want to change it.

Subtitle

Although every chart needs a title, a subtitle is optional. Again, the factors that were important considerations for a chart title apply here as well. Note, however, that the subtitle is usually written in smaller letters than the chart title.

Footnote

A footnote tells the viewer the source of the data used to construct the chart. My preference is for every chart to have a foot

35

> ▶ **Tip:** Generally, you should use subtitles to provide a summary of the data presented in a chart. Your subtitles can gently nudge the readers toward the conclusion you want them to reach.

note. First, stating the source of the chart data lends credibility to the chart. Second, you never know when you will have to use the chart again. Sometimes it's difficult to remember where the data came from when the chart was produced several years ago. A footnote makes it easier to determine the origin of the data.

The X Axis

After you enter the footnote, the cursor moves to the first row of the column labeled X Axis (see Figure 2-4). Notice that the subheading for this column is "Year," the name we gave the X data in the X Data Type Menu. Because HG knows the nature of the data used on the X axis (from our responses in the X Data Type Menu), it has already filled in the appropriate beginning, intermediate, and ending years for us.

However, that HG cannot always fill these input fields for you automatically. For example, if you specified the Month option as the X data type and then supplied the starting and ending values of 1 and 5, HG cannot be sure what the starting month is. HG will do the best it can and fill in the X Axis column with the numbers "1" through "5" rather than the names of the months. You can, of course, edit the entries in this (and almost any other) field.

In some cases, HG doesn't write anything in the X Axis field. When we created the chart shown in Figure 2-3, we used Name data for the X axis. Because HG had no idea what the Name data might be (it could be anything), it left the X Axis field empty. We then filled it in as follows to "stagger" the labels on alternate lines:

```
1979
|1980
1981
|1982
1983
```

|1984
1985
|1986
1987
|1988

As you recall from the "X Data Types" section, the vertical bar tells HG to display the line of data that follows on the next line down.

Keep in mind that the X Axis column shown in Figure 2-4 is a data input field. As such, each time you type information and press Enter, the cursor moves *down* one line to the next entry in the same input field.

> ▶ **Tip:** HG is easier to use if you organize your data in columns. You should remember this when you are gathering raw data—it could simplify data entry.

After you have typed in the years from 1986 through 1990, the cursor will be positioned below the 1990 entry waiting for the next X Axis entry. However, since you have finished entering the years, you need to move to the next column. The easiest way to do this is to press the Home key and then the Tab key. The Home key moves you back to the first year entry (1979), and the Tab key moves you to the next input field, or column (Series 1 in our example).

The Series Columns

The second column in the Bar/Line Chart Data screen is called the Series 1 field. In our example, this column corresponds to the Expense data for the company. Note that when a bar chart has multiple fields, the fields are displayed on the chart from left to right. Notice in Figure 1-1 that the Expense bar appears to the left of the Income bar.

The Income and Expense data shown in Figure 2-5 are repeated in Table 2-1.

Table 2-1. *Expenses and Income Data for Figure 2-5*

Expenses	Income
58.4	50
61.1	66.7
64.9	70.1
66	79.8
74	92.1

Notice that the Pfeiffer Company becomes profitable in the second year (1987). Because this is one of the major points to be made with this bar chart, we emphasized it by using the subtitle "Profitability in the second year."

The choice of whether to make Series 1 the Expenses or Income data is subjective at best. The Expenses data shows a small increase each year, but this increase is less dramatic than the Income increase. Still, both data series show an upward trend and, with the exception of the first year, Income always exceeds Expenses. Because we are accustomed to reading from left to right, the upward trend of the data suggested placing Expenses in Series 1 and Income in Series 2. This was the order used in Figure 1-1.

In Figure 2-5 we show the same chart, but we have reversed the order of the data so that Income is placed before Expenses.

The reversing of the data series has two effects. First, the income bars are more pronounced than in Figure 1-1. Figure 2-5 places more emphasis on the profitability of the firm. Second, the data shown by the bars in Figure 2-5 has less continuity than that in Figure 1-1. Your eyes move up and down more as you follow the tops of the bars from left to right.

So which is better? Figure 1-1 is easier to read and suggests a smooth upward trend for both data series. I would choose this format if I wanted to present the data without rocking the boat. Figure 2-5 places more emphasis on income and profit growth in the face of steady expenses. I would use this format in a business plan or loan application.

There is no "right" way. Once again, you have to consider the purpose of the chart and who will be reading it. The point is that *the ordering of multiple data series has an impact on how*

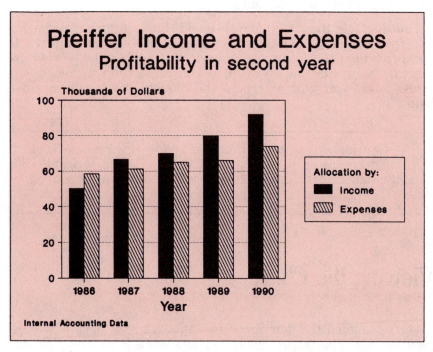

Figure 2-5.   Income data precedes Expenses, reversing their order in Figure 1-1.

39

the chart is perceived. Use the order that fulfills your particular requirements.

How Many Data Series and Data Points?

As you can see in Figure 2-4, HG provides four columns for entering data. The data you enter can be the numbers 0 through 9, plus or minus signs, a decimal point, E for scientific notation, or a forward slash (/) for a fraction (for example, 1/2).

If you need to chart more than four variables, press F9 to display four more input data fields. Therefore, the maximum number of data series (or variables) is 8. Each series can have as many as 240 data points, although Name data is limited to 60 points.

Reversing Two Rows of Data

If you discover that you have reversed the appropriate order for two rows of data, move the cursor to one of the affected rows. If you press the Ctrl and up arrow keys, you will exchange the current row with the row above it. If you press the Ctrl and down arrow keys, you will exchange the current row with the row below it.

> **Caution:** Be careful when using the row-reverse keys. This procedure affects the data for all data series; that is, the data in *all* columns of a specified row will be moved.

40

Viewing the Chart

If you've entered the data listed in Table 2-1, you have now supplied enough information for HG to produce a fairly complete bar chart. To view the chart, simply press F2. HG immediately displays the bar chart on the screen.

Take some time to study the chart you've created. Do you like what you see? If not, what can you do to improve the chart? Although we only have a bare-bones chart at this point, you should be able to critique the title, subtitle, axis labels, and data ordering. We'll add the bells and whistles later.

Ask yourself: Does this chart serve its purpose? Why not create several versions of the chart and ask your boss or a colleague which version they like best and why. This might be best way to pick the "right" chart for the task at hand. HG lets you create several chart variations in a matter of minutes, so why not use this method?

When you finish viewing the chart, press any key to continue where you left off.

 Creating a Basic Bar Chart

1. Press 1.	Selects `Create new chart` option from the Main Menu.

2. Press 3.

Selects the Bar/Line chart option.

3. Select X data type by pressing the first letter of the data type.

Specifies the X axis data type.

4. Enter starting and ending values.

These are optional, depending on the data type.

5. Enter increment.

This is optional, depending on the data type.

6. Enter a title, subtitle, and footnote.

All charts require a title; subtitles and footnotes are optional.

7. Tab to Series 1.

Moves the cursor to the first entry of this data series (row 1, column 1).

8. Enter Series 1 data.

9. Press Home, Tab, Tab.

Moves the cursor to the first entry in Series 2 (row 1, column 2).

10. Enter Series 2 data

11. Press F2.

Displays the chart so you can check your work. □

41

Function Keys

The function keys offer you a powerful means of increasing your efficiency and creativity. If you've been paying attention, you must have noticed that the bottom two lines of the screen list one or more function keys (F1 through F10) that are active at any given point in the program. (If you press Ctrl-F, you can also see the inactive keys.) In the sections that follow, we will discuss the actions of some of the function keys.

F1 Key: On-line Help

You can always press the F1 key to display *on-line help* messages as you run HG. The help messages are *context-sensitive*; that is, the help message displayed varies according to what you are doing in the program when you press F1. In some parts of the program, HG displays several pages (screens) of help text. When multiple help pages are available, use the Pg Dn key to advance to the next help screen and the Pg Up key to review a previous help screen.

When you finish reading a help message, press Esc to return to the point in the program at which you pressed the help key.

F2 Key: Display a Chart

42

The F2 key *displays the chart* you are currently creating. You should use this key often to see how the chart is progressing. HG draws a chart rapidly, so you lose little time if you check your work frequently.

When you finish viewing the chart, press any key to continue where you left off.

F3 Key: The X Data Type Menu

You have already entered information using the X Data Type Menu. However, you might decide that you want to change the X data type, its starting or ending value, or its increment value. If the F3 key is visible near the bottom of the screen, you can press that key to recall the X Data Type Menu and then make the desired changes.

F10 Key: Continue

The F10 key is a "continuation" key that lets you proceed to the next step in the program. Note that the F10 key is *not* the same as the Esc key. As a rule, pressing Esc cancels the current operation. For example, if you are at Step 2 in creating a chart, F10 moves you to Step 3, but Esc returns you to Step 1. However, if you are at the end of a series of chart steps, F10 and Esc might produce the same results.

The remaining function keys, F4 through F9, might not be active at specific times in the program. We will discuss these keys in detail at the appropriate time.

F8 Key: Display Options

When you press the F8 key, the screen displays the first of four pages of chart options, as shown in Figure 2-6. If you scan this figure, you'll notice that you entered most, but not all, of the information on this page earlier.

All four pages of options are discussed at length in the next section.

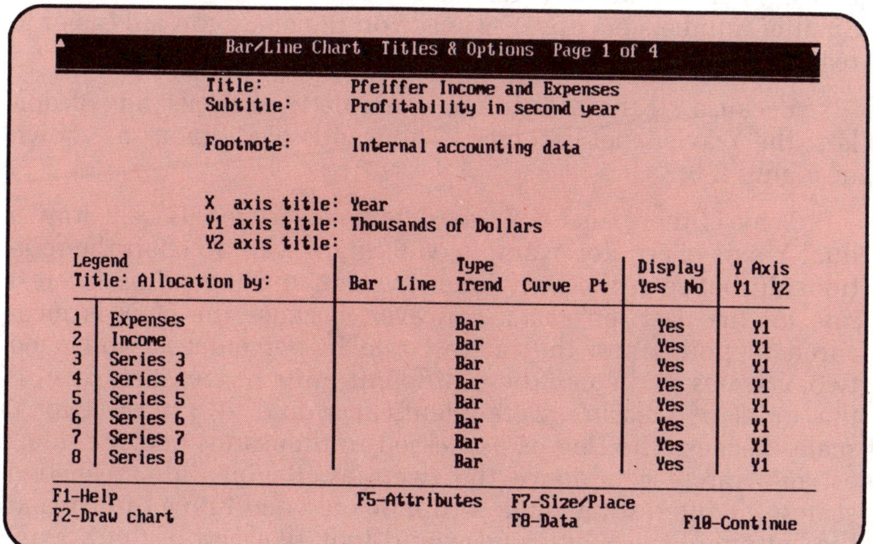

```
▲         Bar/Line Chart  Titles & Options  Page 1 of 4        ▼
              Title:      Pfeiffer Income and Expenses
              Subtitle:   Profitability in second year

              Footnote:   Internal accounting data


         X  axis title: Year
         Y1 axis title: Thousands of Dollars
         Y2 axis title:
 Legend                            Type           Display   Y Axis
 Title: Allocation by:     Bar  Line  Trend  Curve  Pt  Yes  No   Y1  Y2

     1  Expenses                   Bar                     Yes       Y1
     2  Income                     Bar                     Yes       Y1
     3  Series 3                   Bar                     Yes       Y1
     4  Series 4                   Bar                     Yes       Y1
     5  Series 5                   Bar                     Yes       Y1
     6  Series 6                   Bar                     Yes       Y1
     7  Series 7                   Bar                     Yes       Y1
     8  Series 8                   Bar                     Yes       Y1

 F1-Help                    F5-Attributes    F7-Size/Place
 F2-Draw chart                              F8-Data        F10-Continue
```

Figure 2-6.   Page 1 of the Bar/Line Chart Titles & Options Menu

The X Axis Title

If you press the Tab key three times, the cursor will be positioned in the X axis title field near the middle of the screen. Note that you did *not* identify the X axis title when you filled in the X Data Type menu (see Figure 2-2). You only told HG the *nature* of the X axis data. You now need to enter the actual title to be displayed on the chart's X axis in this field. Once again, the data will dictate the appropriate X axis title. In our example, the word "Year" is an adequate title.

The Y1 and Y2 Axes Titles

After you enter the X axis title, HG asks you to enter the Y1 axis title. Keep in mind that you generally have less space for data on the Y axis than you do on the X axis. As a result, the Y axis data is often scaled. In Figures 1-1 and 2-5, the Y axis is scaled to thousands of dollars. Because a large number on the Y axis (such as 50,000) would crowd the chart, the data must be scaled so that a smaller number (such as 50) can be used on the Y axis. Smaller numbers occupy less space on the chart and are easier to read.

44

Because all the data in our example is in thousands of dollars, the Y axis label becomes "Thousands of Dollars," as shown in Figure 2-6.

Why is there also a Y2 axis field—because HG can draw a dual Y axis chart. For example, you might want to chart the relationship between the Dow Jones average and the prime interest rate for the past ten years. However, because the Dow is measured in points and the interest rate in percentages, you need two Y scales to display these different units of measure. Even if the units of measure were identical, you'd still need two Y scales because the Dow is expressed in thousands and the interest rate rarely gets above the twenties. If you didn't use two scales, the interest rate data would be crowded into a tiny area at the bottom of the Y axis and would look like part of the X axis! Figure 2-7 shows the chart using a dual Y axis.

When we created the chart in Figure 2-7, we labeled the Y1 axis "Dow-Jones" and the Y2 axis "Interest Rate." We needed to specify a different title for each axis because the two sets of data are measured in different units.

Because the chart in our example (Figure 1-1) doesn't need a Y2 axis label, leave this field blank. Press the Tab key to advance the cursor to the Legend Title field.

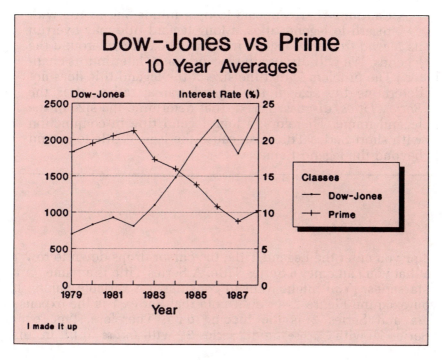

Figure 2-7.   *A dual Y axis chart*

▶ **Tip:** Keep the Y1 and Y2 labels short so that they don't crowd each other, but make them long enough to be informative.

Legend Title

The Legend Title field holds a brief description of the data represented by the bars in the chart. I don't know why, but I struggle with this field. I have a hard time coming up with one or two words that describe *both* data series. If all else fails, you can always use "generic" words such as "classes," "categories," or "series." In Figure 1-1, I used "Allocation by:" for the Legend Title. (I told you I wasn't good at it.) If words fail you completely, merely omit the Legend Title.

> ⊘ **Caution:** There appears to be a minor bug in HG with regard to legend titles: a long legend title may overrun its *legend frame*. (A legend frame is a box drawn around the legends. We will discuss the legend frame later in this chapter.) The problem is that the size of the legend title does not determine the size of the legend frame; rather, it is the *Series Titles*, discussed next, that determine the size of the legend frame. Therefore, a long legend title in conjunction with short Series Titles can cause the legend title to extend beyond the legend frame.

Series Titles

46

After you enter the Legend Title, the cursor drops down to row 1 so that you can enter a Series Title. A Series Title is a name for a data series. (You might want to consider it a variable name.) If you examine Figure 2-4, you'll note that Series 1 is the expense data and Series 2 is the income data. Therefore, type over "Series 1" with Expenses and "Series 2" with Income to fill in this field.

By default, HG is in overstrike mode, so you can type "Expenses" right over the "Series 1" that appears in the first row, as shown in Figure 2-6. Press Enter when you finish typing. The cursor will drop down to the second row (Series 2).

Because the word "Income" is shorter than "Series 1," merely typing "Income" produces the phrase "Income 1." Thus, you might want to clear this line by pressing Ctrl-Del before you enter the second Series Title.

Chart Types: How Data is Graphed

The next field shown in Figure 2-6 is the chart Type, which determines how HG displays the data graphically. The options—Bar, Line, Trend, Curve, and Pt (Point)—fall into three broad categories: bar charts, line charts, and scatter (point) plots.

Press the Tab key to move from the Series Titles column to the Type column. Within this field, you can use the up arrow to move to the first row entry. The default setting is Bar, which results in the data being graphed as a now-familiar bar chart.

▶ **Tip:** The length of your Series Titles has a twofold impact on the chart. First, the size of the legend frame varies directly with the length of the Series Titles. Therefore, short Series Titles produce a small legend frame. As we mentioned earlier, a long Legend Title will likely extend beyond the legend frame, which looks pretty tacky.

Second, if you increase the size of the Series Titles, the legend frame becomes larger. The good news is that the Legend Title probably won't overrun the legend frame. The bad news is that long Series Titles and a big legend frame shrinks the chart itself. After all, there's a limit to the space available for the chart and its elements. You can opt not to have a legend frame, and that forestalls a legend title overrun problem. (It doesn't solve it.) However, you must still strike a balance between the length of the Series names and the size of the chart.

You probably should keep Series Titles as short as possible so that the chart is allocated most of the available space.

47

Two Ways to Select a Chart Type

If you press the right arrow key, the highlight moves to the Line option. If you then press Enter, you are directing HG to draw the Expenses data as a line chart. If you press the right arrow key a second time, you'll advance the highlight to the Trend option, and so on. Use the arrow keys to select the appropriate chart type.

An easier way to select a chart type is to use the pseudo hot keys. The first letter of each chart type is the pseudo hot key; that is, pressing L selects Line, B selects Bar, and so on. Notice that the chart type in row 1 changes as you press a pseudo hot key.

When you press Enter, the highlighted chart type becomes the type of chart HG creates for the specified data series. For example, if you are in row 1 of Figure 2-6 and you select the Trend option, HG automatically inserts the new choice into row 1 of the Type field and then charts the Expenses data as a trend line when it draws the chart.

> ▶ **Tip:** You can use different chart types in a single chart; that is, you can show one data series as a bar chart and another as a line chart. Be careful when you do this, because mixing chart types might confuse the viewer.

Bar Charts. A bar chart is used most often to show changes in a data series over time (a flow variable). Most of the charts presented thus far use time for the X axis. However, a bar chart is also useful for showing the distribution of data at a point in time (a stock variable). For example, you might create a bar chart showing the distribution of the final exam grades for a class.

Line Charts. A line chart is used to emphasize the movement or variability of data over time. In fact, line charts can be boring if the data series does not exhibit pronounced changes. After all, if company sales have been flat for the past five years, most people can picture that data without needing a line chart.

48

Trend Charts. A trend chart is used to show the general movement of data over time. A trend chart uses a *least squares regression* algorithm to produce a line that best represents the movement of the data. A trend chart always produces a straight line. However, HG also plots the actual data points that generate the trend line. If the data points lie close to the line, the trend line is useful for forecasting future movement of the data. (Indeed, regression analysis is a cornerstone of many forecasting models.)

> ▶ **Tip:** Using a trend chart to forecast the movement of a variable is always interesting. However, be aware that HG does *not* provide any support statistics as to how good or bad the trend line fits the data. Also, the trend line does not indicate how far into the future you can expect the trend to continue. However, there are statistical packages available, such as Microstat-II, that you can use in conjunction with HG to provide such supporting data.

Curve Charts. A curve chart attempts to fit a smooth curve through the raw data points. HG uses a *spline* algorithm to generate the curve. This chart is useful for graphing data that exhibits wide variations over time, such as products that show seasonal fluctuations. For example, the demand for gasoline rises in the spring, peaks during the late summer months and then falls off dramatically. The demand for oil follows a similar pattern, but has *two* high points—one during the winter due to the demand for heating oil and the other during the summer driving months. A curve chart can make these cyclical patterns more apparent, especially if you are plotting many data points. (Note that the curve might not pass directly through all of the data points.)

Point (Pt) Charts. A point chart, also called a scatterplot, simply displays the data as dots—the data points are *not* connected by a line. Point plots are useful for showing natural groupings or clusters of data, for identifying trends, or for emphasizing correlations between various data series. A point plot is like a Line plot without the lines between points.

> ▶ **Tip:** The actual type of chart that you select depends upon what you are trying to accomplish. Because it takes only a few seconds to change Chart Types, you should experiment and see how your data looks when graphed on each type of chart.

49

Display

The Display option lets you decide whether or not a given data series will be displayed. In some instances, you will want to enter the data for four or five data series in a single chart and then decide later which of the series you want to show. This option lets you "turn off" those data series that you don't want to display without actually deleting the data. You can then create different charts using different data series by simply turning off the unwanted series.

The Y Axis

The last chart option, Y Axis, determines whether the data is displayed using the Y1 or Y2 axis. The chart in Figure 1-1 shows both Income and Expenses using the Y1 axis. The chart in Figure 2-7, however, shows the Dow-Jones data using the Y1 Axis and the Interest Rate using the Y2 axis.

You will not need to change this option from its default setting of Y1 unless you are using a chart with dual Y axes.

Q Changing a Bar Chart to a Different Chart

1. From the HG Main Menu, press 4.

   Selects the Get/Save/Remove menu so that you can load a chart.

2. Press 1.

   Presents a list of existing charts.

3. Highlight a Bar/Line Type chart and press Enter.

   Loads the selected chart and displays it on the screen.

4. Press the spacebar.

   Ends chart viewing so that you can continue entering data.

5. Press F8.

   Activates Page 1 of the Chart Titles & Options menu.

6. Tab to the Type field.

7. Press the letter of new chart type for the series.

   Depending on the letter pressed, selects a bar line, trend, curve, or point chart.

8. Press F2.

   Displays the new chart. □

50

Bar/Line Chart Titles & Options: Page 2

After you finish entering data and selecting options on Page 1 of the chart Titles & Options menu, press F8 to activate Page 2 and display more chart options.

Bar Styles

Page 2 of the Bar/Line Chart Titles & Options input screen is shown in Figure 2-8. The first field determines the style of bar to be used in the chart. The chart in Figure 1-1 uses the Cluster style of bar. Feel free to experiment with each of the various bar styles using the Pfeiffer Company data.

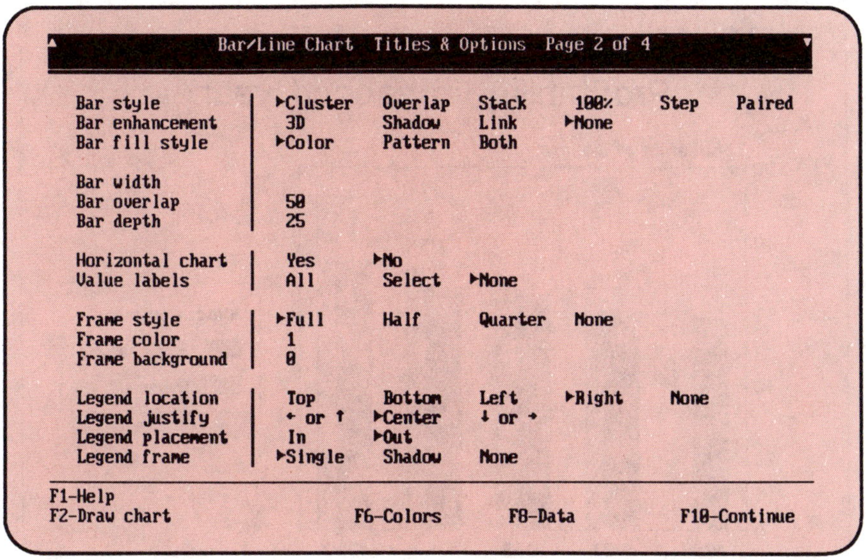

```
┌─────────────────────────────────────────────────────────────┐
│ ▲        Bar/Line Chart  Titles & Options  Page 2 of 4     ▼ │
│                                                               │
│   Bar style          ►Cluster  Overlap  Stack    100%  Step   Paired │
│   Bar enhancement     3D       Shadow   Link    ►None         │
│   Bar fill style     ►Color    Pattern  Both                  │
│                                                               │
│   Bar width                                                   │
│   Bar overlap         50                                      │
│   Bar depth           25                                      │
│                                                               │
│   Horizontal chart    Yes      ►No                            │
│   Value labels        All      Select   ►None                 │
│                                                               │
│   Frame style        ►Full     Half     Quarter  None         │
│   Frame color         1                                       │
│   Frame background    0                                       │
│                                                               │
│   Legend location     Top      Bottom   Left    ►Right  None  │
│   Legend justify      ← or ↑   ►Center  ↓ or →                │
│   Legend placement    In       ►Out                           │
│   Legend frame       ►Single   Shadow   None                  │
│                                                               │
│  F1-Help                                                      │
│  F2-Draw chart              F6-Colors      F8-Data      F10-Continue │
└─────────────────────────────────────────────────────────────┘
```

51

Figure 2-8. Page 2 of the Bar/Line Chart Titles & Options menu

Cluster Bars

A Cluster bar is the most common style of bar. However, cluster bars do not work well with a large number of data points. The chart becomes crowded when there are more than a dozen bars, and much of the visual impact is lost. If you plan to plot more than 12 data points, you should consider an alternate bar style, such as a step bar, or a different type of chart altogether, such as a line chart.

Overlap Bars

In the Overlap style, one set of bars appears in front of another set of bars. Bars are overlapped starting with Series 1 data in the front and ending with the last series in the back. For example, in Figure 2-9, because Expenses is the Series 1 data and Income is the Series 2 data, Expenses appear in the front bars and Income appears in the rear bars. Because of the overlapping, the Expenses bars are shown as full bars, but only part of the Income bars can be seen.

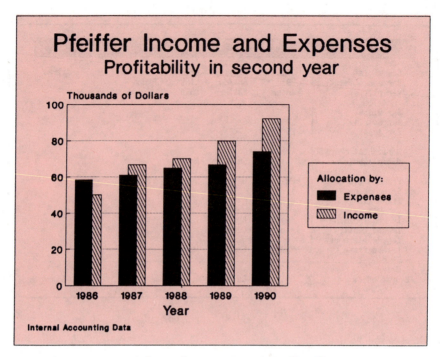

Figure 2-9.   A bar chart using Overlap bars

52

▶ **Tip:** When using Overlap bars, be sure the data series with the smallest values is entered as Series 1 and that data series follow in ascending order. Otherwise, the bars in the foreground will hide the other data bars.

Overlap bars are most effective when you want to emphasize the frontmost data series and when the frontmost data series has smaller values than the other data series.

Stack Bars

In Stack bar style, the series data is placed one on top of another. This makes Stack bars an ideal choice when you want to combine two or more data series in a single bar. For example, you could use Stack bars to show the annual sales data from several different sales offices. If there are four sales offices, the chart would have four bars stacked on top of one another (Series 1 through 4), with the total height showing total sales for the company by year.

> ▶ **Tip:** The Stack bar style lets you summarize data series into a total. Pie charts also show data series combined as a whole, but Stack bars are more effective when you want to graph the summary data for more than two time periods.

100% Bars

The 100% bar style shows each data series proportionally with respect to the total. Thus, the bars in the chart are all the same height, but within bars the portions representing each data series will vary.

53

> ▶ **Tip:** You should use 100% bars when you want to emphasize how the parts of a whole vary over time. Because 100% bars are the same height, they are *not* a good choice when you want to emphasize how the *total* amount varies over time; stacked bars would be a better choice for that.

Figure 2-10 presents the Pfeiffer Company data using 100% bars. Note that the Y axis now shows percentages instead of dollar amounts because the units of measure for both data series must be the same. If the Series 1 data were sales measured in dollars and Series 2 were production figures expressed in tons, a 100% bar would be meaningless. (The Y axis would show the percentage of "tons of dollars!")

Step Bars

Step bars are similar to normal Cluster bars, except that the bars adjoin one another; there is no gap between bars. Step bars are therefore useful when the distribution of the data is continuous rather than discrete. In a discrete distribution, each item is an indivisible unit. A car, for example, is counted in whole units. What does 1.5 cars mean? On the other hand, cloth yardage production is measured continuously, so 1.5 yards of linen does

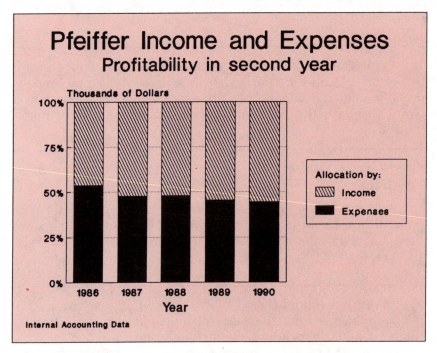

*Figure 2-10. Pfeiffer Company Income and
Expense graphed as 100% bars*

make sense. If you are familiar with statistics, you'll recognize
the normal distribution curve, the *bell curve*, as another example
of continuous distribution. It too can be plotted using Step bars.

▶ **Tip:** Step bars work best with many data points. With a
small number of data points, the chart looks "chunky"
and is not very pleasing to the eye. If your data contains
fewer than 12 points, you might want to use Cluster, Overlap, or Stack bars instead of Step bars.

Paired Bars

Paired bars can be used when the data series have a common X
axis but different Y axes. Figure 2-11 shows the Pfeiffer Company data using Paired bars.

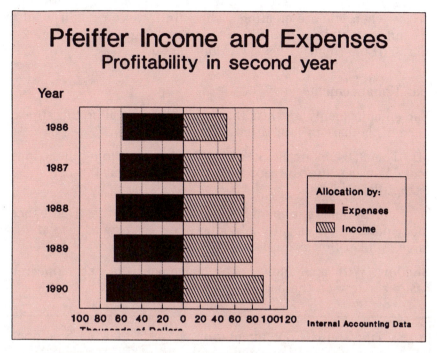

Figure 2-11. Pfeiffer Company Income and Expenses graphed as Paired bars

When Paired bars are used, the *zeropoint* is located at the center of the chart and the two series are scaled outward to the left and right from the center. The Series 1 data is scaled to the left; Series 2 is scaled to the right. Note that you must have activated the Y2 axis for the Series 2 data to create a Paired bar chart. (See the Y Axis field—the last column of Figure 2-6.)

You might think that a Paired bars chart could accommodate only two data series. Not so. If you specify more than two series, HG merely stacks the data on the Paired bars.

> ▶ **Tip:** HG doesn't seem to like negative values when Paired bars are used. To see the (ugly?) impact of negative data, change the first income figure for the Pfeiffer Company to −50. (Be sure the Y Axis field for Income is set to Y2.)

55

Again, HG makes it easy to experiment with different bar styles when you are creating a chart. In fact, you might want to try out each style as you fill in the remaining fields on Page 2 of the Bar/Line Chart Titles & Options menu.

Bar Enhancements

Bar enhancements are just that—they let you alter the appearance of the bars in four different ways:

3D. The 3D enhancement gives the bars a three-dimensional look. You can use this enhancement with all of the bar styles, except Paired bars.

Unlike other bar enhancement alternatives, the 3D enhancement produces a visually pleasing effect even with a relatively large number (for example, 20) of data points.

56

Shadow. With a Shadow bar enhancement the bars appear to cast a shadow on the back "wall" of the chart.

> ▶ **Tip:** The HG documentation suggests that the Shadow enhancement is available only with Cluster, Stack, and 100% bars. In fact, you can also use Shadow with Paired and Overlap bars.

The Shadow enhancement works best when the total number of bars on the chart is relatively small (less than 10). When more than 10 data points are used, the chart looks too "busy," which detracts from the overall impact of the chart.

Link. The Link enhancement (available only with Stack and 100% bars) merely connects adjacent bars with a dotted line. This ties the bars together visually, an effect that diminishes, however, as the number of bars increases.

None. Select the None option if you don't want to use any bar enhancements. This is the default setting for bar enhancements.

The number of data points and the style of bar used are the primary factors that determine whether or not a particular enhancement "works." You should experiment with different bar styles and bar enhancements until you find the combination that presents your data most effectively.

▶ **Tip:** Although the 3D effect is visually more interesting than two-dimensional renderings, it is especially dramatic with Overlap bars, as shown in Figure 2-12. Just a reminder—when using Overlap bars, be sure the data series with the smallest values is designated as Series 1. Otherwise the bars representing this data will be obscured by the bars of the other data series.

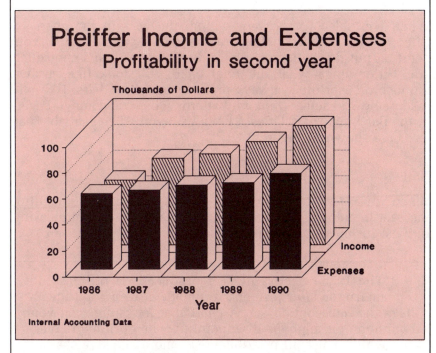

Figure 2-12.   Overlap bars with the 3D enhancement

Bar Fill Style

These options let you display bars in color and alter the pattern HG uses to fill the bars.

Color

When you set the Color option, the bars used in the chart are displayed in color. This option does not let you set the actual colors of the bars. (Setting the bar colors is discussed later in this chapter in the section about Page 4 of the Bar/Line Chart Titles & Options menu.)

Pattern

When you select the Pattern option, the bars in the chart are filled with a hatched pattern rather than a solid color. If your chart output device is not a color device, setting this choice lets you better judge what the final chart will look like because monochrome printers always produce patterned bars. (We will discuss how to select different patterns when we come to Page 4 of the Bar/Line Chart Titles & Options menu.) The available patterns are shown in Figure 2-20.

58

Both

When you select the Both option, HG displays the pattern filling the bars in color. The visual effect of this choice is not pleasing. In most instances, you should select either Color or Pattern.

> ▶ **Tip:** If the chart will be reproduced on ordinary dot matrix or laser printers, it might not be a good idea to have the Color option set. A chart that looks great on your color monitor might be disappointing when printed in black and white. You will probably create more effective charts if you turn the color option off.
>
> On the other hand, if the chart will be displayed on a color monitor or in a slide show, or reproduced on a color printer or film recorder, you will definitely want the Color option turned on. (We will discuss different output devices in a later chapter.)

Bar Width

You can vary the width of bars used in charts from thin (a width of 1) to fat (a width of 100). If you set the value in the Bar Width field to 100, a Cluster bar chart ends up looking like a Step bar chart. Although not displayed on-screen, the default bar width is approximately 50.

> ▶ **Tip:** If you have a large number of data points along the X axis, reducing the bar width will make the chart appear less cluttered. If the number of data points exceeds 30, you should consider using another type of chart, such as a line chart.

Bar Overlap

If you use Overlap bars in a chart, this value determines how much of the second bar is visible. As we mentioned earlier in the chapter, the first data series is shown as a full bar and subsequent data series bars are drawn behind the first bar. If you set the value in the Bar overlap field to 10, about 90 percent of the second bar is visible. If the setting is 90, only a sliver of the second bar is visible.

59

> ▶ **Tip:** If an Overlap bar chart looks crowded, try increasing the Bar overlap value. Less of the second bar will be visible, but the chart will appear to have more open space.

If you specify an Overlap bar with the 3D enhancement, the value in the Bar overlap field determines the spacing between bar rows. In this instance, low values for the Bar overlap will make the rows appear closer together, thereby reducing the 3D effect. Low values also cause the Series Titles to run together.

Bar Depth

The setting in the Bar depth field has meaning only when the Bar Enhancement setting is 3D. The default setting is 25. As the Bar depth value increases, the bars show greater depth in the direction away from the viewer, that is, toward the back of the chart.

▶ **Tip:** As a rule, the depth of a 3D bar should not exceed its height; otherwise, the chart will look "heavy" and "sluggish."

Horizontal Chart

This option lets you rotate the X and Y axes. As a result, the bars are displayed horizontally rather than vertically. One advantage of a horizontal chart is that it can accommodate a larger number of bars without looking crowded. If you will be using a large number of bars, you might want to experiment with this option to see if it improves the appearance of your chart.

60

Value Labels

The Value Labels option lets you place numeric values at the top of the bars. If the Y Axis Label field (discussed later in this chapter) of Page 4 of the Titles & Options menu is set to Yes, you can select the specific bars to be displayed with a numeric value. The default option is None, in which case numeric labels are not displayed.

▶ **Tip:** The All choice for Value Labels will probably cause the numeric values to run together, even with a small number of bars. The chart will then look messy and the numeric values will be difficult to read. If you use numeric labels, consider using them on every other bar or only on those bars that emphasize the point you are trying to make.

Frame Style

The Frame Style option determines the extent of the frame drawn around the bars. Figure 2-13 demonstrates the type of frame that is drawn in each of the three styles.

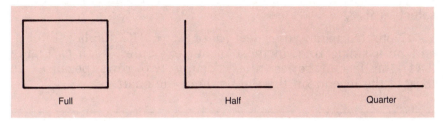

Figure 2-13.   Chart frames drawn in Full, Half, and Quarter styles

The `Full` option draws a box around the bars while the `Half` option only produces the X and Y axes that are common to graphs. The `Quarter` option simply draws the X axis. Most business charts look best with the Full frame style.

Frame Color and Frame Background

61

These options determine the colors that HG uses for the frame and the background of the chart. The default colors are a white frame on a black background. This is a good choice for most charts because of the high contrast, which makes the chart easy to read. Note that the `Frame color` option also determines the color of the grid lines and legend frame (if they are present in the chart).

To experiment with the frame and background colors, press F6. HG then displays a list that lets you choose new colors (see Figure 2-19). Highlight a color by using the arrow keys or mouse to move up or down within the list. Press Enter to select the highlighted color.

If the chart will ultimately be reproduced in color, you should select colors that emphasize the bars, not the background. If the chart will be displayed in black and white, simply use the default setting.

Legend Location

The `Legend location` field lets you place a legend at any of the four edges of a chart by selecting the appropriate option: `Top`, `Bottom`,

Left, or Right. If you don't want to use a legend in the chart, select None.

Note that when you select Top or Bottom, HG displays the legend on a single line. In most of our examples, such as Figure 2-11, the legend series titles occupy two rows because we located the legend on the right side of the chart.

> ► **Tip:** The location of the legend has an impact on the height of the bars in the chart. A legend placed at the top or bottom compresses the bars and can give the chart a "squatty" look. ("Squatty" is a technical term for "not good.") Most charts look best with the legend on the right side of the chart.

62 *Legend Justify*

The Legend justify field lets you position the legend more precisely within the bounds of the location you selected in the previous field. For example, if you selected the Right legend location, the Center justify option will position the legend near the center of the chart (at the right side). The ↑ justify option will place the legend toward the top of the chart and the ↓ option will place it toward the bottom. If you selected either Top or Bottom for the Legend location, the ← option places the legend toward the left side of the chart (at the top or bottom) and the → option moves it toward the right side.

> ► **Tip:** When positioning the legend, be sure it does not crowd the X or Y axis labels. Try to keep as much space as possible between labels.

Legend Placement

You can place a legend within the chart frame (with the In option) or outside it (with the Out option). In all the charts we have created thus far, the legends are placed outside the frame. However, this is a matter of personal preference more than anything else.

> ► **Tip:** The legend takes foreground precedence in the drawing of the chart. Therefore, if you place the legend inside the frame where the bars are normally drawn, the legend will "overwrite" the bars. The nature of the data will often dictate where you should place the legend within the frame. For example, if your data shows a rising trend over time, you might have no choice but to place the legend on the left side of the chart so that the legend does not overwrite the bars.

Legend Frame

If you select a legend frame, HG draws a box around the legend. Two styles of boxes can be used. The Single option draws a single line around the legend. Almost all of the charts we have drawn use this style. The Shadow option also draws a box around the legend but gives a three-dimensional effect by placing a shadow behind the legend. You can see this shadow effect in the legend frame of Figure 2-7.

63

Bar/Line Chart Titles & Options: Page 3

Page 3 of the Titles & Options menu, shown in Figure 2-14, presents additional ways to alter the appearance of a chart. Most of the options on this screen affect the display of the chart axes.

Data Table

The Data Table field lets you display the data used to construct the bars in the chart. In the example shown in Figure 2-15, we selected the Normal option in this field; note that the raw data for the Pfeiffer Income and Expenses chart appears below the chart.

```
┌─────────────────────────────────────────────────────────────────────┐
│ ▲        Bar/Line Chart  Titles & Options  Page 3 of 4           ▼   │
│  ─────────────────────────────────────────────────────────────────  │
│   Data Table        │  Normal    Framed   ▶None                      │
│                                                                       │
│   X  Axis Labels    │ ▶Normal    Vertical   %        None            │
│   Y1 Axis Labels    │ ▶Value     $          %        None            │
│   Y2 Axis Labels    │ ▶Value     $          %        None            │
│                                                                       │
│   X  Grid Lines     │  · · · ·   ──────   ▶None                      │
│   Y1 Grid Lines     │ ▶· · · ·   ──────    None                      │
│   Y2 Grid Lines     │ ▶· · · ·   ──────    None                      │
│                                                                       │
│   X Tick Mark Style │ ▶In        Out       Both      None            │
│   Y Tick Mark Style │ ▶In        Out       Both      None            │
│                     │                                                 │
│                        X Axis    │    Y1 Axis    │    Y2 Axis         │
│  ─────────────────────────────────────────────────────────────────  │
│   Scale Type        │ ▶Linear  Log  │ ▶Linear  Log  │ ▶Linear  Log   │
│   Format            │                                                 │
│   Minimum Value     │                                                 │
│   Maximum Value     │                                                 │
│   Increment         │                                                 │
│  ─────────────────────────────────────────────────────────────────  │
│   F1-Help                                                             │
│   F2-Draw chart                       F8-Data        F10-Continue     │
└─────────────────────────────────────────────────────────────────────┘
```

*Figure 2-14.   Page 3 of the Bar/Line Chart Titles &
Options menu*

If the Framed option had been selected, this same data table
would appear with frame lines drawn around it. Obviously, the
None option omits the data table from the chart.

> ▶ **Tip:** In most cases, the addition of a data table makes
> the chart appear busy and crowded. Also, the presence
> of a data table reduces the overall size of the chart. If you
> want the viewer to have access to the raw data, consider
> creating a separate chart for the raw data.

The X Axis Labels

The X Axis Labels option lets you alter the orientation of the labels
on the X axis. The Normal (default) option displays the labels
using the values you inserted in the Starting with and Ending with
fields of the X Data Type Menu. In the example shown in Figure
2-2, the starting value is 1986; therefore, the Normal option would
print the label "1986" horizontally.

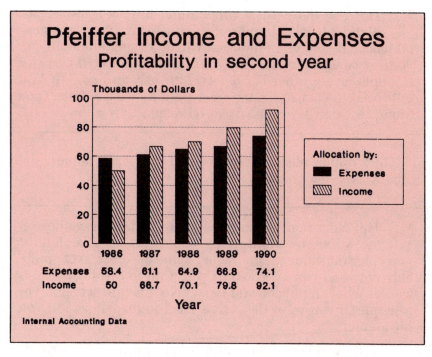

Figure 2-15.   *A bar chart with the Data Table set to Normal*

The Vertical option prints the X axis labels vertically (surprise!); that is, instead of the label "1986" being displayed as:

1986

it would be displayed as:

1
9
8
6

The advantage of the Vertical option is that you can label more bars without crowding the X axis. The disadvantage is that it reduces the vertical size of the chart.

> ▶ **Tip:** Use the vertical orientation only as a last resort. Vertical labels are more difficult to read than horizontal labels. If your chart looks crowded, a better alternative to vertical labels is to label only a limited number of bars (for example, every other bar, every fifth bar, and so on). You will need to change the Increment option of the X Data Type Menu to cause fewer labels to be displayed on the X axis.

The % option places a percent sign after each numeric label on the X axis (for example, 10%).

66

> ▶ **Tip:** Note that HG automatically scales the values on the X axis by multiplying them by 100. Therefore, if you enter the value 50, the scaled value becomes 5000%, probably not what you expected. If you want to display percentages as whole numbers, you must take this into account. For example, if you want the X axis label to display as 50%, you must enter .5.
>
> If, however, you have already entered all of your data as whole numbers instead of decimal fractions, you can fix the chart more easily by changing the scale rather than retyping the data. (We will discuss how this is done later in the chapter.)

The Y1 and Y2 Axes Labels

The fields for Y1 and Y2 Axis Labels are similar to that of the X Axis Labels. By default, the label on the Y axis is a numeric value. The $ option places a dollar sign before each numeric value (for example, $100). The % option places a percent sign after each Y axis value after multiplying the value by 100, just as it did for the X axis value. Selecting the None option omits the values from the vertical axis.

The options for the Y1 and Y2 Axis Label fields are identical. Remember that you must have the Y Axis option on Page 1 of the Titles & Options menu set to Y2 for the Y2 label to be displayed. (See the last column of Figure 2-6.)

> ▶ **Tip:** Use the $ and % options sparingly. If you title the Y
> axes correctly, you will not need dollar or percent
> signs on your labels.

The X, Y1, Y2 Grid Lines

The X Grid Lines, Y1 Grid Lines, and Y2 Grid Lines fields have the
same three options, so we can discuss them as a group. These
options are grids using dotted lines (....), solid grid lines (____),
and no grid lines (None).

Your choice of grid lines will depend upon the data you are
charting. If the general trend of the data is more important than
the specific data values, your chart will be more effective without grid lines. Also note that a dotted grid line provides a frame
of reference for the bars with less intrusion on the chart than a
solid grid line.

67

> ▶ **Tip:** Grid lines extending from the X axis on a bar chart
> are rarely a good idea. After all, variations in the data
> are usually expressed along the Y axis; that is, in the height
> of the bars. Grid lines make those variations more obvious
> to the viewer. The X axis labels should appear without grid
> lines except, of course, if the chart has a horizontal orienta-
> tion. In that instance, you would use X axis grid lines and
> omit the Y axis grid lines.

The X and Y Tick Mark Style

The similarity between the X and Y Tick Mark Style fields lets us
discuss them together. A *tick mark* represents a point on the
chart scale. It gives the viewer a visual frame of reference for the
values used in the chart. The three types of tick marks are
shown in Figure 2-16.

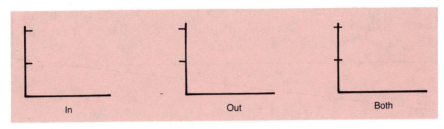

Figure 2-16.   *Tick Mark Style options (Y Axis only)*

The In option positions the tick marks inside the chart frame; the Out option positions the tick marks outside the chart frame; and the Both option displays short tick marks on both sides of the chart frame. Obviously, the None option draws the chart without tick marks.

When you select Out for tick marks on the X axis, the X axis labels are shifted slightly downward. Using Out tick marks for the Y axis helps tie the Y axis values to the chart. When you select the Both option, the tick marks are less obtrusive yet still serve as helpful scale markers.

> ▶ **Tip:** Tick marks are particularly useful when a chart has large gaps between the Y axes labels and there are many data values on the X axis.

Scale Type

The Scale Type field lets you select between Linear and Log scales for each axis. A linear scale is equally spaced over the entire range of the axis. Because a linear scale is used in almost all charts, HG makes it the default scale type.

The Log scale option uses base 10 logarithms for the axis scale. Log scales are suited to data that shows either a geometric or exponential rate of change. Everything from new business ventures to bacterial growth can exhibit rates of change best suited to a Log scale. Because a small portion of a log scale encompasses a wide range of values, log scales can accommodate data over a very wide range.

68

> ⊘ **Caution:** Use log scales only when necessary. Because log scales are not used very often, they might be confusing to your viewers.

Note that you can set the Scale Type options for the X, Y1, and Y2 axes independently.

Format

The Format field lets you determine how the values on the X, Y1, and Y2 axes are displayed. The four basic format entries—comma, number, vertical bar, and exclamation point—can be used individually or combined to display the data in a variety of formats.

69

Comma

The comma format option displays numbers with a comma separating every three digits. For example, if you entered the data 2300500, HG would display it as 2,300,500. The comma makes the axis values easier to read.

> ▶ **Tip:** Normally you would not use axis values large enough to require commas. Recall that large X axis values crowd each other rather quickly and that large Y axis values can shrink the size of the chart itself. Scaling the data typically creates a more readable chart; that is, instead of displaying 2,300,500 on the axis, it is better to use 2.3 with an axis label that reads Millions.

Number

The number format option lets you specify the number of decimal places you want displayed. For example, if you entered 4 in the Format field, the value 1.5 would be displayed as 1.5000. If you don't enter a number in the Format field, no decimal places are displayed, unless the raw data itself contains decimal fractions.

Vertical Bar

You can use a vertical bar (|) to display text before or after a number. For example, if you want to show axis values in German marks, the Format entry

DM |

would display the axis value 25 as follows:

DM 25

If you want to show axis values in Canadian dollars, the Format entry

$| (Can.)

would display the value 25 as:

$25 (Can.)

The Format field entry

$|2 (Can.)

would display the axis value 25 as:

$25.00 (Can.)

70

> ▶ **Tip:** The text to be displayed before or after an axis value should be as short as possible, because HG will reduce the size of the chart to make room for the added text.

If you precede the vertical bar with a number, all axis values are divided by that number. For example, if the Format field for the Y2 axis (Interest Rate) in Figure 2-7 were

100 |

the topmost Y2 axis value would change from 25 to .25, the next value from 20 to .20, and so on.

> ▶ **Tip:** Being able to scale the axis values in this manner can save you a lot of unnecessary typing. For example, if you are charting mil deviations for a machine part, a typical value might be .0015. Typing the decimal point and leading zeros gets old in a hurry. It is much easier to enter the value as 15 and then use
>
>   `10000 |`
>
> in the `Format` field. This displays the appropriate values (including .0015) on the chart, with a lot less typing.

Exclamation Point

If the `Format` field has an exclamation point (!) in it, the axis values are displayed in scientific notation. If the axis value is entered as `1234`, HG displays it as `1.234E + 03`. (Scientific notation expresses numbers in powers of ten.)

71

Additional Format Field Characters

`Format` field entries are not limited to commas, numbers, vertical bars, and exclamation points; HG accepts all 128 characters in the standard ASCII (American Standard Code for Information Interchange) character set. The ASCII character set uses the numbers 0 through 127 to represent various alphanumeric characters. However, IBM developed an extended character set for the PC that includes the values from 128 to 255. HG also accepts *some* of these extended characters in your charts. For example, if you want to precede a value with the symbol for the British pound, hold down the Alt key and type `156` on the numeric keypad. When you release the Alt key, the British pound sign will appear in the Format field.

There are several characters in the IBMEC set that would be useful for constructing charts, but they are not available in HG. For example, not all of the Greek letters used in mathematics and statistics are available. The symbols for infinity and the square root sign would also be useful. Alas, HG rejects most of them.

> ⊘ **Caution:** Not all characters in the IBM extended charac-
> ter (IBMEC) set can be used in a chart. As a rule, none of
> the character graphics symbols can be used. The following
> numbers *cannot* be entered into the Format field: 155, 157-159,
> 169-172, 176-224, 234-237, 249-250, 252-253, and 255. Note
> that although you might be able to generate some of these
> characters in the Format field, HG cannot use them in your
> chart.

Minimum and Maximum Values

These two fields let you set the minimum and maximum values
that appear on the chart, thereby overriding the automatic scaling done by HG.

A word of warning: One of the classic methods of distorting
data is the "broken axis" technique. For example, the last 30
days of the Dow-Jones averages are less dramatic if you chart
them with a scale that ranges from 0 to 3,000 than if you chart
them with a range from 2400 to 2800. If the scale starts at 0, the
Dow-Jones averages will look fairly flat, but if the scale starts at
2400, the averages might well look like a roller coaster!

TV commercials and even major network news programs
use this technique to emphasize a point when it would look less
dramatic otherwise. If you decide to set the minimum and maximum values yourself, you should be prepared to explain why.

It is probably obvious that the minimum value must be less
than the maximum value. Also, the minimum value must be less
than the smallest value in the data series.

Increment

The Increment field determines the frequency with which an axis
label is displayed. If you find that the axis labels run together,
such as on an X axis with many annual data points, simply use a
larger increment. For example, the X axis in Figure 2-7 (Dow
Jones vs Prime) uses an increment of 2; the first X axis label is
1979, followed by 1981, and so on. If we wanted the Y1 axis
labels in this same figure to increase by 750 instead of the cur-

rent increment of 500, we would set the Increment value to 750 in the Y1 column.

Exercise caution, however. Using Figure 2-7 as an example, if you set the Y1 increment value to 1000, the Y1 axis labels become 1, 2, and 3. This causes much of the impact of the chart to be lost because a Dow-Jones of 1, 2, or 3 doesn't make much sense, given that it is usually expressed on a scale of 0 to several thousand. You might have to experiment a bit to find the balance between too many labels crowding the screen and too few labels making the data meaningless.

Bar/Line Chart Titles & Options: Page 4

The final page of the Titles & Options menu is shown in Figure 2-17. The top half of the page is identical to the first page of the Titles & Options menu. (Compare Figure 2-6 with Figure 2-17.)

```
▲        Bar/Line Chart  Titles & Options  Page 4 of 4        ▼

          Title:        Pfeiffer Income and Expenses
          Subtitle:     Profitability in second year

          Footnote:     Internal Accounting Data

          X  axis title: Year
          Y1 axis title: Thousands of Dollars
          Y2 axis title:
     Legend                    Cum     Y Label   Color   Marker/    Line
     Title: Allocation by:     Yes  No  Yes  No            Pattern   Style

     1   Expenses              No      No        2       1          1
     2   Income                No      No        3       2          1
     3   Series 3              No      No        4       3          1
     4   Series 4              No      No        5       4          1
     5   Series 5              No      No        6       5          1
     6   Series 6              No      No        7       6          1
     7   Series 7              No      No        8       7          1
     8   Series 8              No      No        9       8          1

     F1-Help                   F5-Attributes  F7-Size/Place
     F2-Draw chart             F6-Colors      F8-Data           F10-Continue
```

Figure 2-17. Page 4 of the Bar/Line Chart Titles & Options

There are, however, several options appearing in the top half of the page that we have postponed discussing until now.

These options concern the size and placement of the chart titles and labels.

F7 Key: Title Size and Placement Options

If you press F7, you will activate a small submenu of options that let you alter the size and placement of the chart titles. This submenu can be seen in the upper left corner of Figure 2-18.

Size	Place			Bar/Line Chart Titles & Options Page 4 of 4	▼
8	L ▸C	R	Title:	Pfeiffer Income and Expenses	
6	L ▸C	R	Subtitle:	Profitability in second year	
6	L ▸C	R			
2.5	▸L C	R	Footnote:	Internal Accounting Data	
2.5	▸L C	R			
2.5	▸L C	R			
4	▸C		X axis title:	Year	
3	▸▸ ↓		Y1 axis title:	Thousands of Dollars	
3	▸▸ ↓		Y2 axis title:		

| | X labels | Cum | Y Label | Color | Marker/ | Line |
	Y labels ion by:	Yes No	Yes No		Pattern	Style
1	Expenses	No	No	2	1	1
2	Income	No	No	3	2	1
3	Series 3	No	No	4	3	1
4	Series 4	No	No	5	4	1
5	Series 5	No	No	6	5	1
6	Series 6	No	No	7	6	1
7	Series 7	No	No	8	7	1
8	Series 8	No	No	9	8	1

F1-Help			
F2-Draw chart	F5-Attributes	F7-Size/Place	
	F6-Colors	F8-Data	F10-Continue

Figure 2-18.   Title Size and Placement Options submenu

The same size and placement options are available for both titles and labels, so we will discuss them together.

Text Size

The Size field refers to the size of the title, subtitle, footnote text, and axes labels. The number entered in this field determines the percentage of the total chart space that will be used for displaying the title, subtitle, and so on. For example, if you enter 8 in the Size field next to the Title option, about eight percent of the vertical chart space will be used to display the title. This is not an exact correspondence, but it is fairly close.

The range of acceptable values for the size of a title is between 0 and 20. Also, the numbers entered can be fractional values (for example, 6.5 is an acceptable entry for the Size field).

> ► **Tip:** The size of the text alters the size of the chart. Try setting the text size for the title to 40 to see the affect on the chart size.

In most cases you will want the title size to be larger than any other title or label on the chart. The default sizes shown in Figure 2-18 will work well for most charts. Again, the chart medium will influence your choice of a text size. (For example, a chart reproduced as a slide for viewing by a large audience needs a larger text size than a printed chart.)

Notice that the X and Y label fields are empty in Figure 2-18. Although HG does not show a default value in these fields, the default size for both the X and Y labels is 3. These two fields affect the size of the label on either axis, and you can change these sizes as needed.

75

Text Placement

The options for text placement (the Place field) are:

► left side of the chart (L)
► centered (c)
► right side of the chart (R)

These options are self-explanatory. Sometimes, however, it might seem as if these options aren't working. For example, if you have used a long title name, changing the title placement has no visible impact on the chart. If you think about it, this makes sense. If a long title fills up the available title space, left or right justification has no effect on the title's placement— there's no room to shift it left or right!

Likewise, if you have used a large text size, the placement options might not have any visible effect on the placement of the chart title. If you want to alter the title placement in such cases, you will either have to shorten the title or select a smaller text size.

After you place the title, subtitle, and footnote, you can change the placement of the Y1 or Y2 axis titles. (The X axis title is always centered.) The two options for the Y1 and Y2 axis titles are → and ↓ . If you select →, the label is printed left to right in a normal fashion. If you select ↓ , the labels are printed from top to bottom. Therefore, if the label for the Y1 axis is "lbs" and you select →, the label is displayed as

lbs

If you select ↓ , the same label would appear as

l
b
s

The ↓ provides a means of using a longer axis title without reducing the size of the chart itself. The disadvantage is that vertically oriented labels are more difficult to read.

This completes the discussion of the text-size and placement options available by pressing F7. To remove this submenu, press F7 again or press F2 to redraw the chart. After HG redisplays the chart, the F7 submenu is deactivated.

Cumulative Option (Cum)

The Cum field, the first column in Page 4 of the Titles & Options menu, lets you show cumulative totals on the chart. The default setting is No. If you change this to Yes for a data series, the chart displays a running total of the data for that series. This means that each series value is added to all previous values and the resulting total is displayed on the chart.

For example, if the cumulative option is set to Yes for the Series 1 data shown in Figure 2-4, the first cumulative total shown on the chart would be 58.4. The second total shown would be 119.5 (58.4 plus the second value of 61.1) and so on for all values in the series.

> ▶ **Tip:** Cumulative totals are not used very often, so it is a good idea to state in either the title or subtitle that the chart is displaying cumulative totals.

Y Label Option

This Y Label field determines whether or not the exact Y value of each bar in the series will be displayed at the top of the bar. For this option to have any effect, the Value Labels option from Page 2 of the Titles & Options menu (Figure 2-8) must be set to Select, rather than All or None.

If the Value Label option from Page 2 is set to None, no bar values will be displayed, even if the Y Label option on this page (4) is set to Yes. If the Value Label option from Page 2 is set to All, all bar values will be displayed even if the Y Label option is set to No. Table 2-2 shows how the Value Label settings from Page 2 interact with the Y Label field on Page 4.

77

Table 2-2. **Affects of Value Label and Y Label Settings on the Y Value Display**

Setting of Value Label	Setting of Y Label	Result
All	Yes	Y values displayed
All	No	Y values displayed
Selected	Yes	Y values displayed
Selected	No	Y values not displayed
None	Yes	Y values not displayed
None	No	Y values not displayed

It should be apparent from Table 2-2 that if the Value Label field is set to None, no values are shown at the top of the bar. If the Value Label is set to All, the values are shown regardless of how the Y Label field from Page 4 is set. Therefore, the Y Label field only has an impact when the Value Label from Page 2 is set to Select, in which case, the Y Label field determines whether or not the values are shown.

> ► **Tip:** Showing the Y values usually results in a cluttered chart. If you want the viewer to have access to the raw numbers, consider placing them in another chart or table.

Color

The Color option lets you select the bar colors. Ignore this option if the chart will be printed in black-and-white. If the chart will be reproduced in color, press F6 to display the Color Selection submenu, as shown in Figure 2-19.

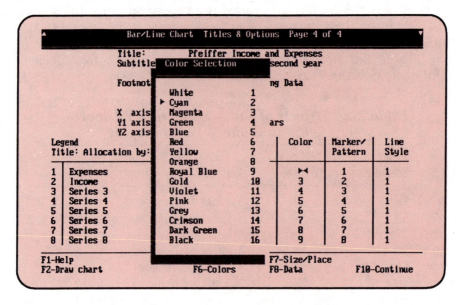

Figure 2-19.   The Color Selection +submenu

Use the arrow keys or mouse to move up and down within the list of available colors. Pressing Enter automatically inserts the number of the color into the Color column on Page 4 for the selected data series. If you decide not to change any of the default colors in the Color column, press F6 a second time to remove the Color Selection submenu from the screen.

Marker/Pattern

If you are drawing line or point charts, this option determines the marker, or symbol, used to indicate data points on the chart. If you are drawing bar charts, this option determines the pattern used to fill the bars.

Marker

If you are drawing a line or point chart, the number entered into this field determines the style of marker used for the points. There are 13 available markers, as shown in Table 2-3.

Table 2-3. HG Marker Styles

No. for Marker Field	Resulting Marker
0	none
1	.
2	+
3	✳
4	□
5	×
6	◇
7	△

The style of marker selected is a matter of personal preference. If there are a large number of points being plotted, use a small marker style (for example, 1). If multiple lines are being drawn, select marker styles that have noticeably different shapes (for example, 1 and 7). If the actual points are not as important as the trend or shape of the line, consider using no marker at all (0).

Line Style

This option determines the style of line drawn in the chart. It only affects line, trend, and curve charts, which are selected in the Type column of Page 1 of the Titles & Options menu (see Figure 2-6). The line style options are presented in Table 2-4.

***Table 2-4. Styles of Lines for Line, Trend,
and Curve Charts***

Number	Resulting Line Type
1	Solid line, thin
2	Solid line, thick
3	Dotted line
4	Dashed line

If you want to emphasize one line relative to others, make the line thick and the others thin. A common practice in statistics is to plot the actual data with a thin solid line and show the trend (or regression) line as a dotted line. This reinforces the fact that a trend line is based on projected rather than actual data. If you use dotted or dashed lines in a chart that has grid lines, the chart might confuse the viewer. Consider turning off the grid lines.

80

Pattern

This option is also affected by the Bar Fill Style setting on Page 2 of the Titles & Options menu. If Bar Fill Style is set to either Pattern or Both, the number you enter here will determine the pattern used to fill the bars. There are 12 patterns available, as shown in Figure 2-20.

Note that if you set the Bar Fill Style to Color, entering a Pattern number here has no impact on the chart.

Select Title Attributes

When you were using Page 1 of the Titles & Options menu (Figure 2-6), you might have noticed that the F5 key was active. (Recall that available function keys are displayed at the bottom of the screen.) This key lets you change the title attributes, that is, the way in which a title is displayed. The F5 key operates in a consistent manner for virtually all of the chart types, so we will explain how to select title attributes as a series of Quick Steps.

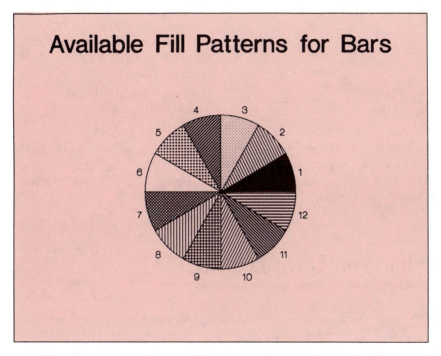

Figure 2-20. The 12 fill patterns for bars

Q Selecting Title Attributes

1. Press F8.   Activates the Titles &
                                Options menu.

2. Position cursor on title to
   be changed using the
   mouse or Tab, Home, or
   End keys.

3. Press F5 or Shift-F5.   F5 affects one letter at a
                                time; Shift-F5 affects the
                                entire line.

4. Tab to the desired attribute
   on the F5 menu at the
   bottom of the screen.

81

5.	Press spacebar.	Selects (or cancels) the specified attribute. (Pressing the spacebar also advances the number in the Color field.)
6.	Press Enter.	Ends title attributes selection. □

Note that these Quick Steps apply to the titles on all charts, not just bar and line charts. You can tell that an attribute (Bold, Fill, and so on) is selected by the small triangle that appears before the attribute.

What You Have Learned

82

You now know how to use all of the options associated with bar and line charts. Along the way, you also saw how a bar chart can be changed to a line chart by simply changing the Type field to Line, Trend, Curve, or Point). You should now be comfortable with how the HG menus work and understand how to edit values in the chart.

You should experiment with different types of charts as you go along; you will quickly discover just how easy it is to create a variety of charts. You might find that a chart you thought would be presented best as a bar chart has greater impact in another form. HG makes it so easy to experiment there's little reason not to. If you've created a bar or line chart, merely press Esc and select Create New Chart from the Main Menu. HG will ask if you want to use the old data. Simply answer Yes and you can use the same data from the old chart to create a new chart.

Chapter 3

Importing and Exporting Data

In This Chapter

▶ *Importing Lotus graphs and data*
▶ *Importing ASCII data files*
▶ *Importing PFS:GRAPH charts*
▶ *Exporting pictures*
▶ *Exporting metafiles*

This chapter shows you how to import data files from other programs and how to export data to programs. There are two major advantages to importing and exporting data rather than typing it directly into HG or another program: it's faster, and it's less likely to introduce errors into the data. Both of these advantages derive from the fact that you don't have to retype the data. Always use the HG import and export facilities whenever you can.

Most of the sections in this chapter discuss the various import options of the HG Import/Export menu. However, we will also briefly show you how to use this menu to export data.

Importing a Lotus Graph

Although you can use Lotus 1-2-3 to create graphs, most people agree that HG has graphics capabilities that far surpass the features you will find in Lotus. However, you can still use your Lotus graph as a starting point and then use HG to transform it into a more polished chart.

From the HG Main Menu, use the mouse, arrow keys, or pseudo hot keys to highlight Import/Export and then press Enter to display the menu. Pressing the hot key (5) also displays the menu, which is shown in Figure 3-1.

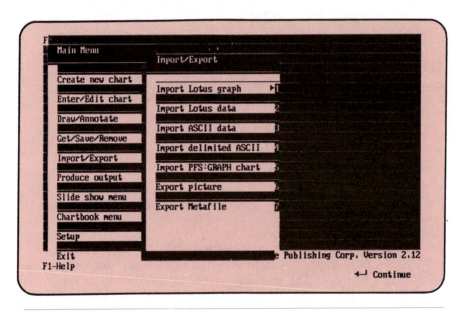

Figure 3-1.   The Import/Export menu

Selecting a Lotus Graph File

To import a Lotus graph from Release 1A or Release 2, select the Import Lotus graph option (1) from the Import/Export menu. HG then displays a Select Worksheet input screen similar to the one shown in Figure 3-2.

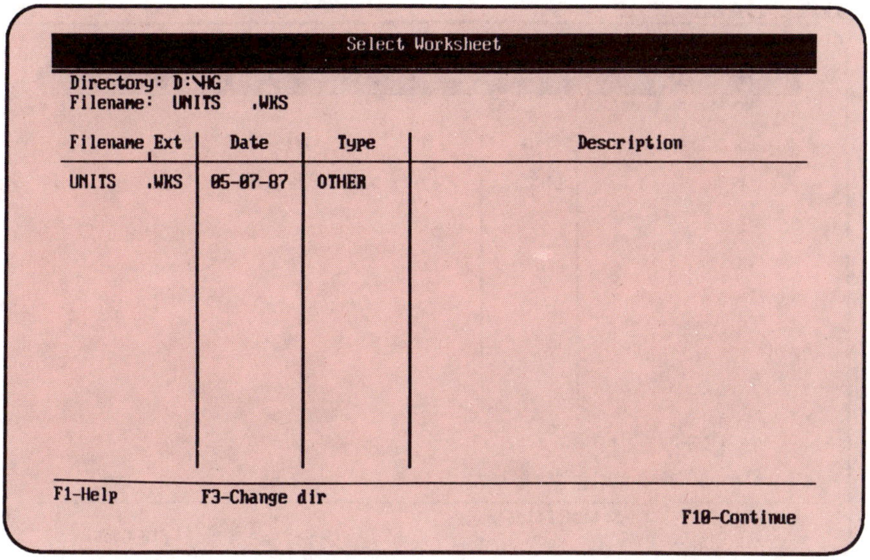

```
                              Select Worksheet

        Directory: D:\HG
        Filename:  UNITS    .WKS

        Filename Ext  |  Date   |  Type   |          Description

        UNITS   .WKS  | 05-07-87 | OTHER   |




        F1-Help          F3-Change dir

                                                       F10-Continue
```

Figure 3-2. The Select Worksheet screen

By default, HG searches only the current working directory for data files. However, when you supplied setup information in Chapter 1, HG let you specify another directory in which it should look for import files. If you entered a directory name in the Import directory field of the Default Settings screen (see Figure 1-3), pressing the F3 key will display that directory name in the first field of the Select Worksheet screen. (If you did not specify an import file directory during the setup process, HG displays the current working directory.)

If you need to specify a different directory, press the up arrow once, enter the new directory name, and press Enter. We will assume that your working directory contains the sample data file UNITS.WKS and that your screen looks similar to Figure 3-2.

Select the file sample Lotus data file UNITS.WKS by highlighting the name and pressing Enter. Your screen will then resemble Figure 3-3.

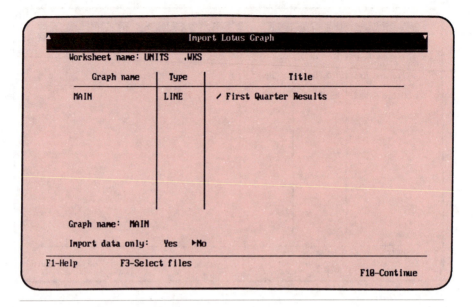

Figure 3-3.   The Import Lotus Graph screen

A Lotus graph file can contain several graphs. If multiple graphs exist in a file, HG will display a list of them on the screen. (Note that the sample data file contains only one graph.) You can use the mouse or arrow keys to highlight the graph you want to use. Because our sample Lotus file only has one graph, HG has already inserted the name MAIN in the Graph Name field (near the bottom of the screen). Press Enter to select this graph.

Import Data Only

The last field on the screen, Import data only, lets you specify if you want to use only the data in the file or all of the available information. Because we want to use the entire graph, select the No option.

HG immediately draws a line chart on the screen using the imported information. Examine this chart closely: Line charts with so few data points are usually not very effective. In the following sections, we will use the techniques presented in Chapter 2 to add a little class to this chart.

Q **Importing a Lotus Graph**

1. From the HG Main Menu, press 5.	Selects the Import/Export menu.
2. Press 1.	Selects the Select Worksheet screen.
3. Type or highlight the desired Lotus data file name and press Enter.	Selects a Lotus file.
4. Type or highlight the desired Lotus graph name and press Enter.	Selects a graph from Lotus file that contains multiple graphs.
5. Press N.	Uses the entire graph (not just the data) to draw the chart.
6. Press Esc.	Ends viewing of the Lotus graph. □

87

Refining a Lotus Graph

After you finish viewing the chart, pressing a key will return you to the HG Main Menu. Because we want to edit the chart currently in memory, press 2 to select the Enter/Edit chart option. (Don't press E or you will exit the program.) Selecting Enter/Edit chart displays the familiar Bar/Line Chart Data screen. The discussions in Chapter 2 have already familiarized you with all of these fields and options. Therefore, let's quickly make a few changes in the Lotus chart to enhance its appearance; use the following sequence of keystrokes:

1. Press F8.	Turns on the Options menu.
2. Press PgDn.	Displays Page 2 of the Titles & Options menu.
3. Press O.	Highlights the Overlap Bars option.
4. Press Enter.	Selects the Overlap Bars option.
5. Press 3.	Highlights the 3D enhancement.

6. Press PgUp.	Returns to Page 1 of the Titles & Options menu.
7. Press Tab eight times.	Moves the highlight to the Type field.
8. Press B.	Changes the chart from Line to Bar.
9. Press Enter.	Moves to Series 2.
10. Press B.	Changes to a Bar.
11. Press Enter.	Moves to Series 3.
12. Press B.	Changes to a Bar.
13. Press F2.	Displays the chart with your changes.

If you've followed these instructions, your chart should look like the one shown in Figure 3-4.

88

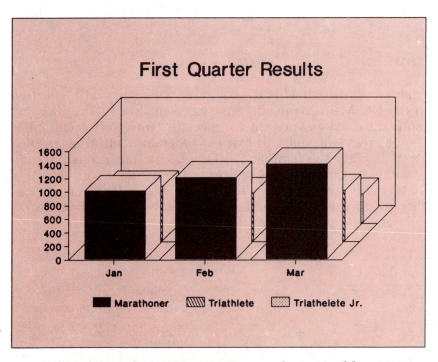

Figure 3-4.   The UNITS.WKS sample Lotus file as a 3D chart with overlapping bars

This chart has several problems. First, the bars are so wide that the entire chart looks heavy. Second, and more important, the viewer cannot really see much of the Triathelete Jr. sales information. The Marathoner sales figures hide many of the details about the other two product lines. Let's correct these problems.

Reducing the Size of Bars

First, let's reduce the "weight" of this chart. To do so, press any key to remove the chart from the screen. Then press the PgUp key to display Page 2 of the Titles & Options menu. Press the Tab key until the highlight is in the Bar width field. Now type the number 40.

When you press F2 again to view the chart, you will notice that it looks a little better now because the bars are not as wide as they were before. The Marathoner data series, however, still dominates the chart.

89

Exchanging Data Series

In Chapter 2, we suggested that you enter the smallest data series first and the largest data series last. Unfortunately, when you are importing data, you have little choice about the order in which data is read into HG. Such is the case with the UNIT.WKS file. Obviously, you need to exchange the Marathoner data series with the Triathelete Jr. data series. HG includes a feature that lets you easily make this exchange.

To reverse the positions of two data series, move the cursor to the first field that you want to exchange. In our example, press the Tab key until the cursor is in the Marathoner column of the Bar/Line Chart Data screen. (If the Titles & Options menu is on the screen, press F8 to return to the Bar/Line Chart Data screen.)

With the cursor in the Marathoner column, press F4. This displays the Calculate input screen, as shown in Figure 3-5.

Note that the cursor is in the Legend field and that HG has inserted the name of the data series you want to exchange. Press the Tab key to advance the cursor to the Calculation field. Now type the following:

```
@EXCH(#3)
```

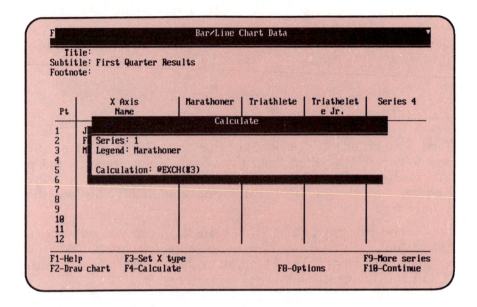

Figure 3-5.   The Calculate input screen

The calculation command @EXCH tells HG to exchange the data in the current column (that is, Marathoner, or Series 1) with the contents of column three (that is, Triathelete Jr., or Series 3). When you press Enter, HG immediately returns to the Bar/Line Chart Data screen; however, notice that columns 1 and 3 have now been exchanged. Now press F2 to display the edited chart and view the results of this data exchange.

As you can see in Figure 3-6, the chart has more open space, the bars are less dominating, and all three data series can easily be viewed at one time. Recall the original line chart and our first version of this bar chart; notice how effective this chart is and how easy it is for the viewer to understand the data. Sometimes a simple exchange of data series can make a great difference in the overall appearance of a chart.

Press Esc to return to the Main Menu. You can save the chart or continue to experiment with it by adding further enhancements.

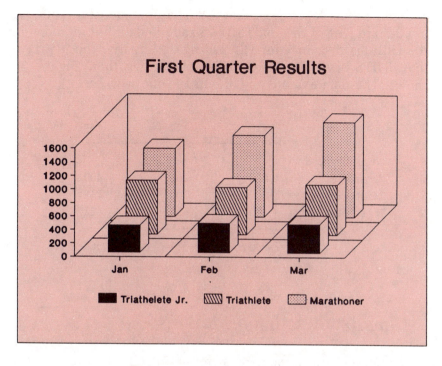

Figure 3-6.   The results of exchanging data series with the @EXCH command

91

Importing Lotus Data

As you gain experience with HG, you will probably stop using Lotus to make charts. Instead, you will import Lotus data directly and create your charts from within HG. This section will show you how easy it is to import data directly from Lotus WKS files.

If you use Lotus, you know that a Lotus worksheet is arranged as a matrix—letters represent columns and numbers represent rows. Figure 3-7 shows the general format used in a Lotus worksheet.

Each element of the matrix formed by the rows and the columns is called a *cell*. Each cell has a unique name defined by its row-column position. For example, cell B1 contains the entry Jan and cell D6 contains the value 422. The numbers shown in Figure 3-7 are part of the UNITS.WKS sample data file included on the Utilities disk in your HG package. (Actually, the matrix in the UNITS.WKS file is considerably wider than Figure 3-7 shows. The data extends to column I in the worksheet.)

	A	B	C	D
1		Jan	Feb	Mar
2		------------------------------		
3	Units Shipped			
4	Marathoner	1,000	1,200	1,400
5	Triathelete	800	700	743
6	Triathelete Jr.	400	431	422
7		------------------------------		
8	Totals	2,200	2,331	2,565

Figure 3-7.   Format for a Lotus worksheet

92

Getting Ready to Import a WKS File

Now that you know the general format of a Lotus file, you can start the process of importing a WKS data file.

> ⊘ **Caution:** To import a Lotus WKS file, you must *first* establish the type of chart you will be creating. Therefore, before you import the data, you *must* select the Create new chart option from the Main Menu and enter a chart type.

Select the Create new chart option from the HG Main Menu. Now select the Bar/Line option. When you press Enter, HG displays the familiar X Data Type menu. You don't need to fill in any fields now, so press Esc until you return to the Main Menu.

Now select the Import/Export option (5) from the Main Menu to display the Import/Export menu, as shown in Figure 3-1. Select the Import Lotus data option (2). At the Select Worksheet input screen, you must specify which file you want to import. Let's continue using the Lotus sample data file; select the UNITS.WKS file from the list, as shown in Figure 3-2.

Q Importing a Lotus Worksheet File

1. From the HG Main Menu, press 1.   Selects the `Create new chart` menu.

2. Select a chart type.   Establishes a chart form into which HG imports the data.

3. Press Esc.   Returns you to the Main Menu.

4. Press 5.   Selects the `Import/Export` menu.

5. Press 2.   Displays the Select Worksheet screen.

6. Type the name of a Lotus data file and press Enter, or select a WKS file from the list on the screen.   Selects the desired worksheet file.

☐

93

Import Lotus Data Screen

After you have selected a file, HG displays the Import Lotus Data screen, as shown in Figure 3-8. Your screen will be similar to the figure, but not exactly the same: I filled in the data fields so that you can see how the entries relate to what you learned in Chapter 2.

Title

You can, of course, enter a new title for the data you are importing. On the other hand, you might find it easier to merely import the title from the WKS file. For example, look at the data in the Lotus file shown in Figure 3-7. You could use the name in cell A3 (`Units Shipped`) as the title of your chart. To do so, simply type the following:

    `\A3`

in the `Title` field. The leading backslash tells HG to insert the *contents* of the following cell (A3) from the WKS file into the `Title` field. (If you omit the backslash, HG merely titles the chart as `A3`, which is not what you want.)

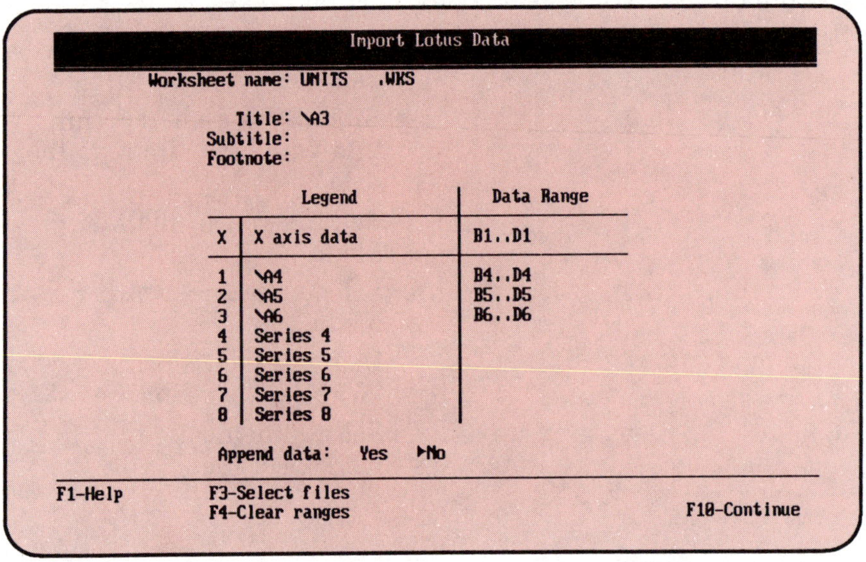

```
                      Import Lotus Data

         Worksheet name: UNITS    .WKS

                 Title: \A3
             Subtitle:
             Footnote:

                    Legend              │  Data Range

              X │ X axis data           │  B1..D1
             ───┼───────────────────────┼──────────
              1 │ \A4                    │  B4..D4
              2 │ \A5                    │  B5..D5
              3 │ \A6                    │  B6..D6
              4 │ Series 4               │
              5 │ Series 5               │
              6 │ Series 6               │
              7 │ Series 7               │
              8 │ Series 8               │

              Append data:    Yes   ►No

   F1-Help        F3-Select files
                  F4-Clear ranges                    F10-Continue
```

94

Figure 3-8. The Import Lotus Data screen

Data Range

Press the Tab key to position the cursor in the Data Range field, that is, the last column in row X. Now, refer to Figure 3-7. The data that we will use in the chart starts in column B and continues through column D. The X axis labels for those columns appear in columns B1 through D1. To enter this information into the HG chart, type the following into the Data Range field for the X axis:

    B1..D1

You can think of the two periods between the cells as representing the words *through cell*. Therefore, the entry in the X Data Range field means: "The X data range is from cell *B1 through cell D1.*" After you press Enter, the cursor will move to the first row of the Data Range field. However, because we want to use legends with the data series, press the Shift-Tab key combination to move the cursor back one field. If you have done this correctly, your cursor will be in the Legend column at the location of \A4 in Figure 3-8.

Setting the Legend Titles

The titles that we want to use as legends appear in column A of Figure 3-7. Specifically, we want to use cells A4, A5, and A6 which correspond to Marathoner, Triathelete, and Triathelete Jr. Enter the three legend titles (\A4, \A5, and \A6) into the first three data series in the Legend column, as shown in Figure 3-8.

⊘ **Caution:** Remember, to tell HG to import the *contents* of cells in the data file as legend titles, you must precede each of the specified cells with a backslash. For example, you would enter \A4 in the Series 1 position in the Legend column.

Setting the Y Data Ranges

95

Our last task is to tell HG which cells hold the actual data values we want to chart. Again, referring to Figure 3-7, you can see that cells B4 through D4 contain the Marathoner data. Therefore, in row 1 of the Data Range column, you must enter the following:

    B4..D4

It should also be clear that the remaining two data series have the following ranges:

    xB5..D5
    B6..D6

After you enter these values in rows 2 and 3 of the Data Range column, your version of the Import Lotus Data screen will look identical to Figure 3-8.

Appending Data

HG now knows how you want to organize the data it will be reading from the WKS file. Because we won't be using any more data, press the End key to skip the other Series numbers and move to the last field on the screen, Append data.

The Append data option lets you add data from one WKS file to the current file. For example, if you must update one of your charts each month with new data from a Lotus WKS file, you could start your work with last month's chart and merely append the new data to it. Because we are creating a totally new chart, select the No option in this field. HG then activates the disk drive, reads the specified data into the chart, and displays the familiar Bar/Line Chart Data screen, as shown in Figure 3-9.

```
┌─────────────────────────────────────────────────────────────────┐
│                      Bar/Line Chart Data                       ▼ │
│ ████████████████████████████████████████████████████████████████ │
│    Title: Units Shipped                                          │
│ Subtitle:                                                        │
│ Footnote:                                                        │
│                                                                  │
│        │  X Axis    │ Marathon │ Triathle │ Triathle │ Series 4 │
│     Pt │   Name     │   er     │   te     │  te Jr.  │          │
│     1  │ Jan        │  1000    │  800     │  400     │          │
│     2  │ Feb        │  1200    │  700     │  431     │          │
│     3  │ Mar        │  1400    │  743     │  422     │          │
│     4  │            │          │          │          │          │
│     5  │            │          │          │          │          │
│     6  │            │          │          │          │          │
│     7  │            │          │          │          │          │
│     8  │            │          │          │          │          │
│     9  │            │          │          │          │          │
│    10  │            │          │          │          │          │
│    11  │            │          │          │          │          │
│    12  │            │          │          │          │          │
│                                                                  │
│ F1-Help        F3-Set X type                      F9-More series │
│ F2-Draw chart  F4-Calculate           F8-Options  F10-Continue   │
└─────────────────────────────────────────────────────────────────┘
```

Figure 3-9. *The Bar/Line Chart Data screen after importing data from a Lotus file*

Press F2 to view the chart. You can now use the methods discussed in Chapter 2 to modify the chart and experiment with further enhancements.

▶ **Tip:** If you want to see how the Append data option affects a chart, simply repeat the previous procedures in this section after you finish viewing the current chart. Your chart will essentially be the same, but it will have twice as many data points.

Importing ASCII Data

Many programs create data files that are not compatible with the Lotus format. However, these programs can often save information in ASCII format. Almost all word processors, spreadsheet programs, and data base programs either store information in ASCII format or can write their information to an ASCII file. If you have a program that you want to use with HG, check the program's documentation to see if it can write data to an ASCII file.

> ▶ **Tip:** You can tell if a file stores information in ASCII format by using the DOS TYPE command to display the file's information on the screen. If only letters and numbers are displayed, the file is an ASCII file; if the computer beeps or generates unusual symbols and characters such as "happy faces," the file is not an ASCII file.
>
> You can also recognize ASCII files by looking for certain file name extensions. File names that end with ASC, TXT, DOC, or DAT extensions are often ASCII files. For example, in the HG package, UNITS.ASC is an ASCII file.

97

To import an ASCII file, return to the HG Main Menu and select the Create new chart option (1). Press 3 or highlight the Bar/Line chart option and press Enter. You could press Esc now (as you did when you imported a Lotus data file), but instead, select Name from the X Data Type Menu and then press F10. (This leaves the Starting with, Ending with, and Increment fields empty for now.)

Fill in the top three fields of the Bar/Line Chart Data screen so that they read as follows:

```
   Title: Units Shipped
Subtitle: Quarterly Results
Footnote: Internal Audit Data
```

Now press Esc to return to the HG Main Menu. You are now ready to import the ASCII data.

Select the Import/Export option (5) from the Main Menu. At the Import/Export menu (see Figure 3-1), select the Import ASCII data option (3). When HG displays the familiar Select File screen, select the UNITS.ASC file included on the Utilities disk of the HG package.

Q **Importing an ASCII Data File**

1. From the HG Main Menu, press 1.	Selects the Create new chart option.
2. Select a chart type.	Establishes a chart form into which HG imports the data.
3. Press Esc twice.	Returns you to the Main Menu.
4. Press 5.	Selects the Import/Export option.
5. Press 3.	Displays the Select File screen.
6. Type the name of an ASCII file and press Enter, or select an ASCII file from the list on the screen.	Selects the desired ASCII file and displays the Import ASCII Data screen.
7. Fill in the appropriate fields in the Import ASCII Data screen.	Completes the formatting of the ASCII data for HG. ☐

Import ASCII Data Screen

After you select a file name (in this case, UNITS.ASC), HG displays the Import ASCII Data screen, as shown in Figure 3-10.

The numbers at the left side of the screen are line numbers, and the numbers across the lower part of the screen are column numbers. (In Figure 3-10, the line numbers range from 1 through 13 and the columns range from 1 through 6.) The contents of the ASCII data file appears in the box outlined by the line and column numbers. Note that the cursor is near the bottom of the screen in the Read data by field.

Read Data By

This field determines how the data is to be read. To have HG read the data by shoe type (that is, set the X Data Type to Mara-

98

thoner and the other shoes), you would select the Line option. If you want the data to be read by time period (that is, Jan and so on), you would select the Column option.

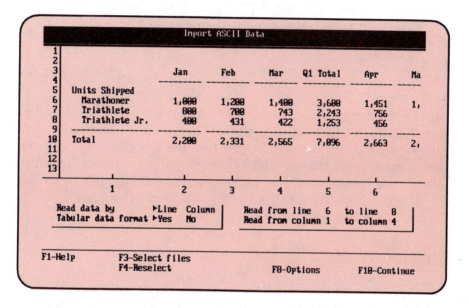

Figure 3-10.   The Import ASCII Data screen

> ▶ **Tip:** HG requires that each column be separated by three or more blank spaces. If your file does not conform to this format, all is not lost. Simply exit from HG, load the file into your favorite word processor, insert the necessary blank spaces between columns, and resave the file in ASCII format.

In this example, we want to emphasize the product line rather than the month, so let's have HG read the data by Line. Press L and then press Enter.

Read From Line

This field determines the first line of the file that HG will read as data. Looking at Figure 3-10, you can see that the Marathoner data starts in line 6. Press **6** and then press Enter.

To Line

This field determines which line marks the end of the data. Figure 3-10 shows that line 8 is the last line (that is, Triathelete Jr.). Note that the default number in this field is three digits long. Remember, press the Ctrl-Del key combination to erase the entire entry in a field. After you delete the default number, type the ending line number for this file (**8**) and then press Enter.

100

Tabular Data Format

Most of the time the data in your files will be organized in table format; if it is, select the **Yes** option in this field. However, some of the charts that you will be creating do not use numeric data (for example, text charts); in these case, select the **No** option. (If you specify **No** in this field, HG numbers the columns to reflect the character count in the file rather than the column count.) In our current example, select the **Yes** option.

Read From Column

This is simply the starting column from which HG will read the data. Because we want the product names to appear in the chart, specify **1** and press Enter.

To Column

This field determines where HG stops reading the data. In our example, we will read only the first quarter data, so type **4** and press Enter.

> ▶ **Tip:** If you want to see the columns and lines more
> clearly, press F8; this highlights the data box region. If
> you've filled out several fields incorrectly, press F4 to clear
> all fields so that you can start over.

The Import Title and Legends Menu

After you enter the number for the last field on the Import ASCII
Data screen, HG displays a menu near the middle of the screen
(see Figure 3-11).

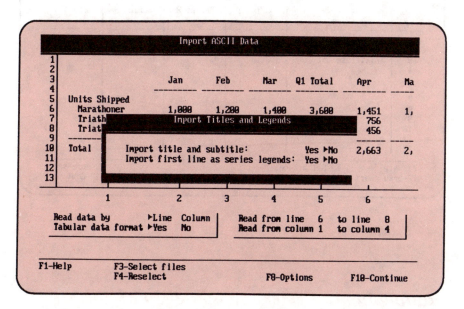

101

Figure 3-11. The Import Titles and Legends menu

The first field asks whether you want to import the title and
subtitle from the data file. Because you have already entered a
title, select No.

The second field, lets you import the first line of the data as
series legends. If the first line to be read from the file contains
the legends for the data, select the Yes option. However, because
we started with line 6 (the Marathoner data), you must select No.

Note that if you had specified line 3 as the starting line
instead of line 6, you could have used this option. However, you

then would have had to delete lines 4 and 5 before you displayed the chart; otherwise, HG would have inserted into the chart the dashes from line 4 and the words Units Shipped from line 5.

After you select No for this field, HG displays the Bar/Line Chart Data screen shown in Figure 3-12.

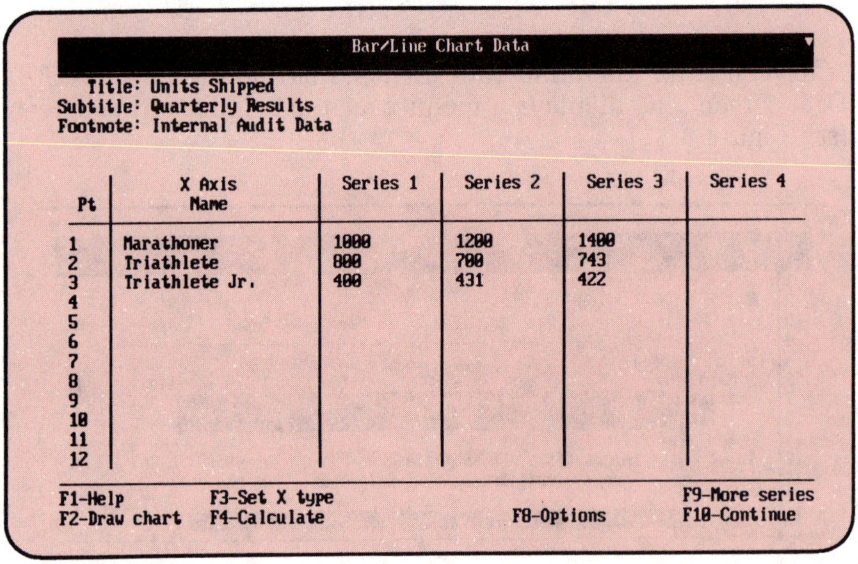

102

```
                        Bar/Line Chart Data                          ▼

    Title: Units Shipped
 Subtitle: Quarterly Results
 Footnote: Internal Audit Data


            X Axis      Series 1    Series 2    Series 3    Series 4
    Pt      Name

    1    Marathoner      1000        1200        1400
    2    Triathlete       800         700         743
    3    Triathlete Jr.   400         431         422
    4
    5
    6
    7
    8
    9
   10
   11
   12

 F1-Help         F3-Set X type                            F9-More series
 F2-Draw chart   F4-Calculate              F8-Options     F10-Continue
```

Figure 3-12.   The Bar/Line Chart Data screen after importing an ASCII file

Adding the Data Series and Legend Titles

Press F8 to activate the Bar/Line Chart Titles & Options menu. Press the Tab key until the cursor is at Series 1 of the Legend Title column. Erase Series 1 and type Jan in its place. Tab to Series 2 and replace it with Feb, and replace Series 3 with Mar. The completed screen is shown in Figure 3-13.

You have now imported and entered all of the information that HG needs to draw the chart. When you display the chart, your finished work will look similar to that shown in Figure 3-14.

Take a few moments to polish the chart a bit. For example, you might try moving the legend inside of the chart, locating it above the Triathelete Jr. data. (The Triathelete Jr. sales are small enough so that the legend will not interfere with the bars.) Notice that placing the legend inside the chart results in a larger chart. With a little experimentation, you should be able to produce a satisfactory chart for almost any audience.

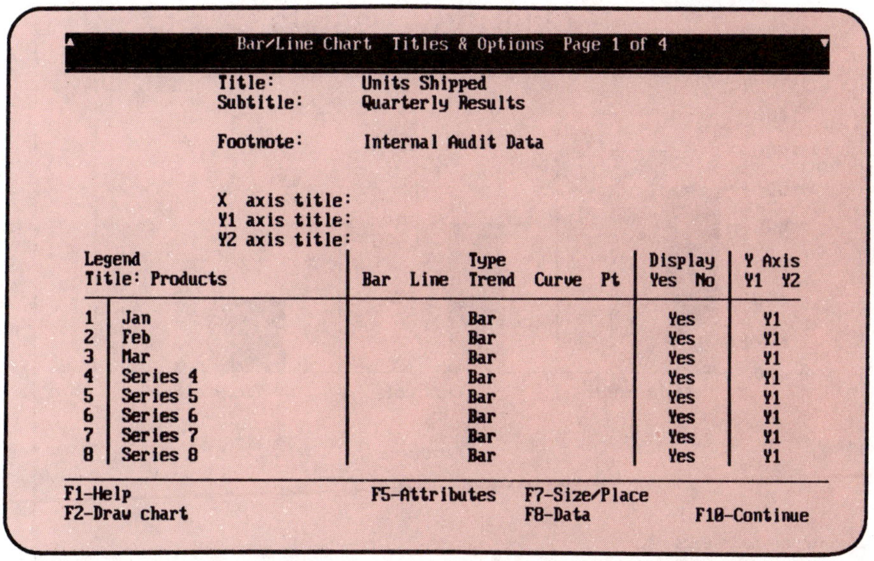

```
▲                Bar/Line Chart  Titles & Options  Page 1 of 4          ▼

                 Title:           Units Shipped
                 Subtitle:        Quarterly Results

                 Footnote:        Internal Audit Data


          X  axis title:
          Y1 axis title:
          Y2 axis title:
     Legend                              Type              Display  Y Axis
     Title: Products        Bar  Line  Trend  Curve  Pt   Yes  No   Y1  Y2

       1  | Jan                           Bar               Yes        Y1
       2  | Feb                           Bar               Yes        Y1
       3  | Mar                           Bar               Yes        Y1
       4  | Series 4                      Bar               Yes        Y1
       5  | Series 5                      Bar               Yes        Y1
       6  | Series 6                      Bar               Yes        Y1
       7  | Series 7                      Bar               Yes        Y1
       8  | Series 8                      Bar               Yes        Y1

     F1-Help                     F5-Attributes    F7-Size/Place
     F2-Draw chart                               F8-Data         F10-Continue
```

Figure 3-13.   The completed Bar/Line Chart Data Titles & Options menu for an imported ASCII file

103

Importing Delimited ASCII Data Files

Many programs do not create ASCII data that is oriented in a tabular format; instead, they generate ASCII files in which data is written as a series of *fields*. In such data files, each field is separated by a character called a *delimiter*. Common delimiters are commas or blank spaces. Figure 3-15 shows a typical delimited ASCII data file.

In Figure 3-15 commas separate, or delimit, each field. The same file written in tabular format would resemble the file shown in Figure 3-16.

The information is the same, but programs can often write delimited files more easily than they can write tabular ASCII files. This is the main reason why delimited ASCII files are more common than tabular ASCII files.

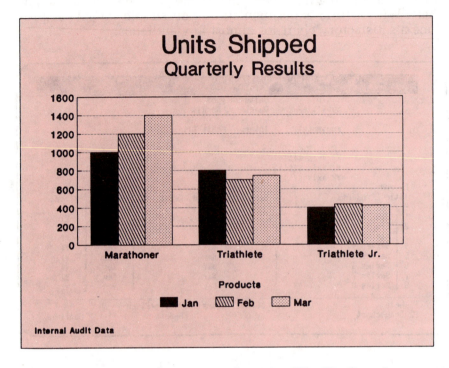

Figure 3-14.   The imported ASCII file displayed as a bar chart

```
"","1985","1986","1987"
"Agriculture",29.6,26.6,29.1
"Nonagriculture",183.5,190.6,223.7
"Manufacturing",145.4,148.7,171.5
```

Figure 3-15.   An example of a delimited ASCII data file

Note how the delimited ASCII file in Figure 3-15 encloses all character (string) data in double quotation marks. Also note that the first character string in the file is an empty string: This blank field allows the years to align properly (see Figure 3-16) over the corresponding data columns. That is, 1985 aligns with 29.6 for Agriculture, and so on.

	1985	1986	1987
Agriculture	29.6	26.6	29.1
Nonagriculture	183.5	190.6	223.7
Manufacturing	145.4	148.7	171.5

Figure 3-16. A tabular ASCII data file

Carriage-Return/Line-Feed Pairs

One character cannot be seen in Figure 3-15—the "carriage-return/line-feed" sequence that appears at the end of each line of data. A carriage-return character is a non-printing ASCII character (number 13) that repositions the cursor at the start of the line. A line-feed character is a non-printing ASCII character (number 10) that causes the cursor to move to the next line.

Although you might not have thought about it, each time you press Enter, the keyboard sends out the carriage-return/line-feed pair of characters. The result you see on the screen is that the cursor moves to the start (carriage-return) of the next line (line-feed). In a delimited file, this carriage-return/line-feed sequence is often used to mark the end of a data record. Therefore, even though you cannot see these end-of-record makers, you need to understand that they exist whenever data appears on a new line.

105

In Figure 3-15, the second line in the file actually contains the following character sequence:

```
"Agriculture", 29.6,26.6,29.1<CR><LF>
```

in which `<CR>` is the carriage-return character and `<LF>` is the line-feed character.

 Tip: You can always use a word processor to create a delimited ASCII file for use with HG.

To create a chart using a delimited ASCII file, first select the type of chart you want to create. For now, let's use the familiar Bar/Line chart. Next, press Esc to return to the Main Menu and select the Import/Export option (5). At the Import/Export submenu, select the Import delimited ASCII option (4). Then select the name of the delimited ASCII file that you want to import.

To practice importing this type of file, you can create a sample data file using the information and format shown in Figure 3-15. Use your word processor to enter the data, but be sure to save the file in ASCII format.

The ASCII Delimiters Menu

After you select a delimited ASCII file name, HG displays the ASCII Delimiters menu (see Figure 3-17). This menu lets you specify which characters are used to delimit the data.

106

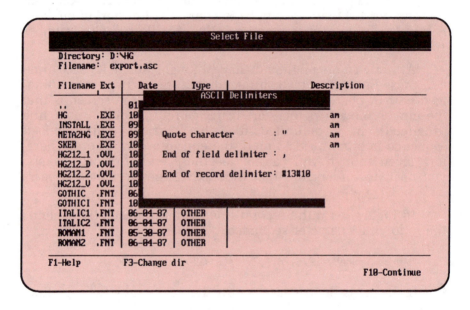

Figure 3-17. The ASCII Delimiters menu

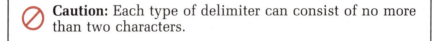 **Caution:** Each type of delimiter can consist of no more than two characters.

Quote Character

The first field lets you specify which character in the file marks text data (non-numeric characters). In most instances, the double quotation mark is used to enclose text data, so HG inserts it as the default delimiter. Some programs use a single-quote character as the delimiter for text data. Type the appropriate choice and press Enter.

End of Field Delimiter

This field lets you specify which ASCII character separates one field from another in the file. The most common delimiter is the comma, as shown in Figure 3-15. However, some programs use a blank space, a semicolon, or a colon to separate fields. Type the appropriate choice for your file and press Enter.

107

> ▶ **Tip:** If you don't know which characters are used as delimiters in an ASCII data file, use your word processor to examine the file. If you do not have a word processing program, use the DOS TYPE command to display the file on the screen.

End of Record Delimiter

The end-of-record delimiter marks the end of one related sequence of numbers. In Figure 3-15, each record starts on a new line, so you can be reasonably sure that the end-of-record marker is the carriage-return/line-feed pair (CR/LF) of ASCII characters. Appendix A lists the entire ASCII character set; notice that the line-feed character has the decimal value 10 and that the carriage return has the decimal value 13. HG inserts these values as the defaults for this field.

Notice that each value in the field is preceded by a pound sign (#). If you must enter different values, you must type the pound sign before specifying the decimal value of any non-printing ASCII character to be used as a delimiter.

Press the F10 key to continue to the next menu.

First Record as Series Legends

HG now presents another small menu that lets you import the first record as series legends for the chart (see Figure 3-18). Typical ASCII files include column headings associated with the data, as is the example shown in Figure 3-15. If your file looks similar to Figure 3-15, select the Yes option; otherwise select No. Note that you can always enter the series legends in the Titles & Options menu.

108

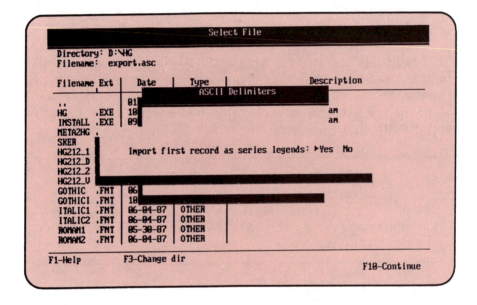

Figure 3-18.   The Import series legends menu

After you supply this last piece of information, HG reads the file and then displays the Bar/Line Chart Data screen. You can now press F2 to view the chart. Then, you can modify the chart using the features we discussed in Chapter 2.

Importing *PFS:GRAPH* Charts

If you've previously created a chart using *PFS:GRAPH*, you can import it into HG using the Import PFS:GRAPH chart option (5) of the

Import/Export menu. When you select this option, HG presents the usual file selection menu that lets you import the appropriate *PFS:GRAPH* chart.

At the field that asks if you want to import the data only, select the No option (you want the entire file) and then press F10. Because a *PFS:GRAPH* disk file can contain only one graph (unlike a Lotus graph file), you don't need to insert any further information. After you display the chart, you can use any of HG's features and enhancements to modify it as you see fit.

Exporting a Picture File

After you create a chart with HG, you can export it for use by other programs in two different formats. Export a *picture* when you want to incorporate the chart directly into a document created by the *PFS:Professional Write* word processor. This feature lets you easily include charts in written reports. Selecting the Export picture option (6) from the Import/Export menu displays the Export picture menu.

109

Directory

This input field lets you save the data file to a drive or subdirectory other than the current data directory. If you want to use the current directory, skip this field.

> *⃠* **Caution:** Picture files can be quite large, often requiring storage space exceeding 200 KB. Before you export a picture file, be sure your disk has enough available free space.

Picture Name

Enter the name that you want to give to the picture file. Note that this file name should include a file extension (for example, TEST.EPS, TEST.PLT, and so on).

> ▶ **Tip:** If you are exporting a picture to *Harvard Professional Publisher* you do not need to add a file name extension. HG automatically adds the IMG extension to the file.

Picture Quality

This field lets you select between standard or high quality output. If you select Standard, the output file is smaller and takes less time to create. However, the chart lacks the details and resolution that it has when you select the High option. You should experiment with both modes to see how they affect your charts and to find out what impact they have on your specific hardware and software environment.

110

Format

You can export a picture in one of three formats: Professional Write (PFS), Encapsulated Postscript, or HPGL. Select the appropriate response. (If you select the Professional Write option, HG also asks you to specify a printer and to answer whether or not the printer is capable of producing color output.)

> ▶ **Tip:** If the picture you are exporting will eventually be used in the HPGL or Postscript format, you should change the font to something other than Executive or Square serif. Select the Setup option from the Main Menu, and change the font at the Default Settings screen.

Press F10 when you finish making your selections.

> **Caution:** Be prepared to wait. HG can take several minutes to generate a picture file.

Exporting a Metafile

A *Metafile* is a graphics file format that can be used with a growing number of programs, such as *Freelance Plus*, *Manuscript*, and *SuperImage*. Metafiles represent an attempt to create a graphics image file format that can be used in a variety of hardware environments.

Ø **Caution:** If you want to use the Metafile format, you must first install the META.SYS and GSSCGI.SYS device drivers so that they are available when you start your computer. These device drivers are required to support the Virtual Device Interface (VDI) necessary to use Metafiles. See Appendix D in the HG manual for instructions about installing these VDI drivers.

111

To export a Metafile, select the Export Metafile option (7) from the Import/Export submenu.

Metafile Name

The first field on Export Metafile screen lets you enter the name you want to give to the Metafile. If you don't add a file name extension, HG automatically adds the CGM extension (for example, TEST.CGM) because most programs that use Metafiles use CGM as the default extension.

Use Harvard Graphics Font

To use the Metafile font, select the No option in this field. If you select Yes, HG uses its own fonts when it creates the Metafile. However, if you select Yes, the Metafile will be larger and it will take slightly longer to process because it will contain additional overhead to support the HG fonts.

Press F10 to write the Metafile to disk.

What You Have Learned

The import facilities of HG let you easily move data to HG from other programs. This can save you a lot of time and frustration because you won't have to retype the data previously stored on disk by other programs. After you have imported the data, you can use all of HG's features and enhancements to fine-tune the chart.

HG's export facilities are equally easy to use. However, you will often need to readjust your charts to produce the proper chart effects in the program that receives the HG export file. Each program uses its own fonts, line styles, color choices, and enhancements; these intangibles can substantially alter the way a HG file looks in another program.

112

Chapter 4

Pie Charts

In This Chapter

▶ *Matching the proper data to a pie chart*
▶ *Creating pie charts*
▶ *Generating multiple pie charts*
▶ *Using different types of pie charts*

Pie charts are commonly used to show how the parts of a data series relate to each other. Therefore, most people use pie charts to show ratios or percentages. This chapter not only demonstrates how to use HG to create effective pie charts, it also lets you know *when* to create pie charts.

When To Create a Pie Chart

You use a pie chart to show how the whole of "something" is distributed among its parts. For example, you might show how total company sales are divided by sales regions, how total expenditures break down according to expense categories, or how much each car model contributes to total car sales. If you consider these examples, you will see that pie charts are properly used with stock data.

Recall our discussion of stock and flow data types from Chapter 1. In the world of data, stock types are the snapshots and flow types are the movies. Stocks capture data at a moment in time, and flows give us a view data throughout time.

A pie chart should show how some quantitative measure is distributed at a point in time. If the quantity is a flow variable that has a time subscript, you probably don't want to present the data in a pie chart. For example, consider the pie chart in Figure 4-1. The viewer can interpret this chart in two ways.

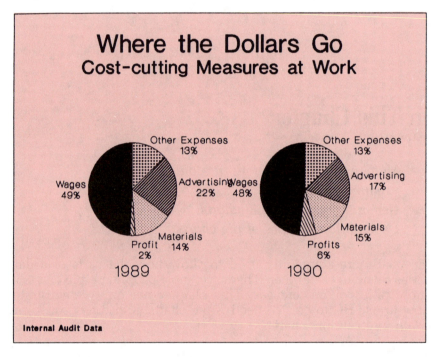

Figure 4-1. *A first attempt at a two-pie chart*

The first interpretation leads to the conclusion that the company reduced most of its expenses and that profits increased. However, the chart doesn't show what happened to the *absolute* numbers for the two years. For example, if 1990 sales were only 25 percent of 1989 sales, the company actually had lower profits in 1990.

This demonstrates a fundamental problem of using this type of information in a two-pie chart—the viewer naturally makes a comparison over the two-year period. The result is a flow conclusion derived from stock data. That is, a conclusion is drawn for the period from 1989 *through* 1990, but the data actually represents the information *at* 1989 and *at* 1990. Depending upon the underlying numbers, the *apparent* conclusion might be completely misleading.

A second interpretation of the chart is possible if the viewer is interested only in the amount of change between categories for the two years. If that is the viewer's only interest, Figure 4-1 is acceptable. However, most business people want to know both the amount of change from year to year *and* the total expenditures. In such cases, other chart types might be a better choice; for example, a stacked bar chart could show all of this information.

Keep in mind the following information and advice when you use pie charts:

115

▶ Pie charts are best used to show how a total is distributed among its parts (for example, it displays percentages or ratios).

▶ Pie charts that use flow data often cause viewers to arrive at misleading conclusions.

▶ Avoid using multiple pies in the same chart, especially if the data varies widely in magnitude or is separated by long periods of time.

▶ Too many *slices* make a pie chart cluttered and difficult to read.

▶ Ask yourself: "Would some other type of chart illustrate my point more effectively?"

With those tips and caveats in mind, let's discuss how to create a pie chart.

Creating a Pie Chart

To create a pie chart, first select the `Create new chart` option (1) from the HG Main Menu. Next, select the `Pie` chart option (2). HG immediately displays Page 1 of the Pie Chart 1 Data screen, similar to that shown in Figure 4-2.

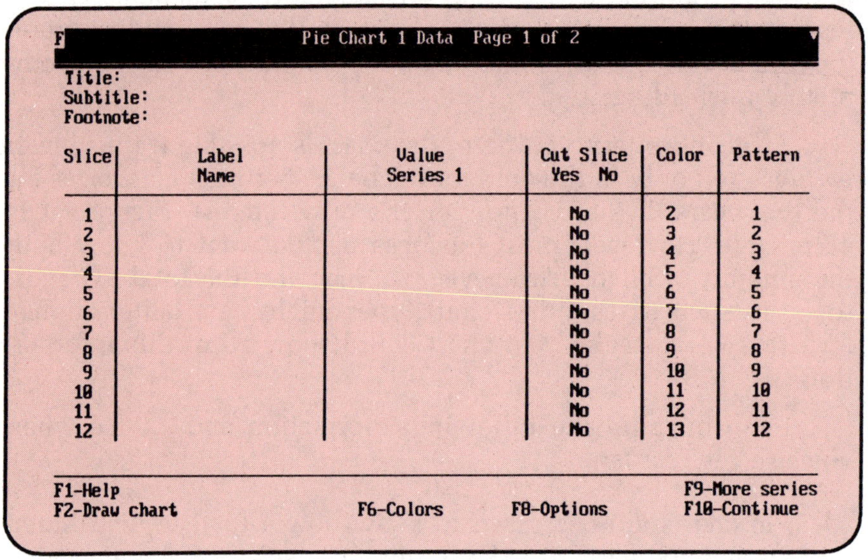

Pie Chart 1 Data Page 1 of 2					

Title:
Subtitle:
Footnote:

Slice	Label Name	Value Series 1	Cut Slice Yes No	Color	Pattern
1			No	2	1
2			No	3	2
3			No	4	3
4			No	5	4
5			No	6	5
6			No	7	6
7			No	8	7
8			No	9	8
9			No	10	9
10			No	11	10
11			No	12	11
12			No	13	12

F1-Help
F2-Draw chart   F6-Colors   F8-Options   F9-More series
                                                               F10-Continue

Figure 4-2.   The Pie Chart 1 Data screen

To use HG to create the examples presented in this chapter, enter the following information into the corresponding fields on Page 1 of the Pie Chart 1 Data screen:

Title: Gross Tax Receipts, 1986
Subtitle:
Footnote: I.R.S. (Billions of Dollars)

Label Name	Value Series 1
Personal Income	416.6
Employment	244.4
Corporation	80.4
Estate and Gift	7.2
Excise	33.7

After you have entered this information, press F2 to view the pie chart. It will look similar to the one shown in Figure 4-3. Now, save the chart so that you can use it later without having to re-enter the data.

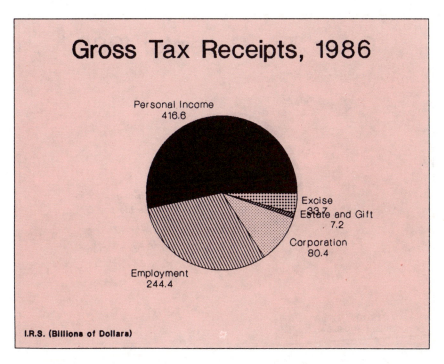

Figure 4-3 content:

Gross Tax Receipts, 1986

Personal Income
416.6

Excise
33.7

Estate and Gift
7.2

Corporation
80.4

Employment
244.4

I.R.S. (Billions of Dollars)

Figure 4-3.   A first attempt at a pie chart

117

This is not a very good chart. The first, and most noticeable, problem is that the Estate and Gift label and the Excise label overlap. Let's try to fix this problem. Press a key to return to Page 1 of the Pie Chart 1 Data screen.

Cut Slice

The Cut Slice column lets you offset pieces of a pie chart relative to the other slices. This serves to emphasize one or more slices of a pie. For example, to emphasize the corporation tax in the example chart, use the Tab key to move the cursor to row 3 of the Cut Slice column. Press Y to select the option. This offsets the corresponding Corporation data, as shown in Figure 4-4.

As you can see in Figure 4-4, cutting a slice out of the pie is not the solution for improving our chart. Press any key to return to the Pie Chart 1 Data screen.

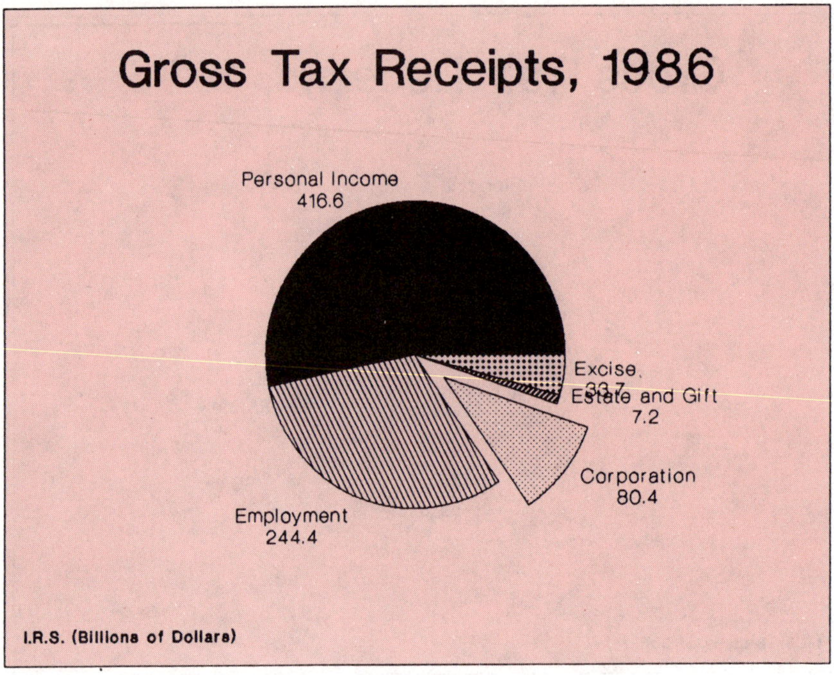

Gross Tax Receipts, 1986

Personal Income
416.6

Excise
33.7
Estate and Gift
7.2

Corporation
80.4

Employment
244.4

I.R.S. (Billions of Dollars)

Figure 4-4.   Using the Cut Slice option to emphasize data

118

> ▶ **Tip:** Although you can offset all slices of a pie, doing so will lessen the visual impact of individual slices and make the chart look somewhat disorganized.

Color

You can change the colors that HG uses to draw the pie chart. Press F6 to display a menu that lists the sixteen available colors (see Figure 4-5). Note that if you print the chart on a standard black-and-white printer, changing the colors has no effect on the final look of the chart.

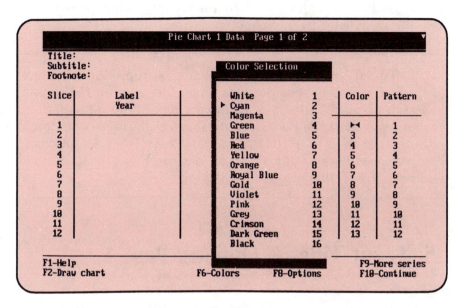

Figure 4-5.   The HG Color Selection menu

▶ **Tip:** If you are producing the chart for a color output device, select your colors carefully. Dark colors tend to emphasize a slice. Also, the HG manual warns that four percent of all males are red-green color blind, so you should not use these two colors together in a chart.

Pattern

The pattern you select for the chart is especially important when you are producing the chart for a standard non-color printer. Figure 2-20 in Chapter 2 shows all of the available pattern styles from which you can make your selections.

If you decide to change pattern styles, try to have another person view your work before you set the final patterns. Some people actually get vertigo from certain heavily-lined patterns, which create a *moire* effect. Also, try to alternate heavy and light line patterns for greater contrast.

Because we are working with a single pie chart, press F8 to go directly to the Pie Chart Titles & Options menu. We'll discuss the second page of the Pie Chart Data screen when we create a two-pie chart later in this chapter.

> ▶ **Tip:** If your final chart will not be reproduced on a color device, consider turning off the color for HG's on-screen display so that you can experiment with a "pattern-only" pie chart. To do so you must select the Pattern option in the last field on Page 1 of the Pie Chart Titles & Options screen (see Figure 4-6). (We will discuss this procedure in detail later in this chapter.)

Pie Chart Titles & Options: Page 1

The options available for pie charts are much the same as those discussed in Chapter 2 for bar and line charts. Because of this similarity, we will concentrate only on new pie-chart elements in this section. Figure 4-6 shows Page 1 of the Pie Chart Titles & Options screen.

Titles, Subtitles, and Footnotes

You can enter or modify the title, subtitle, and footnote for a pie chart exactly as you would with a bar or line chart. If you need to review these procedures, consult the "Titles," "Subtitles," and "Footnote" sections in Chapter 2.

The only new fields on this Titles & Options screen are Pie 1 title and Pie 2 title. As you would expect, these fields let you enter titles for two pie charts. (In Figure 4-1, we titled the two pies 1989 and 1990.) Note that HG positions the titles below the pies by default. To specify that the titles be above the pies, press the F7 key, which displays a size and placement submenu.

Notice in Figure 4-7 the up and down arrows to the left of each pie title field. In the figure, the ↓ symbols next to both pies are active. This is the default mode that displays the titles

below the pies. Use the arrow keys to highlight the correct
option (↑ to display the title above and ↓ to display the title
below), and then press Enter to change the title position. Note
that if your title is two lines long you can also place one line
above the chart and one line below.

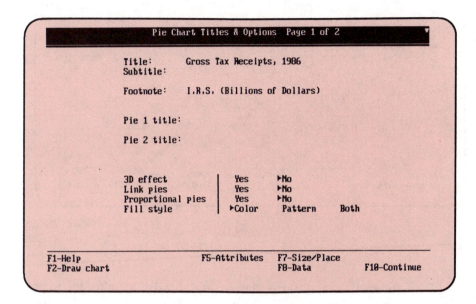

┌───┐
│ Pie Chart Titles & Options   Page 1 of 2   ▼ │
│   │
│   Title: Gross Tax Receipts, 1986   │
│   Subtitle: │
│   │
│   Footnote: I.R.S. (Billions of Dollars)   │
│   │
│   │
│   Pie 1 title: │
│   │
│   Pie 2 title: │
│   │
│   │
│   3D effect   │ Yes   ▶No   │
│   Link pies   │ Yes   ▶No   │
│   Proportional pies│ Yes   ▶No   │
│   Fill style   │ ▶Color   Pattern   Both   │
│   │
│   F1-Help   F5-Attributes   F7-Size/Place   │
│   F2-Draw chart   F8-Data   F10-Continue │
└───┘

Figure 4-6.   Page 1 of the Pie Chart Titles &
Options screen

⊘ **Caution:** If you decide to place the pie titles above the
pies, be sure to leave enough room between the chart
title and the individual pie titles. Also remember that your
charts tend to look "crowded" when the pie titles appear
above the pies.

3D Effect

Activating the 3D effect option causes HG to display the pie in
three dimensions. For example, Figure 4-8 shows the tax
receipts pie chart drawn in three dimensions.

121

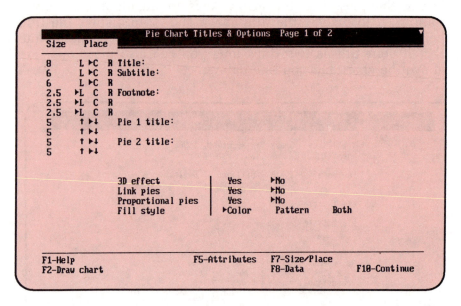

Figure 4-7.   Pressing F7 displays a submenu for changing the size and position of a title

The three-dimensional enhancement rarely adds much to a pie chart and, in fact, can be misleading. Part of the problem is that HG creates the effect by adding depth to the front sections of the pie. This makes these sections appear larger than they really are. For example, In Figure 4-8, the "rim" of the pie gives the illusion of depth, but the Personal Income section of the pie appears smaller than it would without the 3D effect. Under most circumstances, you probably should avoid using the 3D effect with pie charts.

▶ **Tip:** Another disadvantage of 3D pie charts is that you cannot cut a slice out of a pie displayed with the 3D effect.

We will discuss the next two fields, Link pies and Proportional pies, later in this chapter because they are meaningful only when you are displaying two pies in the same chart.

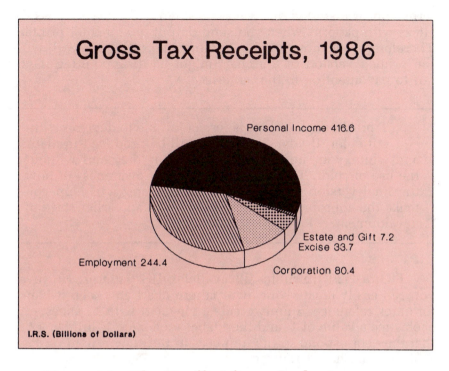

Figure 4-8. The 3D effect for a pie chart

Fill Style

You can use one of three options to distinguish each pie section: Color, Pattern, or Both.

Color

If your system has a color monitor, as you create a pie chart, HG will display each pie slice on the screen with a different color. However, if the chart is destined for a standard non-color printer, the Color option has no impact on the final chart.

Pattern

Your choice of patterns is important for several reasons. First, some pattern combinations are difficult to view. We already mentioned the moire effect that makes some closely-spaced patterns appear distorted or "wavy". Second, HG always draws the slices with patterns when you send output to non-color printers. Therefore, even though color is more interesting to work with, the printed version of the chart might be disappointing if you fail to pay attention to the patterns.

> ▶ **Tip:** Although a chart is less enjoyable to develop without color, if your final chart will be produced in black and white, you should consider creating the chart without the use of color. This will heighten your awareness of how the final version of the chart will look and will help you make the appropriate design decisions at an earlier stage of development.

124

Figure 2-20 illustrates all available HG patterns. However, you can easily create your own pattern chart and keep it handy for quick reference. Simply create a pie chart with 12 slices, give each slice a value of 1, and then label each slice 1 through 12 so that they correspond to the numbers in the Pattern field on Page 1 of the Pie Chart 1 Data screen.

> ▶ **Tip:** Avoid placing dark patterns next to other dark patterns. Heavy patterns side by side often prevent the viewer from distinguishing between pie slices and also can make the chart look lopsided. Always alternate light and dark patterns.

Both

This option draws the pie chart using both patterns and colors for each slice. The only time this option affects the output is if you are using a color printer or other type of color device. I think most viewers will find this option creates charts that are too "busy."

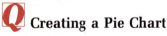 **Creating a Pie Chart**

1. Press 1.   Selects the Create new chart option.

2. Press 2.	Selects the Pie chart option and displays Page 1 of the Pie Chart 1 Data screen.
3. Enter a title, subtitle, and footnote.	Gives the chart a name and lets HG display other pertinent information.
4. Tab to the Label Name field and enter a label for each slice.	Labels what the data in each slice represents.
5. Press Tab; then press ↑ until the cursor is in the first row of the Value Series column.	Moves the cursor to the first series data field.
6. For each slice, type the appropriate data and press Enter.	Enters the data series values for the pie chart.
7. Press F2.	Displays the pie chart. ☐

125

Pie Chart Titles & Options: Page 2

The second page of the Pie Chart Titles & Options screen gives you great control over the details of the final pie chart. Page 2 is presented in Figure 4-9.

Chart Style

This option lets you display the data either as a pie chart or as a column chart. A column chart is similar to the stacked bar chart we created in Chapter 2. For now, let's create a pie chart. However, later in this chapter we will show you a use for the column chart.

Sort Slices

If you set this option to Yes, HG sorts the slices and presents them in descending order, with the largest slice at the top. Figure 4-10 shows the same pie chart shown in Figure 4-3, but after the slices have been sorted. Notice how the slices decrease in value going in a counter-clockwise direction.

Pie Chart Titles & Options	Page 2 of 2						
	Pie 1				**Pie 2**		
Chart style	▶Pie	Column			▶Pie	Column	None
Sort slices	▶Yes	No			Yes	▶No	
Starting angle	340				0		
Pie size	50				50		
Show label	▶Yes	No			▶Yes	No	
Label size	3				3		
Show value	▶Yes	No			▶Yes	No	
Place value	▶Below	Adjacent	Inside		▶Below	Adjacent	Inside
Value format							
Currency	Yes	▶No			Yes	▶No	
Show percent	Yes	▶No			Yes	▶No	
Place percent	▶Below	Adjacent	Inside		▶Below	Adjacent	Inside
Percent format							

F1-Help	
F2-Draw chart	F8-Data F10-Continue

*Figure 4-9.   Page 2 of the Pie Chart Titles &
Options screen*

▶ **Tip:** Sorting the slices of a pie chart often prevents labels from overwriting each other. Notice in Figure 4-10 that the sorting of the pie slices makes the Estate and Gift label *almost* readable.

Starting Angle

Because we read from top to bottom, the slice at the top of a pie chart receives the most attention. Unfortunately, the top slice might not be the one you want to call attention to. The Starting angle field lets you specify an angle (in degrees) by which you can *rotate* the slices of the pie. This enables you to place any given slice at the top of the pie. Figure 4-11 illustrates the results of rotating a pie.

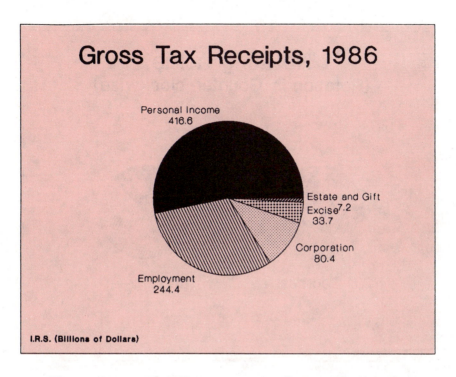

Figure 4-10. The Figure 4-3 pie chart with sorted slices

127

Look at the pie on the left. Notice that the left edge of the dark pie slice is vertical (at the 12 o'clock position). Formally called a *0 degree angle of rotation*, this is HG's default setting.

The pie on the right shows the same slice after changing the angle of rotation to 45 degrees. The angle of rotation starts at 0 degrees; increasing the angle rotates the pie the number of specified degrees in a counter-clockwise direction.

Figure 4-12 shows Figure 4-10 after we rotated the pie 340 degrees. Notice the slight improvement in the readability of the Estate and Gift value (7.2); it's not perfect, but it's better. Remember, you can use both the Sort slices and Starting angle options to improve the legibility of text and values on a chart.

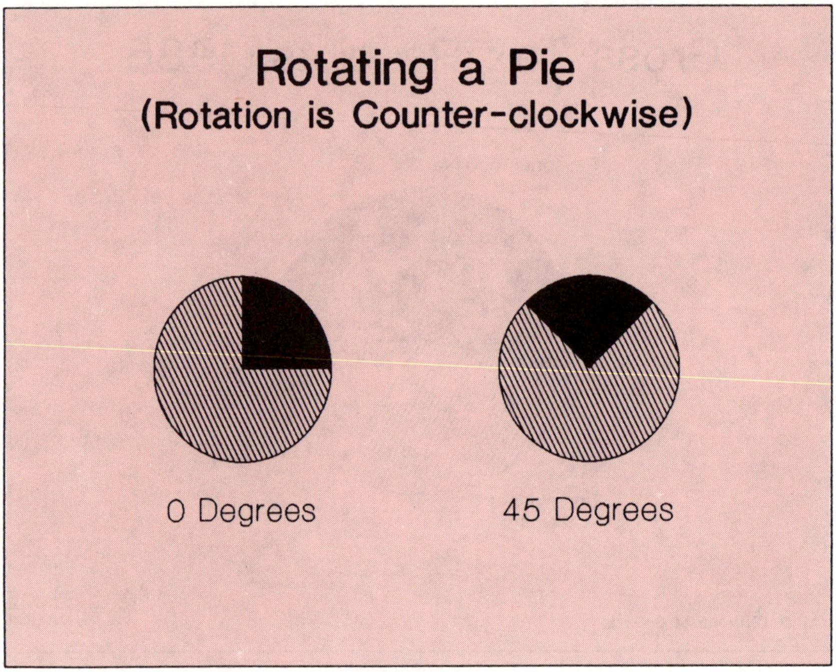

Figure 4-11. *Increasing the angle of rotation*

Q **Sorting and Rotating a Pie Chart to Enhance Readability**

1. Press F2.	Displays the chart. Check labels for readability. If text or values overlap, use the following steps.	
2. Press any key.	Displays the Pie Chart 1 Data screen.	
3. Press F8.	Activates the Titles & Options menu.	
4. Press PgDn.	Selects Page 2 of the Titles & Options menu.	
5. Press Tab.	Moves the cursor to the Sort slices field.	
6. Press Y.	Sets Sort slices to Yes.	
7. Press F2.	Displays the chart. Did sorting improve it? If not, redisplay Page 2 of the Titles & Options screen.	

8. Press Tab until the cursor is in the Starting angle field.	Lets you specify an angle of rotation.
9. Enter an angle.	Rotates the chart a specified number of degrees.
10. Press F2.	Displays the chart. If the chart's appearance is not improved, repeat steps 8, 9, and 10 until you produce the desired effect. □

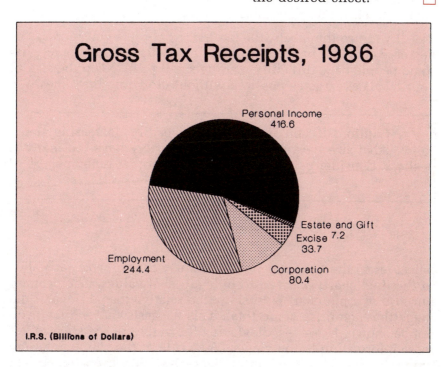

Gross Tax Receipts, 1986

Personal Income
416.6

Estate and Gift
7.2
Excise
33.7

Employment
244.4

Corporation
80.4

I.R.S. (Billions of Dollars)

Figure 4-12.   The Figure 4-10 pie chart after rotation

Pie Size

The Pie size field corresponds to the percent of the chart that the pie itself will occupy. The default setting is 50, meaning that the pie takes up a little less than 50 percent of the screen. The values in this field can range from 0 to 100. A value of 0 displays no pie in the chart. In most cases, the default value is best. However, if you will be using the chart as part of a slide show, you might want to increase the pie size. Increasing the size of the pie can also be helpful when some of the individual slices are relatively small.

Show Label and Label Size

If you set the Show label option to No, HG omits the labels associated with each pie. The default setting displays the labels.

If you use the labels, the Label size field lets you increase or decrease the size of the displayed characters. Don't forget that some people have difficulty reading small print. Keep the size of your labels as large as possible without crowding the slices.

130

> Ø **Caution:** If you find yourself steadily decreasing the label size on a pie chart, you probably have too many slices. Consider using your data in some other type of chart.

Show Value

Select Yes in the Show value field to display the value of each slice in the final chart; select No to hide all label values. The primary purpose of a pie chart is to show the relative magnitudes of the items that comprise some total. This suggests that values need not be shown. However, displaying the values of the slices gives more information to the viewer. As a rule, if the values interfere with other labels (as they do in Figure 4-3), they probably should be omitted; otherwise, they should be displayed.

Place Value

If you select the Yes option for Show value, you can display label values in one of the following three positions:

Below	Displays the values below the labels
Adjacent	Displays the values at the end of the labels
Inside	Displays the values inside the slices

Figure 4-12 uses the `Below` option. Changing the setting to `Adjacent` results in the chart shown in Figure 4-13.

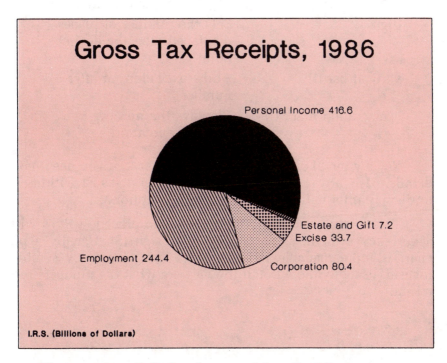

Figure 4-13.   Label values positioned with the Adjacent option

When you compare Figures 4-12 and 4-13, notice that using the `Adjacent` option makes the chart more readable.

> ⊘ **Caution:** Be careful when you select the `Inside` option. HG does not create a "hole" in the slice when it displays the value. Therefore, numbers on dark slices are "invisible" when displayed on a standard printer.

Value Format and Currency

The Value format option behaves exactly as was discussed in the "Format" section of Chapter 2. Recall that the four basic options are:

comma (,)	Places a comma in numbers at the specified location
digit	Sets the number of places displayed after the decimal point
vertical bar (|)	Adds text before or after a number
exclamation mark (!)	Displays the number in scientific notation

132

Review the "Format" section of Chapter 2, if you need more details. Also, always remember that you can press F1 within HG to display information about any field or option.

The Currency option simply tells HG to precede values with a currency symbol, such as the dollar sign ($). Usually a pie chart is more readable if you do not use a currency symbol. Instead, use a footnote to tell the viewers what the numbers represent.

Show Percent, Place Percent, and Percent Format

These three fields correspond to three earlier fields on the screen (Show value, Place value, and Value format), except that they display, place, and format *percentages* rather than the actual values. Their actions, however, are the same.

If you want to show the percent that each slice represents of the total pie, select Yes for the first option. Note that the default selection is No. You can place the percentages below or adjacent to the labels or inside the slices. The Percent format options are the same as the Value format options that we discussed in the previous section.

> ▶ **Tip:** HG will let you position values and percentages at
> the same place on a chart. For example, you can set
> Show value and Show percent to Yes and then set both Place value
> and Place percent to Below. Although HG will display the
> chart, the resulting jumble will look awful. The chart will
> look less crowded if you display *only* values or *only* per-
> centages.

Whether you decide to use percentages or values depends
upon the purpose of the chart. If you want to show your viewers
the breakdown of a total without revealing the actual numbers,
use percentages. Percentages can convey information without
providing unnecessary details.

On the other hand, if you want the reader to be able to
analyze the data, then display the values themselves. If the chart
is an analytical tool that must convey the maximum information
(and you don't care if it looks cluttered), consider presenting
both the values and the percentages.

133

Always remember that a non-color printer can obliterate
any numbers that appear within a dark pie slice.

This completes our discussion of single-pie pie charts. In
the rest of the chapter, you will learn how to create a chart that
displays two pies, and we will discuss some techniques that you
can use to make pie charts more interesting and more readable.

Creating Two-pie Pie Charts

Designing a pie chart that displays two pies is not much different
than the process you used to create a single-pie chart. In fact, the
process is identical except that you must also enter labels and
values for the second pie. Rather than repeat our previous discussions, let's concentrate on those options that differ when you create a two-pie chart.

In the example that follows, you will create a second pie
that uses only the Excise value and the Estate and Gift value
from Figure 4-3. This process shows you more than just how to

design a two-pie chart. The example also illustrates how the previously discussed options affect charts using two pies, and, more importantly, it shows you how to solve a problem that is common to pie charts—displaying slices that are "too small."

Pie Chart 1 Data: Page 1

Let's use the data from the example Gross Tax Receipts pie chart as the basis for our new two-pie chart. Figure 4-14 shows the completed Pie Chart 1 Data screen for the first pie. Note that most of the information is the same as shown in Figure 4-2, except that we removed the Excise and the Estate and Gift labels and values. Instead, the Label Name field for the fourth slice is now blank and the fourth Value Series 1 data field now contains the combined values of the Excise and Estate/Gift fields (7.2 + 33.7 = 40.9).

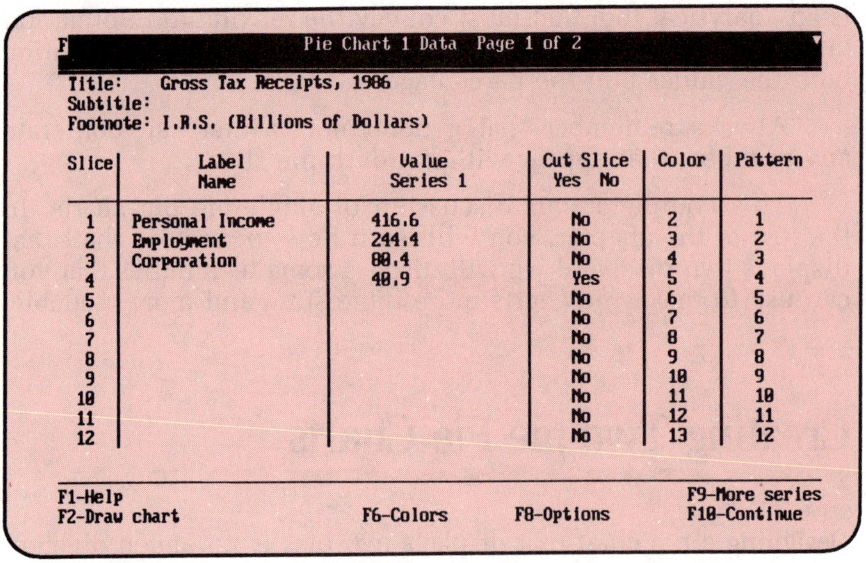

134

```
F                    Pie Chart 1 Data   Page 1 of 2                      ▼
 Title:    Gross Tax Receipts, 1986
 Subtitle:
 Footnote: I.R.S. (Billions of Dollars)

 Slice│       Label          │   Value    │ Cut Slice │ Color │ Pattern
      │       Name           │  Series 1  │ Yes  No   │       │
      ─────────────────────────────────────────────────────────────────
   1    Personal Income         416.6          No         2        1
   2    Employment              244.4          No         3        2
   3    Corporation              88.4          No         4        3
   4                             40.9          Yes        5        4
   5                                           No         6        5
   6                                           No         7        6
   7                                           No         8        7
   8                                           No         9        8
   9                                           No        10        9
  10                                           No        11       10
  11                                           No        12       11
  12                                           No        13       12

 F1-Help                                              F9-More series
 F2-Draw chart              F6-Colors    F8-Options   F10-Continue
```

Figure 4-14.   The Pie Chart 1 Data screen with changes

If you look closely at Figure 4-14, you will also notice that the new entry for Slice 4 has the corresponding Cut Slice field set to Yes. You will understand why this change is necessary when we link the two pies together.

Pie Chart 2 Data: Page 2

Page 2 of the Pie Chart 2 Data screen includes the same fields as Page 1; however, all of the data in this screen applies to the second pie. Simply press the PgDn key to advance to this second data screen, and enter the data shown in Figure 4-15. As you can see, we merely moved the last two labels and values in the original data screen (Figure 4-2) and placed them into the second pie.

135

```
F                      Pie Chart 2 Data   Page 2 of 2
Title:    Gross Tax Receipts, 1986
Subtitle:
Footnote: I.R.S. (Billions of Dollars)

Slice|       Label        |     Value    | Cut Slice | Color | Pattern
     |       Name         |    Series 2  |  Yes  No  |       |

  1   Estate and Gift          7.2           No         2       1
  2   Excise                  33.7           No         3       2
  3                                          No         4       3
  4                                          No         5       4
  5                                          No         6       5
  6                                          No         7       6
  7                                          No         8       7
  8                                          No         9       8
  9                                          No        10       9
 10                                          No        11      10
 11                                          No        12      11
 12                                          No        13      12


F1-Help                                              F9-More series
F2-Draw chart           F6-Colors      F8-Options    F10-Continue
```

Figure 4-15.   Page 2 of the Pie Chart Data screen

Pie Chart Titles & Options: Page 1

Now that we have split our tax data into two pies, we need to tell HG to link the pies together. To do so, first press F8. This displays Page 1 of the Pie Chart Titles & Options screen, as shown in Figure 4-16.

The only entry we need to change in this screen is the Link pies field. Press Tab until the cursor is in this field, and then press Y to change the option to Yes. The two pies are now "linked." To view the linked-pie chart, press F2. The resulting chart will look similar to Figure 4-17.

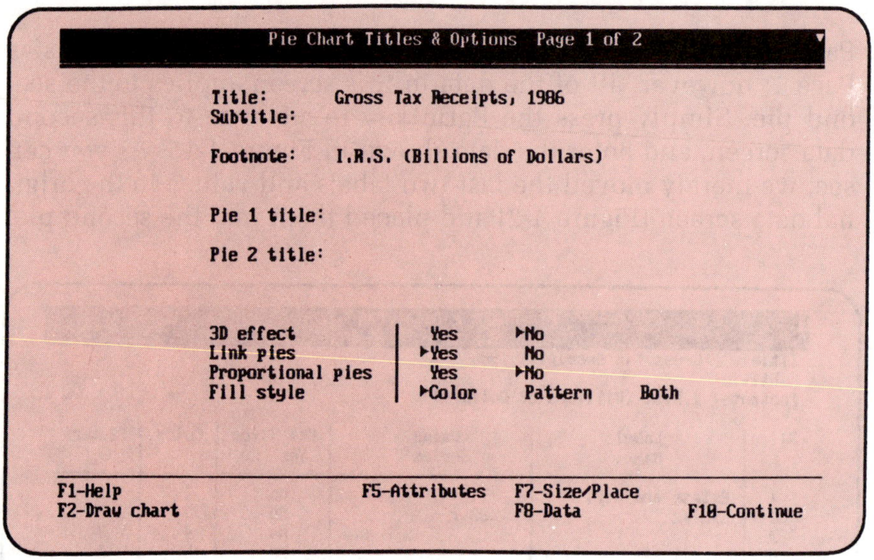

```
                Pie Chart Titles & Options   Page 1 of 2                ▼

          Title:       Gross Tax Receipts, 1986
          Subtitle:

          Footnote:    I.R.S. (Billions of Dollars)


          Pie 1 title:

          Pie 2 title:



          3D effect       │   Yes     ▸No
          Link pies       │  ▸Yes      No
          Proportional pies │ Yes     ▸No
          Fill style      │  ▸Color    Pattern     Both



    ────────────────────────────────────────────────────────────
    F1-Help                    F5-Attributes    F7-Size/Place
    F2-Draw chart                               F8-Data           F10-Continue
```

136

*Figure 4-16.   Page 1 of the Pie Chart Titles &
Options screen*

    Although we indeed created a linked pie chart, it has some
serious problems. Notice how the Excise label interferes with the
Corporation label, thus making the labels and values difficult to
read. To correct this, we need to move the Corporation slice out
of the way of the label in the second pie.

Reordering the Data

First, let's try reordering our data. Press the spacebar to remove
the chart from the screen and restore Page 1 of the Pie Chart
Titles & Options screen.

Turn Off Slice Sorting

Press the PgDn key to advance to Page 2 of the Titles & Options
screen. If you didn't change any of the settings that we used in
our earlier examples, the Sort slices field for Pie 1 should be set
to Yes. Turn off the sorting feature by moving the cursor to this
field and pressing N.

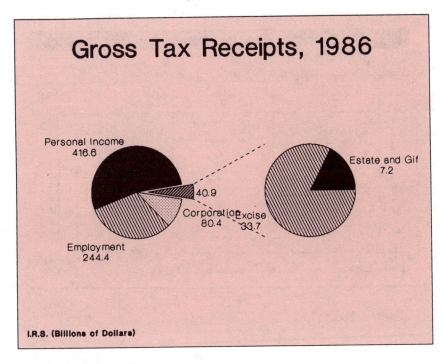

Figure 4-17.   A first attempt at creating a linked-pie chart

137

If the Sort slices option for pie 2 is set to Yes, press the Tab key to advance to the Sort slices option in the Pie 2 column, and press N to change the entry to No.

Reducing the Size of a Pie

Press Enter twice to advance to the Pie size field. We need to make the second pie slightly smaller for two reasons. First, the Estate and Gift label is so long that it crowds the right edge of the chart. Second, making the second pie smaller reinforces the viewer's impression that Pie 2 represents a smaller value than Pie 1. Change the value in the Pie size field to 40. Now press F8 to return to the Page 1 of the Pie Chart 1 Data screen (*not* the Titles & Options screen).

Let's try to improve the chart by reordering the data. Look at Figure 4-18, and reorganize the data on your screen to match the data shown in the figure.

```
┌──────────────────────────────────────────────────────────────────┐
│              Pie Chart 1 Data  Page 1 of 2                    ▼    │
│  Title:    Gross Tax Receipts, 1986                                │
│  Subtitle:                                                         │
│  Footnote: I.R.S. (Billions of Dollars)                           │
│                                                                    │
│  Slice│      Label          │    Value      │ Cut Slice │ Color │ Pattern │
│       │      Name           │    Series 1   │ Yes  No   │       │         │
│  ─────┼─────────────────────┼───────────────┼───────────┼───────┼─────────│
│    1  │ Personal Income     │    416.6      │    No     │   2   │    1    │
│    2  │ Corporation         │     88.4      │    No     │   3   │    2    │
│    3  │ Employment          │    244.4      │    No     │   4   │    3    │
│    4  │                     │     48.9      │    Yes    │   5   │    4    │
│    5  │                     │               │    No     │   6   │    5    │
│    6  │                     │               │    No     │   7   │    6    │
│    7  │                     │               │    No     │   8   │    7    │
│    8  │                     │               │    No     │   9   │    8    │
│    9  │                     │               │    No     │  10   │    9    │
│   10  │                     │               │    No     │  11   │   10    │
│   11  │                     │               │    No     │  12   │   11    │
│   12  │                     │               │    No     │  13   │   12    │
│                                                                    │
│  F1-Help                                           F9-More series  │
│  F2-Draw chart          F6-Colors      F8-Options  F10-Continue    │
└──────────────────────────────────────────────────────────────────┘
```

Figure 4-18. Reordering the Corporation data

> ▶ **Tip:** There is an easy way to reorder chart data. In our example, we want to exchange rows 2 and 3. First, move the cursor to the line you want to move (to the Label Name field in line 2) and then press the Ctrl-↓ key combination. This instantly exchanges the data in lines 2 and 3.
>
> If you want to exchange the data in the other direction (for example, to move row 3 to row 2), merely move the cursor to line 3 and then press Ctrl-↑. These key sequences let you easily move any line to a new position.

If you have followed the previous instructions, and your screen matches Figure 4-18, you are ready to redisplay the linked-pie chart. When you press F2, HG draws the chart shown in Figure 4-19.

The preceding steps have cured most of the problems of the pie chart shown in Figure 4-17. However, you might want to try another alternative.

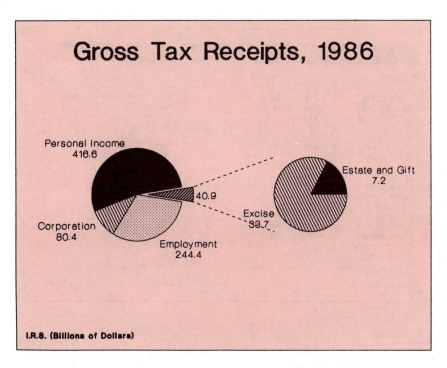

Figure 4-19. The modified linked-pie chart

139

Treating a Slice as a Column

After you finish viewing the chart, press the spacebar to return to the Pie Chart 1 Data screen. Press F8 to activate the Titles & Options screen, and press the PgDn key to advance to Page 2. In the first field of the screen, Chart style, move the cursor to the Pie 2 column, press C, and then press Enter. This changes the chart style from Pie to Column. If the Sort slices field in the Pie 2 column is set to No, change it to Yes. These changes result in the screen shown in Figure 4-20.

When you finish making these changes, press F2 to display the results of your work. Your chart should look similar to Figure 4-21.

```
┌──────────────────────────────────────────────────────────────────┐
│▲          Pie Chart Titles & Options   Page 2 of 2                 │
│████████████████████████████████████████████████████████████████  │
│                                                                    │
│                        Pie 1          │        Pie 2                │
│                 ──────────────────────┼──────────────────────      │
│ Chart style     ►Pie    Column        │   Pie   ►Column   None      │
│ Sort slices     Yes    ►No            │  ►Yes    No                 │
│ Starting angle  0                     │   0                         │
│ Pie size        50                    │   50                        │
│                                       │                             │
│ Show label      ►Yes    No            │  ►Yes    No                 │
│ Label size      3                     │   3                         │
│                                       │                             │
│ Show value      ►Yes    No            │  ►Yes    No                 │
│ Place value     ►Below  Adjacent  Inside │ ►Below  Adjacent  Inside │
│ Value format                          │                             │
│ Currency        Yes    ►No            │   Yes   ►No                 │
│                                       │                             │
│ Show percent    Yes    ►No            │   Yes   ►No                 │
│ Place percent   ►Below  Adjacent  Inside │ ►Below  Adjacent  Inside │
│ Percent format                        │                             │
│ ─────────────────────────────────────────────────────────────     │
│ F1-Help                                                            │
│ F2-Draw chart                         F8-Data        F10-Continue  │
└──────────────────────────────────────────────────────────────────┘
```

Figure 4-20.   Changing Pie 2 to a column chart

This is an acceptable chart. The labels and values are easy to read and understand. The transformation of the second pie into a column also adds a little diversity and interest to the chart.

Hiding a Pie Slice

We can still make one minor improvement to the chart shown in Figure 4-21. If we could ''hide'' the cut slice of the pie, the chart would look less cluttered and the meaning of the column would become more apparent.

To hide a slice, return to Page 1 of the Pie Chart 1 Data screen. Press the Tab key until the cursor is in the Color column (see Figure 4-18). Press the ↓ key until the cursor is in the row in which Cut slice is set to Yes (that is, row 4). Change the color number from 5 to 0.

When you press F2 to view the chart, it should resemble Figure 4-22. Note that the unlabeled Cut slice no longer appears on the chart.

140

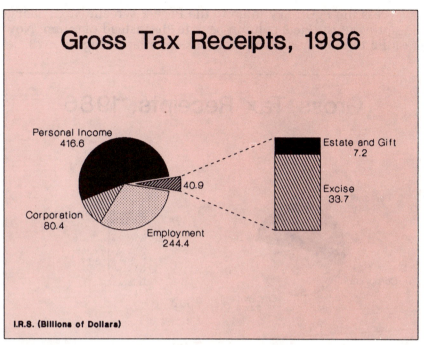

Figure 4-21. *A pie and column chart*

> ▶ **Tip:** If you set the color for a pie slice to 0, HG no longer displays the slice on the chart. This is an easy way to "remove" a slice from a pie without actually erasing the data for the slice.

Proportional Charts

There remains one pie chart option that we have not used—Proportional pies. This option is one of the four "enhancement" fields at the bottom of Page 1 of the Pie Chart Titles & Options screen (see Figure 4-16). If you want to try this option, press the End key to move to the bottom of the screen and then use the arrow keys to place the cursor in the Proportional pies field. Press Y key to select the option.

Press the PgDn key to go to the Page 2 screen. Next, change the setting in the Pie 2 column back to Pie instead of Column. Now, press F2 to display a chart that looks similar to Figure 4-23.

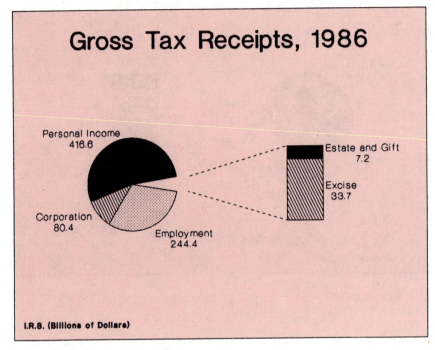

Figure 4-22. *Hiding a pie chart slice*

Although the chart is not pretty, it *is* a proportional pie chart. In most cases, people have difficulty judging how much larger one pie is than another. For that reason, proportional pie charts are less effective than some alternatives.

F5 Key: Character Attributes

If you've examined each screen closely, you've probably noticed that the F5 key has been active during several different data screens. Whenever HG lists F5 at the bottom of the screen, pressing this key displays a small one-line menu on the last line of the screen (see Figure 4-24). The F5 key lets you set the *attributes* for printed characters in all of the HG chart types. The five available attribute options are: Fill, Bold, Italic, Underline, and Color.

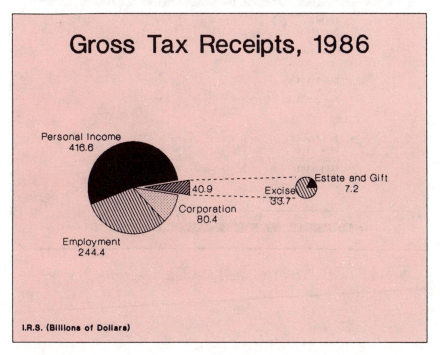

Figure 4-23. *A chart that uses proportional pies*

143

Changing Attributes

Before you press F5, move the cursor to the first character in the field that you want to change. Now, press F5 to display the attributes menu at the bottom of the screen. Notice that the cursor changes color as soon as you press F5.

If you continue to press F5, the cursor will move from left to right across the characters in the field at which the cursor is positioned. This enables you to change a single character, several characters, or the entire line.

> ▶ **Tip:** The fastest way to change the attributes for an entire line of text is to press the Shift-F5 key combination. This tells HG that all characters on the line will be set to the new attribute.

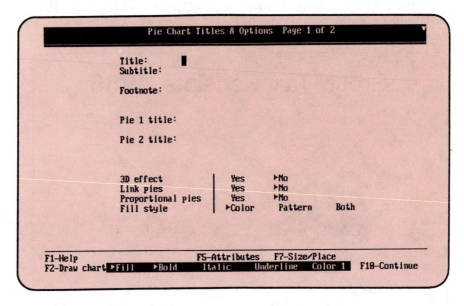

Figure 4-24. The F5 menu for setting printing attributes

Selecting an Attribute

After you highlight the appropriate characters, use the Tab key to move from one attribute in the menu to the next. (Shift-Tab moves to the previous choice in the list.) When the cursor is at the attribute you want to use, press the spacebar. The small marker that appears immediately to the left of that attribute signifies that it is now active. If you press the spacebar while the cursor is at an already active attribute, HG turns off that attribute.

> ⊘ **Caution:** If the cursor is at the Color attribute field, pressing the spacebar does *not* select Color; instead, it increases the specified Color number by 1. To select a new color, press the spacebar until you display the proper color value (or type that value into the Color field), and then press Enter.

When you finish making your selections, press Enter. HG will now use the new attributes for the selected characters or text.

Attribute Effects

Figure 4-25 shows the effects of selecting each attribute. (The Color attribute has multiple attributes, as explained below.)

145

Figure 4-25.   Character attributes

The actual appearance of an attribute varies according to the font that you are currently using. By default, HG uses the Executive font, so the following comments assume that HG is using the Executive font and that the other attributes are turned off.

Fill	A thin, straight character
Bold	A "hollow" character
Italic	A thin character slanted to the right

Underline	An underlined Fill character
Color	A character displayed in the selected color

Multiple Attributes

You can use multiple attributes for characters. For example the word "Color" in Figure 4-25 uses the attributes Fill, Bold, and Color 5. The default attributes (used in all the chart examples presented thus far) are Fill and Bold, which results in a thick, filled-in letter. You can achieve some interesting effects by using different combinations. Keep in mind, however, that the purpose of the text is to convey information to the reader. Overusing different character attributes can detract from a chart.

146

What You Have Learned

In this chapter, you learned how to recognize the appropriate data for a pie chart. Pie charts commonly show how the parts of a data series relate to each other; therefore, pie charts usually depict ratios or percentages. You learned how to create pie charts, two-pie charts, linked-pie charts, and proportional-pie charts. The many examples in the chapter illustrated common problems that you will encounter as you create your pie charts; more importantly the chapter also showed you how to correct these problems, sometimes presenting more than one acceptable solution.

Chapter 5

Area and High/Low/ Close Charts

In This Chapter

- ▶ *Using area and high/low/close charts effectively*
- ▶ *Creating an area chart*
- ▶ *Designing area charts for emphasis*
- ▶ *Creating a high/low/close chart*

In this chapter, you will learn how to construct area and high/ low/close charts. Most of the options that you will use to create these charts were discussed in Chapter 2, "Bar and Line Charts"; if you need to refresh your memory, refer to the appropriate sections. This chapter will concentrate on those options that are unique to area and high/low/close chart types.

When to Use Area and High/Low/Close Charts

Area charts are used primarily to show volume or cumulative totals during a period of time. Therefore, area charts almost always use flow data, or data with a time subscript. For example, an area chart can be an effective means for showing the year-by-year allocation of total revenues to various expense categories and to profit. However, area charts can also be used to emphasize relationships between series of data: We will present such an example later in the chapter.

The use for high/low/close charts is probably obvious. They show the range of data over a given period of time: The high, low, and closing prices of a company's stock is the classic example. However, because these charts typically show more than one high/low range, the data normally spans more than one time period. For example, showing the one-day high/low prices of an issue of stock is not all that interesting; therefore, these charts usually show the high and low values for a week or a month. Used in this manner, high/low/close charts rely on flow data, or data that spans a period of time. Later in the chapter, you will see that high/low/close charts are also effective for creating Gantt and PERT charts.

148

Creating an Area Chart

To create an area chart, first select the Create new chart option (1) from the HG Main Menu. Next, select the Area option (4) from the Create New Chart submenu, as shown in Figure 5-1.

X Data Type Menu

When HG displays the X Data Type Menu, select the appropriate data type. (For more information about this menu, see the "X Data Type Menu" section in Chapter 2.) If you want to follow the examples in this chapter, simply select Name as the X data type and leave the other fields empty. (The data we will be charting starts with 1980 and skips to 1984; entering the years in the X Axis Name field is just as easy as deleting the 1981-1983 rows that HG would create if you specified a starting value of 1980, an ending value of 1987, and an increment of 1.)

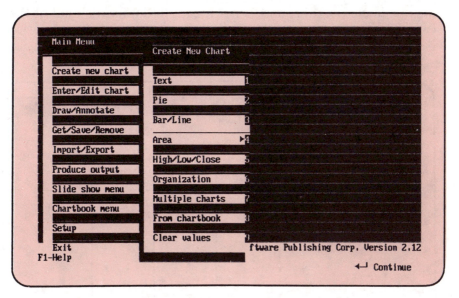

Figure 5-1. The Create New Chart submenu

Area Chart Data

After you enter the appropriate information in the X Data Type Menu, HG displays the Area Chart Data menu, which is identical to the Bar Chart Data menu discussed in Chapter 2. Fill in the title, subtitle, footnote, and various data fields with the text and values shown in Figure 5-2.

Notice that we entered the largest values (the United States data) as the first data series. This tells HG to display these values on the "bottom" of the chart.

> ▶ **Tip:** HG places Series 1 data at the bottom of the chart, Series 2 on top of Series 1, and so on for all data series that you specify.

After you have entered the data in Figure 5-2, press F2 to display the chart. Notice that the U.S. data exhibits relatively little change and generally has larger values than does the Japanese data. We want our example to show that U.S. unit labor costs are

149

relatively constant when compared with those of Japan. Unlike most area charts, this chart is *not* meant to depict the total of the two data series: Its purpose is to show the change in one series relative to the change in another series.

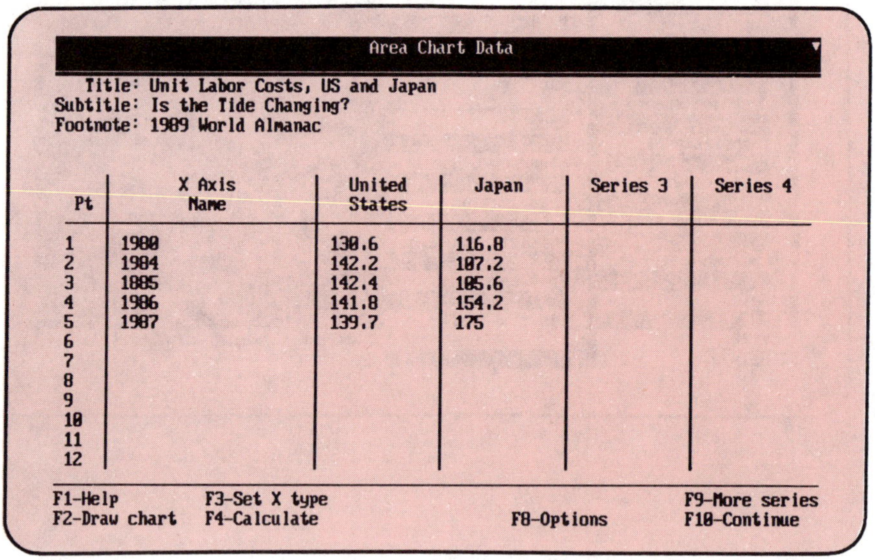

```
┌─────────────────────────────────────────────────────────────────┐
│                        Area Chart Data                         ▼ │
│    Title: Unit Labor Costs, US and Japan                         │
│ Subtitle: Is the Tide Changing?                                  │
│ Footnote: 1989 World Almanac                                     │
│                                                                  │
│            X Axis        United     Japan    Series 3  Series 4  │
│       Pt   Name          States                                  │
│       1   1980           130.6      116.8                        │
│       2   1984           142.2      107.2                        │
│       3   1985           142.4      105.6                        │
│       4   1986           141.8      154.2                        │
│       5   1987           139.7      175                          │
│       6                                                          │
│       7                                                          │
│       8                                                          │
│       9                                                          │
│      10                                                          │
│      11                                                          │
│      12                                                          │
│                                                                  │
│  F1-Help        F3-Set X type                     F9-More series │
│  F2-Draw chart  F4-Calculate         F8-Options   F10-Continue   │
└─────────────────────────────────────────────────────────────────┘
```

Figure 5-2.   A completed Area Chart Data menu

▶ **Tip:** If you are creating an area chart to show change, place the data with the fewest fluctuations in Series 1. This approach lets you emphasize the variations of the next data series.

⊘ **Caution:** HG limits your data series to a maximum of 100 data points. It is unlikely that you will be plotting that many points, so this restriction should not cause a problem.

Now that you've seen the basic chart, let's try to improve it. Press F8 to display Page 1 of the Area Chart Titles & Options menu.

Area Chart Titles & Options: Page 1

Figure 5-3 shows the first page of the Titles & Options menu for the data that we entered earlier. Note that we filled in the X axis title field with Year and the Y1 axis title field with US Dollars, but we left the Legend Title field blank.

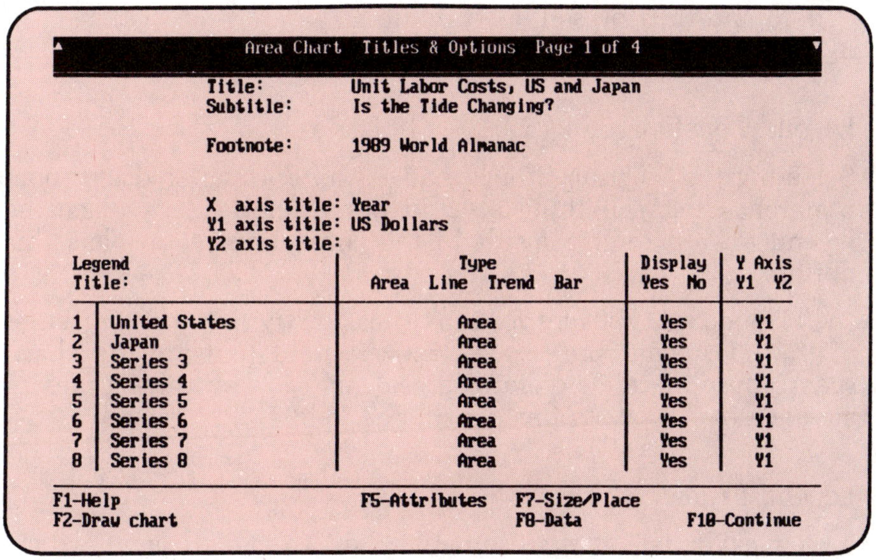

```
▲          Area Chart  Titles & Options  Page 1 of 4              ▼
             Title:        Unit Labor Costs, US and Japan
             Subtitle:     Is the Tide Changing?

             Footnote:     1989 World Almanac


             X  axis title: Year
             Y1 axis title: US Dollars
             Y2 axis title:
     Legend                          Type           Display | Y Axis
     Title:                 Area  Line  Trend  Bar   Yes  No | Y1  Y2

       1 │ United States          Area            Yes        Y1
       2 │ Japan                  Area            Yes        Y1
       3 │ Series 3               Area            Yes        Y1
       4 │ Series 4               Area            Yes        Y1
       5 │ Series 5               Area            Yes        Y1
       6 │ Series 6               Area            Yes        Y1
       7 │ Series 7               Area            Yes        Y1
       8 │ Series 8               Area            Yes        Y1

 F1-Help                    F5-Attributes   F7-Size/Place
 F2-Draw chart                             F8-Data         F10-Continue
```

Figure 5-3. Page 1 of the Area Chart Titles & Options menu

The Series 1 data is labeled United States and the Series 2 data is labeled Japan. Let's not change any of the other settings on this page. Press the PgDn key for the Page 2 of the Titles & Options menu.

The Area Chart Titles & Options: Page 2

We'll use most of the default settings on this page, with the exception of the legend fields. Press the Tab key until the cursor moves to the Legend Location field.

> ▶ **Tip:** If you feel comfortable with the other cursor movement keys, you can use them to move to this field more quickly; for example, press the End key and then press either ↑ or the Shift-Tab combination until the cursor is at Legend Location. Of course, if you have a mouse, you merely have to position the cursor in the Legend Location field and then press the left button.

Legend Location

Selecting the location of a legend is more a matter of personal preference than anything else. In our example, let's place the legend toward the right side of the chart. Press R to select this option.

152

The default settings for the Legend justify field (in the center of the chart) and the Legend placement field (outside the chart) seem appropriate. Therefore, press the Tab key three times to advance the cursor to the Legend Frame field.

Legend Frame

In our example, let's try something different—a legend with a single frame line. Press S until the you select the Single option. Now, check your screen against the completed Page 2 Titles & Options menu shown in Figure 5-4.

> ▶ **Tip:** If you will be using legends in related charts, be sure that their type and placement is consistent from one chart to the next.

We will use all of the defaults on Page 3 of the Titles & Options menu. Press the PgDn key twice to advance to Page 4 of the Titles & Options menu.

The Area Chart Titles & Options: Page 4

We will also use all of the defaults on Page 4 of the Titles & Options menu; however, before you display the chart, notice

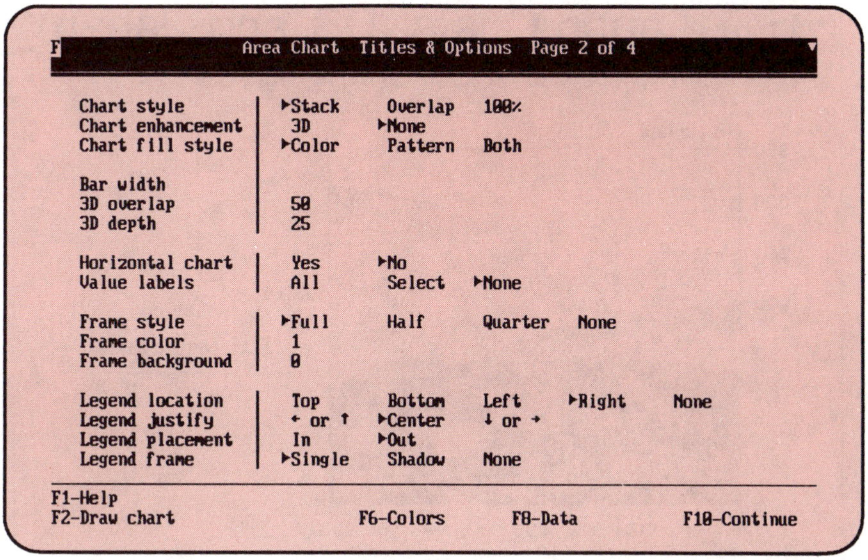

```
┌──────────────────────────────────────────────────────────────────┐
│ F▌     Area Chart  Titles & Options  Page 2 of 4               ▼ │
│                                                                    │
│   Chart style       │▶Stack    Overlap   100%                      │
│   Chart enhancement │ 3D       ▶None                               │
│   Chart fill style  │▶Color    Pattern   Both                      │
│                     │                                              │
│   Bar width         │                                              │
│   3D overlap        │ 50                                           │
│   3D depth          │ 25                                           │
│                                                                    │
│   Horizontal chart  │ Yes      ▶No                                 │
│   Value labels      │ All      Select    ▶None                     │
│                                                                    │
│   Frame style       │▶Full     Half      Quarter   None            │
│   Frame color       │ 1                                            │
│   Frame background  │ 0                                            │
│                                                                    │
│   Legend location   │ Top      Bottom    Left     ▶Right   None    │
│   Legend justify    │ ← or ↑   ▶Center   ↓ or →                    │
│   Legend placement  │ In       ▶Out                                │
│   Legend frame      │▶Single   Shadow    None                      │
│ ─────────────────────────────────────────────────                 │
│ F1-Help                                                            │
│ F2-Draw chart              F6-Colors    F8-Data      F10-Continue  │
└──────────────────────────────────────────────────────────────────┘
```

153

Figure 5-4. The completed Page 2 of the Area Chart Titles & Options menu

that the Page 4 lets you display the data as cumulative totals. You might want to experiment with this option (set the Cum column to Yes) to see the impact it has on the way HG presents the data.

This page also lets you select the colors and patterns that will be used when the chart is printed or displayed. To select different colors, use the Tab key to advance to the Color field and then press F6 to list the color options. The available patterns are the same as those for bar and pie charts.

> ▶ **Tip:** The default patterns specified by HG are well-conceived because they start with darker (solid) patterns and increase to lighter patterns. Placing the darker patterns near the bottom of an area chart makes the chart appear more "stable" because the data appears to be resting on a solid base.

Now press F2 to display the results of your selections. The area chart will look like the one shown in Figure 5-5.

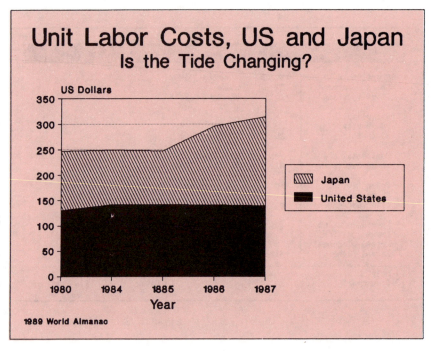

Figure 5-5. **The completed example area chart**

Although the finished chart does its job and shows that unit labor costs in Japan are rising at a faster rate than they are in the United States, the chart is pretty boring. Area charts tend to look flat, especially when the data does not vary as much as it does in our example chart. A few minor changes can make this chart much more interesting. The next section will show you how to experiment with different options to make the chart better.

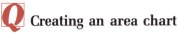 **Creating an area chart**

1.	At the Main Menu, press 1.	Selects the Create new chart option.
2.	Press 4.	Selects the Area chart option.
3.	Fill out the X Data Type Menu and press Enter.	Enters the proper data type, and, optionally, the starting, ending, and increment values.

154

4. At the Area Chart Data screen, enter a title, subtitle, and footnote.

These fields are optional.

5. Enter the appropriate labels in the X Axis field.

HG displays these labels along the X axis.

6. Press Tab; then press ↑ until the cursor is in the first row of the Series 1 column.

Advances the cursor to the first series data field.

7. Enter Series 1 data.

HG displays this data (usually the largest) at the bottom of the chart.

8. Press Tab; then press ↑ until the cursor is in the first row of the Series 2 column.

Advances the cursor to the second series data field.

155

9. Enter Series 2 data.

This data is usually of major interest to the viewer.

10. Press F8.

Displays Page 1 of the Area Chart Titles & Options menu.

11. Tab to X axis title field and enter a title.

Labels the X axis so that the viewer know what type of data it represents.

12. Enter a title in the Y1 axis title field.

Labels the Y axis so that the viewer know what type of data it represents.

13. Enter legend in the Legend Title field.

This field is optional.

14. Add titles in the Series rows.

Defines the data in the individual series.

15. Press F2.

Displays the chart; check to see if it needs to be modified. □

Improving Your Area Charts

Area charts often appear lifeless because they typically deal with few variables. As a result, they look flat and uninteresting. Adding depth to an area chart, however, can make it visually more appealing.

The Three-Dimensional Option

The first change you might make to an unsatisfactory area chart is to use the 3D option, located on Page 2 of the Titles & Options menu (see Figure 5-4). Change the Chart enhancement field from None to 3D by pressing 3. Next, press the End key to advance to the last field on the page, and change the Legend frame from Single to Shadow (press S). Press F2 to display the three-dimensional chart shown in Figure 5-6.

156

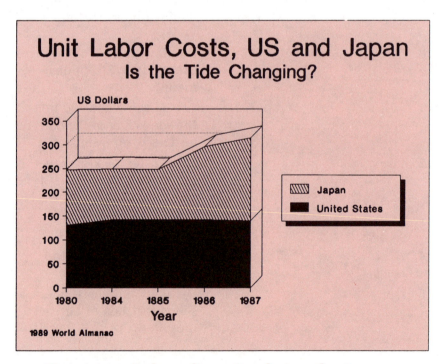

Figure 5-6.   *A three-dimensional area chart*

Now, compare Figures 5-5 and 5-6. Notice how the use of the 3D effect eliminates the flatness of original chart and gives the presentation more drama.

> ▶ **Tip:** As you experiment with the 3D option in your area charts, you will find that this effect is not appropriate for *all* charts. For example, stacked 3D charts are not effective for emphasizing the total of a series of data.

Emphasizing the Values of Two Series

If you want to emphasize the totals for two series, your data might be more interesting if you use an area chart with overlapping bars. To see this effect, first press Esc to return to Page 2 of the Titles & Options menu. Next, press the Home key to advance the cursor to the Chart style field. Finally, press 0 to change the current style from stacked areas to overlapping areas.

157

Exchanging Data Series

With an overlapping style, an area chart displays the first data series *in front* of the second series. Because the US data starts with values that are larger than the Japanese data, you need to exchange the two data series. To do so, press F8 to return to the Area Chart Data menu (see Figure 5-2). At this menu, press the Tab key to advance the cursor to the first data series (that is, the United States data column).

To exchange these series, you need to use one of the calculation options. Press F4 to display the Calculate menu in the middle of the screen. Press the Tab key to advance the cursor to the Calculation field and type:

    @EXCH(#2)

so that your Calculate menu looks like the one shown in Figure 5-7.

As you saw in the "Exchanging Data Series" section in Chapter 3, this command tells HG to exchange the data in the column at which the cursor is positioned (that is, United States) with the column number specified in the calculation (2). When

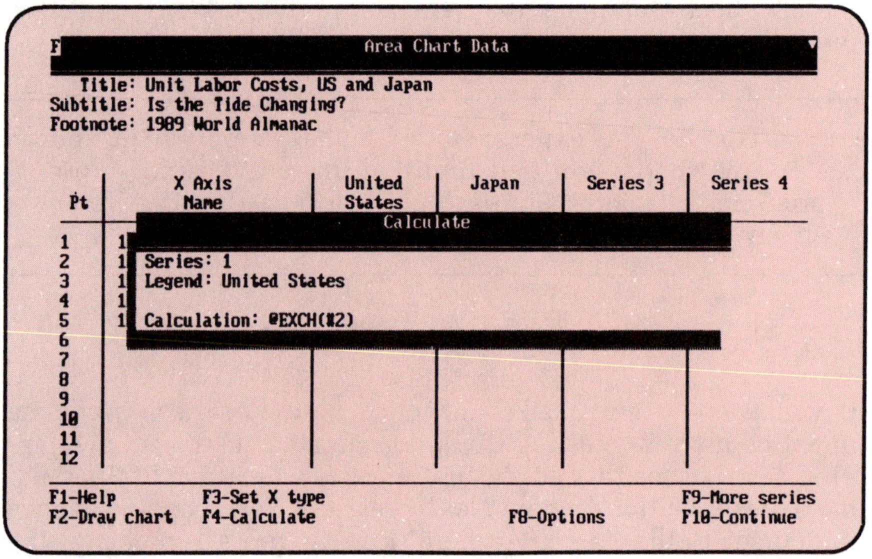

Figure 5-7. Using the Calculate option to exchange data

you press Enter (or F10), HG instantly swaps the data in the Series 1 and 2 columns. This places the smaller Japanese data in front of the U.S. data and makes the chart more readable.

Press F2 to display the revised chart. Figure 5-8 shows the result of these changes.

Figure 5-8 has two big advantages over previous versions of the chart: it is visually more interesting, and it better shows the relative magnitudes of the data. The only disadvantage is that some of the Japanese area hides a portion of the U.S. data in the last year. Still, most viewers would agree that this chart is more effective and dramatic than a "straight" area chart.

Now, save the chart so that you can experiment with it later without having to re-enter the data.

158

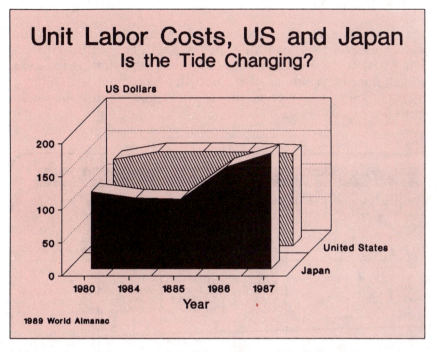

Figure 5-8.   Overlapping areas with the 3D enhancement

Area Charts That Emphasize a Total

In some situations you'll need to show how each series of data contributes to a total. In the following example, we will chart the proportion of pollution abatement costs that are paid by business, government, and individuals. The goal of this chart is to show the relative contribution each segment of society makes to the total pollution-abatement effort. Furthermore, let's assume that we are more interested in the relative contribution of each sector than in the absolute dollar amounts contributed by each sector.

An Example Chart

To create this chart, press 1 at the Main Menu, and press 4 at the Create New Chart submenu. Because we will be plotting consecutive years, at the X Data Type Menu, enter the starting value as 1979, the ending value as 1983, and the increment as 1. Fill in the Area Chart Data menu with the text and values shown in Figure 5-9.

		Area Chart Data			▼
Title: Pollution Abatement Expenditures					
Subtitle: Business Leads the Way					
Footnote: 1989 World Almanac					

Pt	X Axis Name	Business	Government	Personal	Series 4
1	1979	29.008	11.377	5.426	
2	1980	32.283	11.62	6.589	
3	1981	35.545	10.647	8.152	
4	1982	35.61	10.571	8.318	
5	1983	37.619	10.705	9.737	
6					
7					
8					
9					
10					
11					
12					

F1-Help	F3-Set X type			F9-More series
F2-Draw chart	F4-Calculate		F8-Options	F10-Continue

Figure 5-9.   The completed Area Chart Data menu for the example chart

Next, press F8 to display Page 1 of the Area Chart Titles & Options menu. Enter Year in the X axis title field and Billions of Dollars in the Y1 axis title field. In the Legend Title field, enter Spending Source. Finally, enter Business as the name of the Series 1 data, Government as Series 2, and Personal as Series 3.

After you finish entering the sample data, press the F2 key to view the results. As before, this chart is lifeless and unappealing. Let's try to make some improvements.

Area Chart Titles & Options: Page 2

Return to the Titles & Options menu. Press the PgDn key to advance to Page 2. At the Chart style field, change the current setting to the 100% option by pressing 1. Change Chart enhancement to 3D by pressing 3. Now, move the cursor to the Legend location field, and press R to select the Right option. At the Legend frame field, press S to select Single. After you have finished making these changes, the completed input screen should look exactly like Figure 5-10.

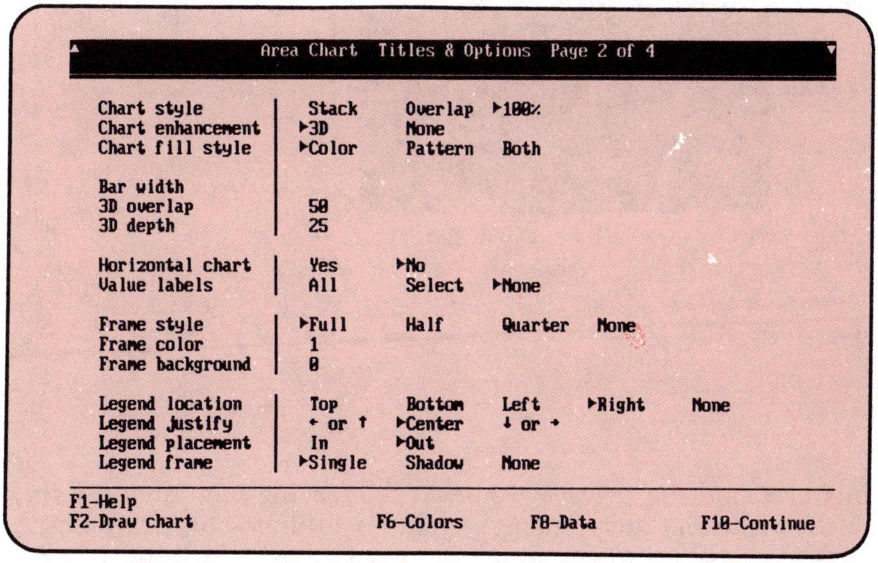

```
                Area Chart  Titles & Options  Page 2 of 4
▲                                                                     ▼

    Chart style       │  Stack      Overlap  ▶100%
    Chart enhancement │ ▶3D         None
    Chart fill style  │ ▶Color      Pattern   Both

    Bar width         │
    3D overlap        │  50
    3D depth          │  25

    Horizontal chart  │  Yes       ▶No
    Value labels      │  All        Select   ▶None

    Frame style       │ ▶Full       Half      Quarter   None
    Frame color       │  1
    Frame background  │  0

    Legend location   │  Top        Bottom    Left    ▶Right    None
    Legend justify    │  ← or ↑    ▶Center    ↓ or →
    Legend placement  │  In        ▶Out
    Legend frame      │ ▶Single     Shadow    None

  F1-Help
  F2-Draw chart                    F6-Colors      F8-Data       F10-Continue
```

Figure 5-10.   Settings for the sample Page 2 Titles & Options menu

161

Now, press F2 to view the resulting chart. Your revised area chart should look similar to Figure 5-11.

Note the percentages on the Y axis. When you selected the 100% option in the Chart style field, HG automatically replaced the dollar values with percentages—exactly what we wanted the chart to show. Because the height of the Y axis represents 100 percent, this type of area chart lets you easily see the relative contribution of each series to the total. We used the 3D effect to make the chart more interesting than its two-dimensional counterpart. Finally, notice how this type of chart emphasizes that

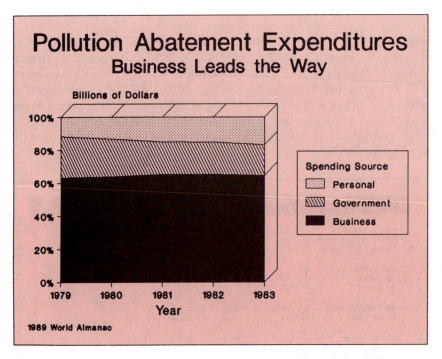

Figure 5-11. **An area chart in which totals are important**

business and the private sector are increasing their share of the costs while the government's share is falling. The 100-percent area chart is perfect for showing such interrelationships.

As long as you have a sample data set entered into HG, you might want to experiment with some of the other Chart Area Titles & Options menus to see if you can find another combination of options that better suits your needs and preferences. When you finish, you might want to save the chart so that you can experiment with it later without having to re-enter the data.

High/Low/Close Charts

High/low/close (referred to as HLC from now on) charts are used to show the range of a data series, usually through time. Rather than create a standard chart that plots stock prices or temperatures, let's devise a chart that will let us monitor a production process to see if there is a correlation between the number of product defects and the time of day.

> ▶ **Tip:** Sometimes you can use multiple graphs to clarify a point. For example, you could first show the pollution abatement costs as a standard area or bar chart. This would give the viewer the raw values—the number of dollars spent. A second chart using a 100 percent area chart would emphasize the point about the rising private costs of pollution abatement. This *raw-refined* approach adds emphasis to a presentation and helps hold the viewer's interest.

First, select the Create new chart option (1) from the HG Main Menu, and then select the High/Low/Close option (5) from the Create New Chart submenu (see Figure 5-1). Next, set the X Data Type field to Name, and leave the Starting with, Ending with, and Increment fields blank.

163

Now, enter the text and values for the sample chart. Figure 5-12 shows the HLC Chart Data menu filled in with the appropriate values.

Next, press F8 to display Page 1 of the High/Low/Close Titles & Options menu. At the X axis title field, enter Time of Day; at the Y1 axis title field, enter Defects; and for the Legend Title, enter Defect Ranges. Enter the Series 1, 2, and 3 titles as Maximum, Minimum, and Average, respectively.

Press the PgDn key to display Page 2 of the Titles & Options menu. Move the cursor to the Legend location field and press R to select the Right option. Finally, change the Legend frame field to Single. Now we're ready to view the chart. Press F2 to display the HLC chart shown in Figure 5-13.

The chart is unacceptable because the X axis values run together. Recall that you can use a vertical bar (|) to stagger data series labels (see the "Name" section in Chapter 2 for details). If the chart is still on your screen, press a key to display the High/Low/Close Chart Data menu. Now, change the values in the X axis column (the hours) to match the column in Figure 5-14.

```
╔═══════════════════════════════════════════════════════════════════╗
║                    High/Low/Close Chart Data                    ▼ ║
║ ┌───────────────────────────────────────────────────────────────┐ ║
║ │                                                                 │ ║
║    Title: Average Defects Per Hour                                ║
║ Subtitle: (Weekly Averages)                                       ║
║ Footnote: Internal Production Data                                ║
║                                                                   ║
║          X Axis      Maximum    Minimum    Average      Open       ║
║   Pt      Name                                                     ║
║                                                                   ║
║   1    8:00 - 9:00    4          1          3                      ║
║   2    9:00 - 10:00   6          2          5                      ║
║   3    10:00 - 11:00  3          1          2.5                    ║
║   4    11:00 - 12:00  5          3          3.5                    ║
║   5    12:00 - 1:00   7          3          3.75                   ║
║   6    1:00 - 2:00    4          1          2.75                   ║
║   7    2:00 - 3:00    7          3          4.5                    ║
║   8    3:00 - 4:00    8          5          6.25                   ║
║   9                                                                ║
║   10                                                               ║
║   11                                                               ║
║   12                                                               ║
║                                                                   ║
║ F1-Help        F3-Set X type                      F9-More series  ║
║ F2-Draw chart  F4-Calculate          F8-Options   F10-Continue    ║
╚═══════════════════════════════════════════════════════════════════╝
```

Figure 5-12.   The completed High/Low/Close Chart Data menu for the example chart

Notice that we also shortened each label to better fit the limited space for X axis labels. When you press F2, HG displays the results of these two changes, as shown in Figure 5-15.

Even though most of the information is the same as before, the resulting chart is much easier to read. Still, we can further refine the chart to make it even clearer.

Q Creating a High/Low/Close chart

1. At the Main Menu, press 1.

   Selects the `Create new chart` option.

2. Press 5.

   Displays the High/Low/Close X Data Type Menu.

3. Fill out the X Data Type Menu and press Enter.

   Enters the proper data type, and, optionally, the starting, ending, and increment values.

4. At the High/Low/Close Chart Data screen, enter a title, subtitle, and footnote.

   These fields are optional.

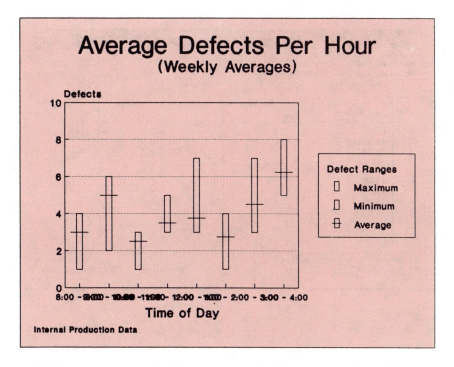

Figure 5-13.   The first version of the example HLC chart

5. Enter the appropriate labels in the X Axis Name field.	HG displays these labels along the X axis.
6. Press Tab; then press ↑ until the cursor is in the first row of the Series 1 column.	Advances the cursor to the first series data field.
7. Enter Series 1 data.	HG displays this data (usually the largest) at the bottom of the chart.
8. Press Tab; then press ↑ until the cursor is in the first row of the Series 2 column.	Advances the cursor to the second series data field.
9. Enter as many data series as you want to chart.	Supplies the values for the X axis of the chart.
10. Press F8.	Displays Page 1 of the Area Chart Titles & Options menu.

```
┌──────────────────────────────────────────────────────────────────────────┐
│ F▐                        High/Low/Close Chart Data                      ▼│
│                                                                            │
│      Title: Average Defects Per Hour                                       │
│   Subtitle: (Weekly Averages)                                             │
│   Footnote: Internal Production Data                                      │
│                                                                            │
│           X Axis          Maximum    Minimum    Average     Open          │
│     Pt     Name                                                            │
│                                                                            │
│     1   8:00              4          1          3                         │
│     2   !9:00            6          2          5                          │
│     3   10:00            3          1          2.5                        │
│     4   !11:00           5          3          3.5                        │
│     5   12:00            7          3          3.75                       │
│     6   !1:00            4          1          2.75                       │
│     7   2:00             7          3          4.5                        │
│     8   !3:00            8          5          6.25                       │
│     9                                                                      │
│     10                                                                     │
│     11                                                                     │
│     12                                                                     │
│                                                                            │
│   F1-Help          F3-Set X type                        F9-More series    │
│   F2-Draw chart    F4-Calculate           F8-Options    F10-Continue      │
└──────────────────────────────────────────────────────────────────────────┘
```

166

Figure 5-14.   Inserting vertical bars to stagger X axis labels

11. Tab to X axis title field and enter a title.

Labels the X axis so that the viewer know what type of data it represents.

12. Enter a title in the Y1 axis title field.

Labels the Y axis so that the viewer know what type of data it represents.

13. Enter legend in the Legend title field.

This field is optional.

14. Add titles in the Series rows.

Defines the data in the individual series.

15. Press F2.

Displays the chart; check to see if it needs to be modified. ☐

Refining the HLC Chart

First, the legend title makes it obvious that the chart is display-ing ranges. Therefore, we can collapse the Maximum and Minimum series labels to simply read Minimum-Maximum for the first series

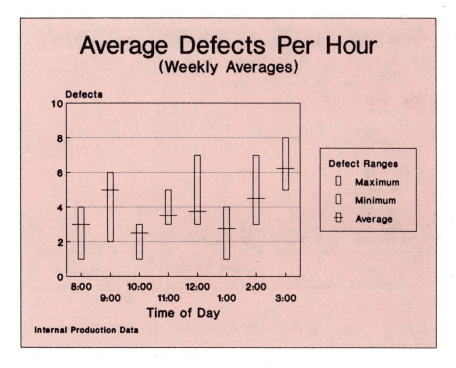

Figure 5-15.   The example HLC with X axis changes

label. To do so, press F8 to display Page 1 of the Titles & Options menu, and then press the Tab key until the cursor is in the first series label field. Change this label to Minimum-Maximum. Next, press Tab to move the cursor to the second series label field, and then erase the entry (that is, Minimum). This procedure will remove this entry from the legend box.

Now, press the PgDn key to advance to Page 2 of the Titles & Options menu. Press the Tab key once to move the cursor to the High/Low style field. Press E to change the option in this field from the default Bar setting to Error bar (see Figure 5-16).

Press F2 to display the final version of the chart, shown in Figure 5-17.

Compare this version of the chart to the original version in Figure 5-13. Notice how the chart in Figure 5-17 is easier to read and looks less cluttered.

```
┌─────────────────────────────────────────────────────────────────┐
│ ▲        High/Low/Close Chart  Titles & Options  Page 2 of 4   ▼ │
│                                                                   │
│     Bar style          │ ►Cluster   Overlap    Stack             │
│     High/Low style     │  Bar       Area     ►Error bar          │
│     Bar fill style     │ ►Color     Pattern    Both              │
│                        │                                         │
│     Bar width          │                                         │
│     Bar overlap        │  50                                     │
│                        │                                         │
│     Horizontal chart   │  Yes     ►No                            │
│     Value labels       │  All      Select    ►None               │
│                        │                                         │
│     Frame style        │ ►Full     Half      Quarter   None      │
│     Frame color        │  1                                      │
│     Frame background   │  0                                      │
│                        │                                         │
│     Legend location    │  Top      Bottom    Left    ►Right  None│
│     Legend justify     │  ← or ↑  ►Center    ↓ or →              │
│     Legend placement   │  In      ►Out                           │
│     Legend frame       │ ►Single   Shadow    None                │
│   ─────────────────────────────────────────────────────────────│
│   F1-Help                                                        │
│   F2-Draw chart           F6-Colors      F8-Data    F10-Continue │
└─────────────────────────────────────────────────────────────────┘
```

Figure 5-16. Setting the High/Low style to Error bar

Variations of HLC Charts

If you tip an HLC chart on it side, you can create a Gantt or PERT chart. These charts, used as scheduling and product management tools, organize people or tasks, usually through time. To create the following PERT example, select the Create new chart option (1)from the Main Menu, and then select the Hi/Low/Close option (5) from the Create New Chart submenu (see Figure 5-1). When HG displays the X Data Type Menu, select Name as the data type and leave the remaining fields blank.

Next, enter the text and values shown in Figure 5-18 into the High/Low/Close Chart Data menu on your screen. When your screen matches the figure exactly, press F8 to display Page 1 of the Titles & Options menu. Enter Week Number as the X axis title, and enter Activity as the Y1 axis title. Now, type the appropriate series labels; for example, type Site Purchase as Series 1, Site Survey as Series 2, and so on (enter all of the series listed in the X axis column in Figure 5-18).

Press the PgDn key to display Page 2 of the Titles & Options menu, tab to the High/Low style field, and press B to select the Bar

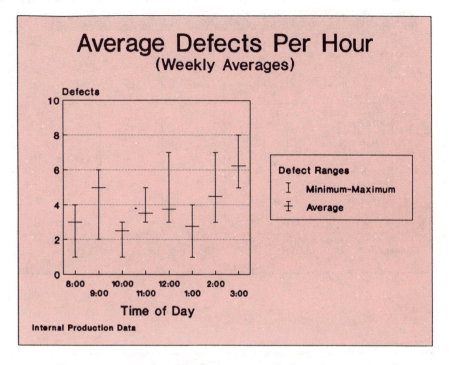

Figure 5-17.   The final version of the HLC example chart

option. Advance the cursor to the Horizontal chart field and press Y; this overrides the default setting (No) and orients the chart so that the X axis appears in the usual Y position (as the vertical axis). Finally, move the cursor to the Legend Location field and press N to select the None option. Figure 5-19 shows the correct settings for Page 2 of the Titles & Options menu.

Now press F2 to view the chart. Your screen should look like Figure 5-20.

The resulting chart is acceptable, but it could be improved. For example, the bars would show up better if they were solid black. (You can do this with the HG Draw/Annotate options, discussed in Chapter 7.) For the moment, however, remember that you can create a useful Gantt or PERT chart simply by laying a HLC chart on its side.

```
┌──────────────────────────────────────────────────────────────────────┐
│              High/Low/Close Chart Data                              ▼ │
├──────────────────────────────────────────────────────────────────────┤
│     Title: New Home Construction Plan                                  │
│  Subtitle: (General Contractor's Weekly Schedule)                      │
│  Footnote: Homeowner's Request                                         │
│                                                                        │
│         X Axis          High        Low        Close       Open        │
│   Pt    Name                                                           │
│                                                                        │
│   1    Site Purchase      1           3                                │
│   2    Site Survey        3           4                                │
│   3    Excavation         4           6                                │
│   4    Foundation Work    6           8                                │
│   5    Framing            9          11                                │
│   6    Roofing           12          14                                │
│   7    Rough Interior    10          15                                │
│   8    Exterior - Windows 13         16                                │
│   9    Interior Finishing 12         17                                │
│  10    Cleanup           16          18                                │
│  11                                                                    │
│  12                                                                    │
│                                                                        │
│ F1-Help        F3-Set X type                          F9-More series   │
│ F2-Draw chart  F4-Calculate              F8-Options    F10-Continue     │
└──────────────────────────────────────────────────────────────────────┘
```

170

Figure 5-18.   Data for the PERT chart example

```
┌──────────────────────────────────────────────────────────────────────┐
│ ▲         High/Low/Close Chart  Titles & Options  Page 2 of 4       ▼ │
├──────────────────────────────────────────────────────────────────────┤
│   Bar style          ►Cluster  Overlap    Stack                        │
│   High/Low style     ►Bar      Area       Error bar                    │
│   Bar fill style     ►Color    Pattern    Both                         │
│                                                                        │
│   Bar width                                                            │
│   Bar overlap         50                                               │
│                                                                        │
│   Horizontal chart   ►Yes      No                                      │
│   Value labels        All      Select    ►None                         │
│                                                                        │
│   Frame style        ►Full     Half      Quarter   None                │
│   Frame color         1                                                │
│   Frame background    0                                                │
│                                                                        │
│   Legend location     Top      Bottom    Left      Right    ►None      │
│   Legend justify      ← or ↑  ►Center    ↓ or →                        │
│   Legend placement    In      ►Out                                     │
│   Legend frame        Single   Shadow    ►None                         │
│                                                                        │
│ F1-Help                                                                │
│ F2-Draw chart             F6-Colors       F8-Data       F10-Continue   │
└──────────────────────────────────────────────────────────────────────┘
```

Figure 5-19.   Settings for Page 2 of Titles & Options menu for the PERT example

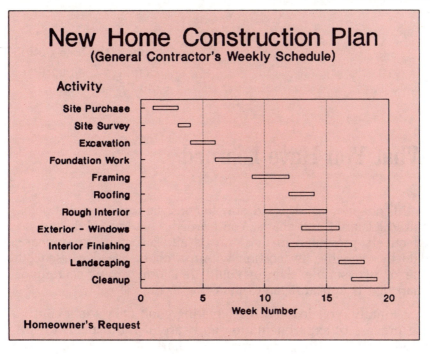

New Home Construction Plan
(General Contractor's Weekly Schedule)

Figure 5-20.   The final PERT chart

Q Creating a Gantt or PERT chart

1. Follow the previous Quick Steps ("Creating a High/Low/Close chart").	Creates a standard High/Low/Close chart.
2. Press F8.	Displays Page 1 of the High/Low/Close Titles & Options menu.
3. Press PgDn.	Displays Page 2 of the Titles & Options menu.
4. Press Tab.	Advances the cursor to High/Low style field.
5. Press B.	Selects the Bar style option.
6. Press Tab twice.	Moves the cursor to the Horizontal chart field.
7. Press Y.	Selects the Yes option.
8. Press Tab 5 times.	Advances the cursor to the Legend location field.

171

9. Press N.	Selects the None option.
10. Press F2.	Displays the chart; modify as needed. □

What You Have Learned

In this chapter, you learned how to construct area, high/low/close, and PERT and Gantt charts. You learned what type of data is most effectively presented in these charts and also how to emphasize data by changing its location within a chart. We discussed how one or two simple changes could transform a dull chart into a chart that is appealing and interesting to the viewer.

172

Finally, you learned that creating good charts is a continuing process of experimentation and careful refinement. Keep in mind that bar, line, pie, and area charts accept similar input data. That means that you should often try using your data with different types of charts. HG makes it easy for you to experiment with different charts until you find the one style that best suits your needs.

Chapter 6

Text and Organizational Charts

In This Chapter

173

▶ *Creating title charts*
▶ *Creating simple list and bullet list charts*
▶ *Creating two- and three-column charts*
▶ *Creating free form charts*
▶ *Creating organizational charts*

Of all the charts HG can produce, text charts are the simplest to create. The charts discussed in this chapter are called *text* charts because they do not use HG's full graphics capabilities; instead, they use written text to convey most of the information. Still, text charts are very useful indeed, and we will provide a variety of ways in which you can use them.

This chapter also shows you how to create effective organizational charts. We discuss organizational charts in this chapter because they share many similarities with text charts.

HG lets you generate six basic types of text charts, as you can see from the Text Chart Styles menu shown in Figure 6-1. (To display this menu, select the `Create new chart` option (1) from the Main Menu, and then select the `Text` option (1) from the Create New Chart menu.) We will discuss these chart styles in the order they appear in the menu.

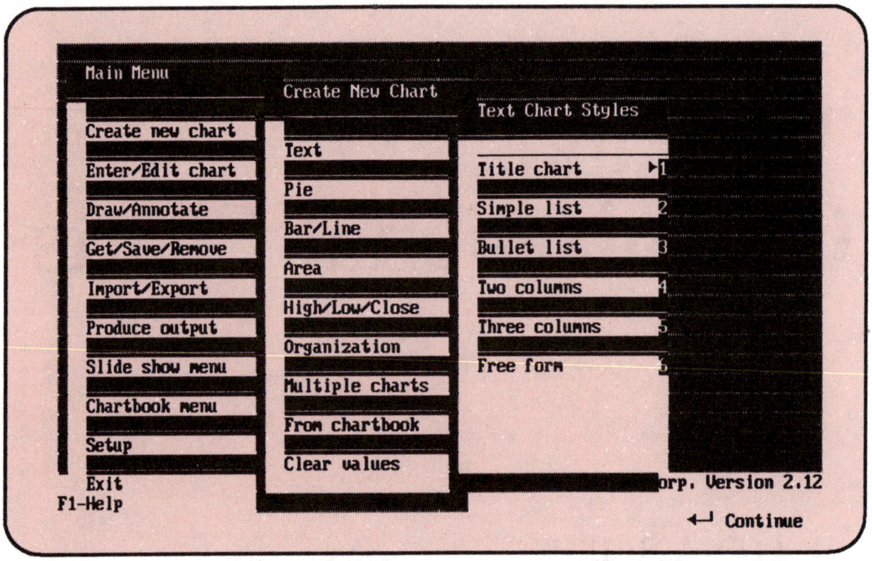

Figure 6-1.   The Text Chart Styles menu

174

Title Charts

When you select the Title chart option (1) from the Text Chart Styles menu, HG presents the Title Chart form shown in Figure 6-2.

Notice how HG divides all title charts into three sections: top, middle, and bottom. Each of these sections can include three lines of text.

Top

A title chart should have a central theme, or purpose, and the top section of the chart should announce that purpose. By default, HG specifies larger letters for the text in the top section than it does for text in the rest of the chart. Larger letters draw attention to the top of the chart and emphasize the chart's purpose.

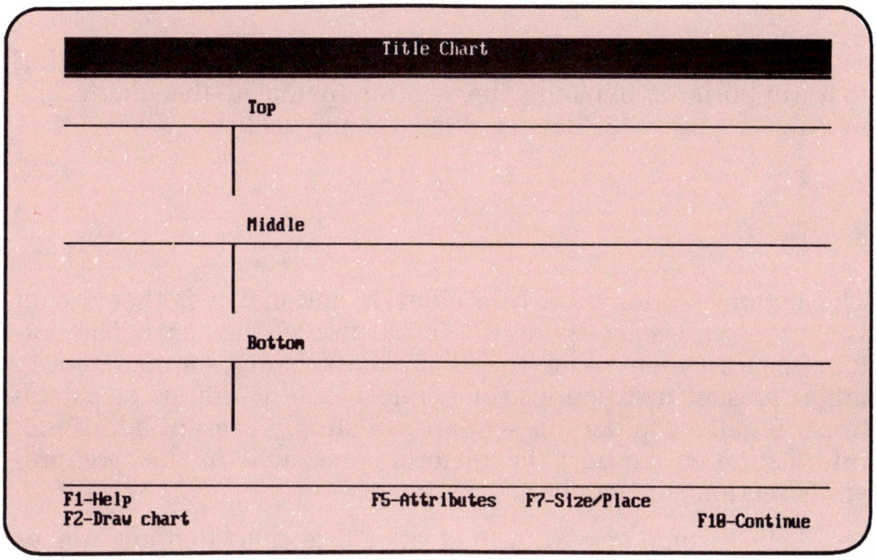

```
                          Title Chart

              Top
              |
              |
              Middle
              |
              |
              Bottom
              |
              |

F1-Help                      F5-Attributes   F7-Size/Place
F2-Draw chart                                       F10-Continue
```

Figure 6-2.   The Title Chart form

> **Tip:** Instead of using capital letters to emphasize a word in a title, change the attribute of the word. Press F5 to display the Attribute menu, and then italicize or underline the word, for example. Capital letters make a chart more difficult to read.

A line in a title chart cannot be more than 60 characters in length. However, if you use the default text size, the length of a text line will be considerably shorter than 60 characters. The best title charts use as few words as possible, so this restriction is usually not a problem.

> **Tip:** All elements in a title chart should be short and concise. You rarely use complete sentences in title charts.

Middle

The middle section of a title chart should contain information that supports or expands the central theme of the chart. The middle text provides details about the top section.

Bottom

The bottom section in a title chart is optional; whether or not you use it varies according to the purpose of the chart. The bottom section might refer to other charts being summarized, it might present instructions, or it might note warnings or exceptions. Finally, the bottom section can simply present additional information to support the material presented in the two previous sections of the chart.

176

Let's assume you want to create a title chart that announces a company meeting. Figure 6-3 shows a completed Title Chart input screen for such a chart.

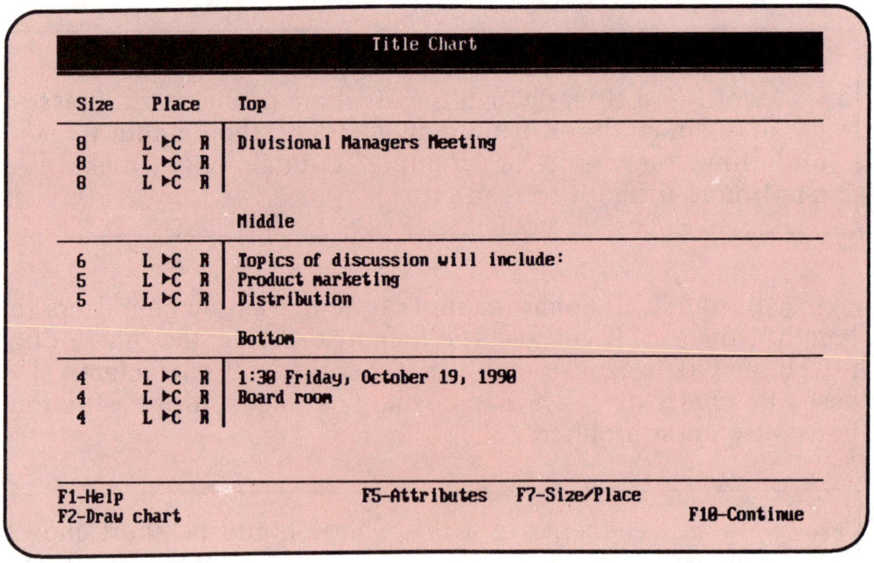

Figure 6-3.   A Title Chart input screen

After you enter the information presented in Figure 6-3, press F2. The resulting title chart is shown in Figure 6-4.

Divisional Managers Meeting

Topics of discussion will include:
Product marketing
Distribution

1:30 Friday, October 19, 1990
Board room

Figure 6-4.   An example of a title chart

177

Let's examine the title chart in Figure 6-4 in more detail. Notice that when you use the default settings, the size of the text decreases from top to bottom. This suggests that the order of importance also decreases from top to bottom. In our example, the central theme is the announcement of the meeting; the list of discussion topics expands upon this theme; and the final section lists the details of when and where the meeting will take place.

Also notice that HG centers text by default. Centering the text in a chart usually produces a balanced and symmetrical look. You can easily change this by pressing F7, which displays the Size/Place menu on the left side of the screen. To make text begin at the left margin, move the cursor to that line in the Place column and press L; to make text end at the right margin, move the cursor to that line in the Place column and press R. You can also change the size of the characters on each line: Simply move the cursor to the appropriate line in the Size column, and type a new number. (Although HG lets you enter any number in the range 1 through 99.9, you probably will find that the default sizes are quite practical for most uses.)

Finally, notice in the example that title charts should keep the narrative short and concise. The chart should have only one main theme (announced in the top section of the chart), and the rest of the chart should merely support that main theme. Because title charts are best used to convey information quickly, they rarely include complete sentences.

178

⊘ **Caution:** If the text at the top of your title chart is more than 30 or so characters, you might have to reduce the size of the characters. Press F7, and change the setting in the Size column to decrease the size of the text.

After making that change, press F2 to view the chart and see whether you need to use correspondingly smaller characters with the remaining text in the chart.

To summarize, good title charts: have one central theme announced at the top of the chart, present information in decreasing order of importance, and use as few words as possible.

Q Creating a Title Chart

1. From the Main Menu, press 1.	Selects Create new chart option.
2. Press 1.	Selects the Text option.
3. Press 1.	Selects the Title chart option and displays the Title Chart input screen.
4. Enter Top text.	Establishes the main theme of the chart.
5. Enter Middle text.	Adds details about the theme.
6. Enter Bottom text.	Adds optional support information about the theme.
7. Press F7.	Lets you change the size and placement of text.
8. Press F2.	Displays the chart. ☐

Simple List and Bullet List Charts

Simple list charts and bullet list charts are nearly identical; in fact, the only difference is that HG inserts a *bullet* (marker) in front of the items in a bullet list. Because of this similarity, we will discuss these two list types together.

Simple Lists

To create a simple list chart, select the Create new chart option (1) from the Main Menu, and then select the Text option (1) from the Create New Chart menu. Now select the Simple List option (2) from the Text Chart Styles menu (see Figure 6-1).

> ⊘ **Caution:** If you entered the previous sample title chart and immediately began this exercise, HG will display a Change Chart Type menu in the middle of your screen. If you want to retain the data from your previous chart so that you can try it in another type of text chart, press Y and then Enter.
>
> If you want to clear the data and create an entirely new chart, press N and then Enter. If you have not yet saved the current chart, HG will display a WARNING message to that effect. To save the chart, press Esc to return to the Main Menu and then follow the "Saving a Chart" Quick Steps in Chapter 1. To erase your earlier data and continue with a new (blank) input screen, press Enter.

Because you will be creating a chart from new data, press N and then Enter at the Change Chart Type menu. You don't need to save the simple title chart example, so when HG displays the WARNING message, press Enter to erase that data. HG now displays the Simple List input screen.

The Simple List input screen is different from most of the screens you've seen so far. Although it presents the standard Title, Subtitle, and Footnote fields, the rest of the screen seems strangely empty. Enter the sample data shown in Figure 6-5 into the Simple List screen (be sure to skip a line between each item in the list). When you finish, press F7 to display the Size/Place menu at the upper left corner of the screen.

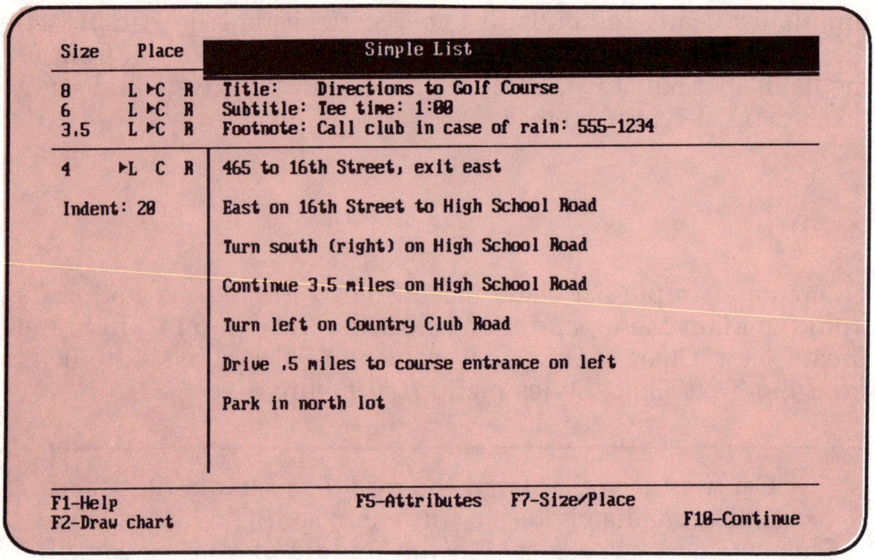

```
  Size    Place  ┌──────────────────Simple List──────────────────────┐
                 │████████████████████████████████████████████████████│
   8      L ▸C R │ Title:    Directions to Golf Course                │
   6      L ▸C R │ Subtitle: Tee time: 1:00                           │
   3.5    L ▸C R │ Footnote: Call club in case of rain: 555-1234      │
                 ├───────────────────────────────────────────────────┤
   4      ▸L C R │ 465 to 16th Street, exit east                     │
                 │                                                   │
 Indent: 20      │ East on 16th Street to High School Road           │
                 │                                                   │
                 │ Turn south (right) on High School Road            │
                 │                                                   │
                 │ Continue 3.5 miles on High School Road            │
                 │                                                   │
                 │ Turn left on Country Club Road                    │
                 │                                                   │
                 │ Drive .5 miles to course entrance on left         │
                 │                                                   │
                 │ Park in north lot                                 │
                 │                                                   │
                 ├───────────────────────────────────────────────────┤
 F1-Help                       F5-Attributes   F7-Size/Place         │
 F2-Draw chart                                          F10-Continue │
```

Figure 6-5.   The Simple List input screen with sample data (after F7 has been pressed)

The F7 key functions the same here as it does with the title chart we discussed earlier: It displays a menu that lets you change the default settings for the chart's text size and placement.

Notice that the largest part of the input screen is devoted to the list of items. As you can see from the Size/Place menu in Figure 6-5, all items in a list share the same size and placement. The only way to change the relative position of the items in a list is to set the Indent field to a value other than 0. In this example, all the items are *left-justified* (begin at the left margin) with an Indent value of 20. (The value is a percentage of the width of the chart.) Press F2 to display the simple list chart shown in Figure 6-6.

Note that we skipped a line between each item in the list so that the finished chart would be easier to read. As far as improving the chart, there's not much to be done. Because the items in the chart look a little too far to the right, you might want to experiment with a smaller indent value. (An indent value of 15 might be a better choice.)

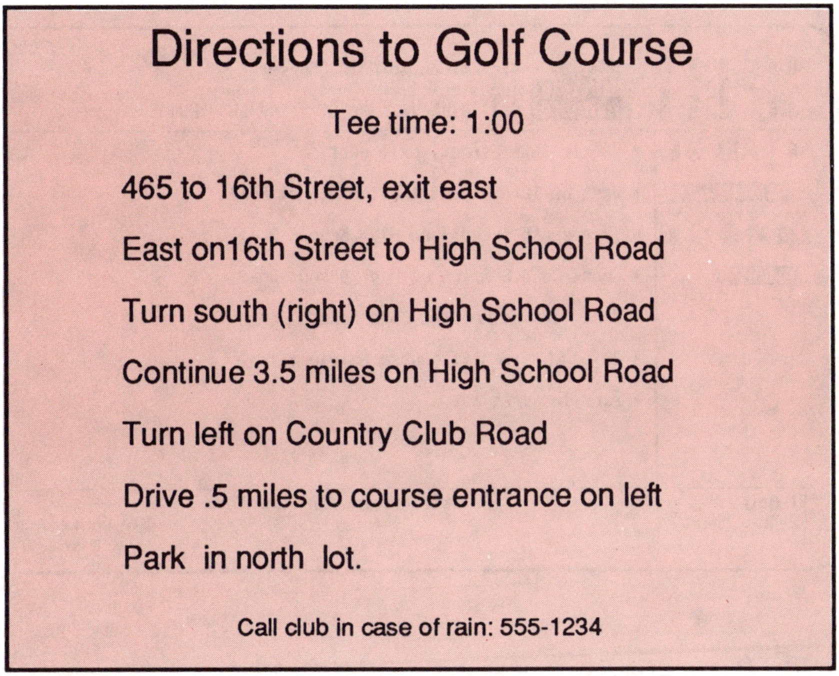

Directions to Golf Course

Tee time: 1:00

465 to 16th Street, exit east

East on16th Street to High School Road

Turn south (right) on High School Road

Continue 3.5 miles on High School Road

Turn left on Country Club Road

Drive .5 miles to course entrance on left

Park in north lot.

Call club in case of rain: 555-1234

Figure 6-6.   An example simple list chart

Bullet Lists

To create a bullet list, select the Create new chart option (1) from the Main Menu, then select the Text option (1), and finally select the Bullet List option (3) from the Text Chart Styles menu. If you want to follow along with our examples, press Y at the Change Chart Type menu: This tells HG to keep the data from the previous chart (Figure 6-6) and insert it into the new Bullet List input screen. If you want to create a new chart, press N and type your own data into the new Bullet List screen.

Bullet Types

Press F7 to activate the Size/Place menu. In addition to the options presented for the simple list chart, HG also includes a Bullet Shape field that lets you select a marker shape or specify that all lines be numbered. This new Size/Place menu option is shown in Figure 6-7.

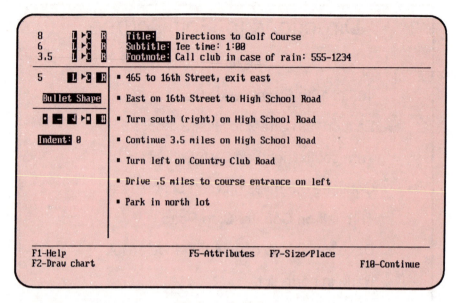

Figure 6-7. The Bullet List input screen (with F7 active)

The selections available in the Bullet Shape field (from left to right) are:

dot
dash
check mark
square
number

The first four bullet types are obvious. However, the last option (#) causes HG to print a number in front of each item in the list. To select an item, advance the cursor to the Bullet Shape field, use the spacebar to specify the appropriate type of bullet marker, and then press Enter.

In our example, we selected the square marker. The resulting bullet list chart is shown in Figure 6-8.

Ctrl-B: Bullets within Bullets

Sometimes you might need to create a bullet list in which major headings use one type of bullet marker and subheadings use

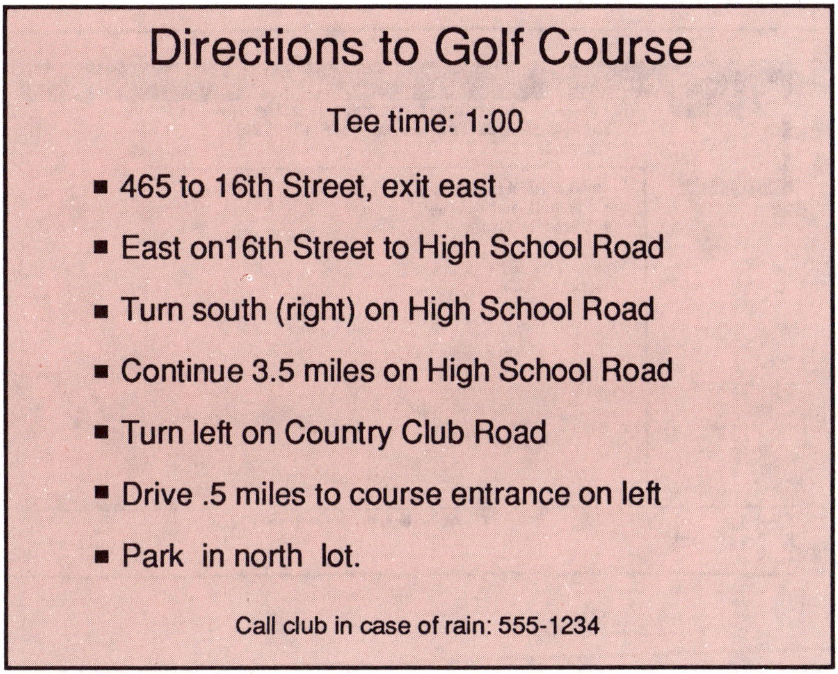

Directions to Golf Course

Tee time: 1:00

- 465 to 16th Street, exit east

- East on16th Street to High School Road

- Turn south (right) on High School Road

- Continue 3.5 miles on High School Road

- Turn left on Country Club Road

- Drive .5 miles to course entrance on left

- Park in north lot.

Call club in case of rain: 555-1234

Figure 6-8.   A sample bullet list chart

183

another type of bullet marker. For example, let's change Figure 6-4 into a "double" bullet list. Enter the data shown in Figure 6-9 into the Bullet List input screen. (Don't try to duplicate Figure 6-9; merely type the data as though you were creating a regular bullet list.) When you finish, use the following Quick Steps to create the double bullet list.

> **Tip:** To create a bullet list, you must separate each item in the list with a blank line. (You create a blank line by pressing Enter when the cursor is in a line that contains no data.) HG does not insert a bullet in front of any text that begins on a line *immediately* below a bulleted item. This lets you create bulleted items that have more than one line of text.

 Creating a Double Bullet List

1. Start with a bullet list.

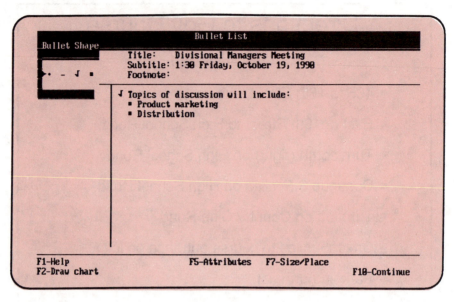

Figure 6-9.   Sample data for a double bullet list.

2. Move the cursor to a blank line and press the Ctrl-Del key combination.	Removes a blank line between items in the list.
3. Repeat step 2 until you erase all blank lines between the secondary bullet lines.	Necessary to insert secondary bullets.
4. Use Tab and arrow keys to move cursor to the start of a line that requires a secondary bullet.	Sets the location at which the bullet will be inserted.
5. If cursor is an underline character, press the Ins(ert) key.	Cancels "overstrike mode," and places HG in "insert mode."
6. Press Ctrl-B.	Displays the Bullet Shape menu.
7. Specify a bullet marker.	This will be the *secondary* bullet marker in the chart.
8. Press Enter.	Selects the bullet marker.
9. Repeat steps 4-8, as necessary.	Sets markers for the rest of the secondary bullet items in the list. □

⊘ **Caution:** If you are adding a secondary bullet to the front of an existing line, be sure you are in "insert mode." If you are not in insert mode, the bullet will overwrite the first character on the line.

If the cursor looks like an underline character, you are *not* in the insert mode. Press the Ins key to toggle to the insert mode. When you are finished inserting bullets (or text), press Ins again to reactivate "overstrike mode."

Press F2 to display the finished version of the sample "double" bullet list chart, as shown in Figure 6-10.

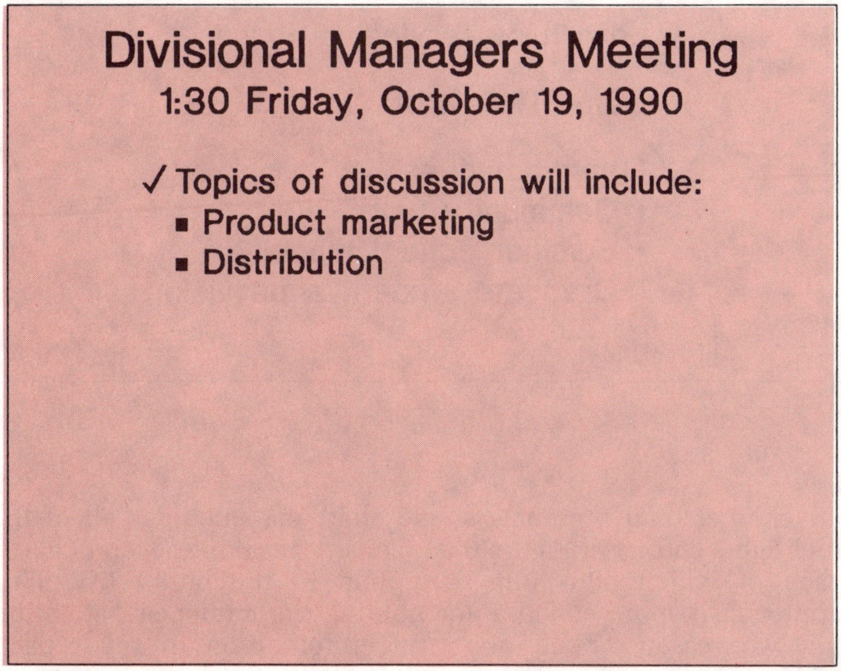

> # Divisional Managers Meeting
> ## 1:30 Friday, October 19, 1990
>
> ✓ Topics of discussion will include:
>   ▪ **Product marketing**
>   ▪ **Distribution**

Figure 6-10.   A "double" bullet list chart

Using Bullet Lists as Part of a Presentation

As you might imagine, bullet list charts can be an effective part of an oral presentation because you can use them to highlight major points. However, you shouldn't present a bullet list filled with ideas before you first discuss those ideas. For example, suppose your presentation uses an HG *slide show* to stress the points shown in Figure 6-11. (A slide show is a sequence of charts displayed during a presentation, as discussed in Chapter 8.)

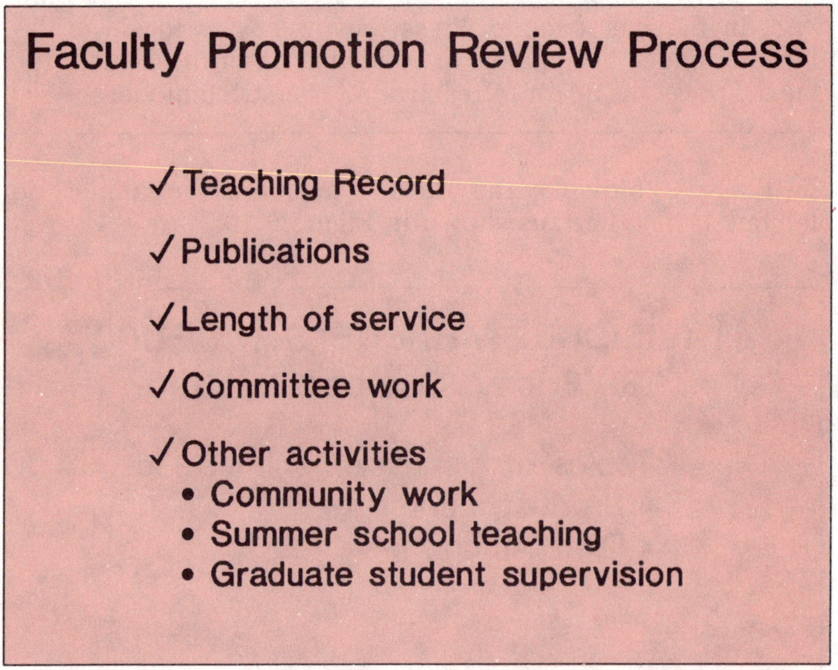

186

Faculty Promotion Review Process

√ Teaching Record

√ Publications

√ Length of service

√ Committee work

√ Other activities
  • Community work
  • Summer school teaching
  • Graduate student supervision

Figure 6-11.   An outline of highlights depicted in a bullet chart

Rather than present a single chart that includes all of the highlights shown in Figure 6-11, consider making several charts, each of which adds one new item to the bullet list. This approach is more effective for holding the audience's attention for two reasons. First, presenting information in small parts makes a presentation easier to understand. Second, if you show all of the highlights at once, the audience might assume that they now know everything about your talk and then tune you out. Instead of using the chart shown in Figure 6-11, consider a sequence of charts, using the progression shown in Figures 6-12 and 6-13:

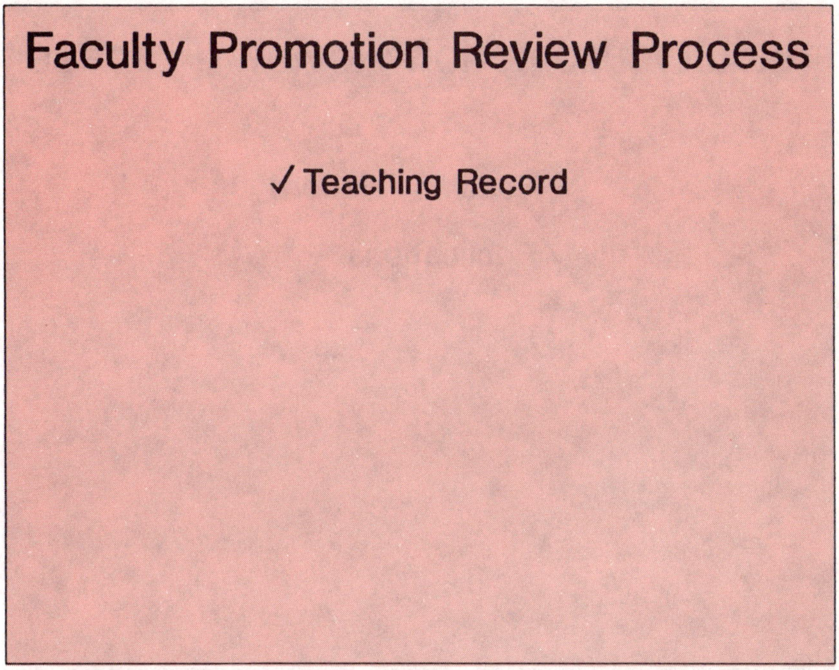

Figure 6-12.   The first bullet list chart in slide show

This method builds to a climactic bullet list chart of highlights that summarizes the entire presentation. As a rule, whenever you create a bullet list for a presentation, consider dividing the chart into several smaller charts and presenting them one at a time; this is a proven method for keeping your audience attentive.

Two- and Three-Column Charts

Two- and three-column charts are virtually the same, the only exception being the addition of the third column. Because of their similarity, we will discuss both types of charts in this section.

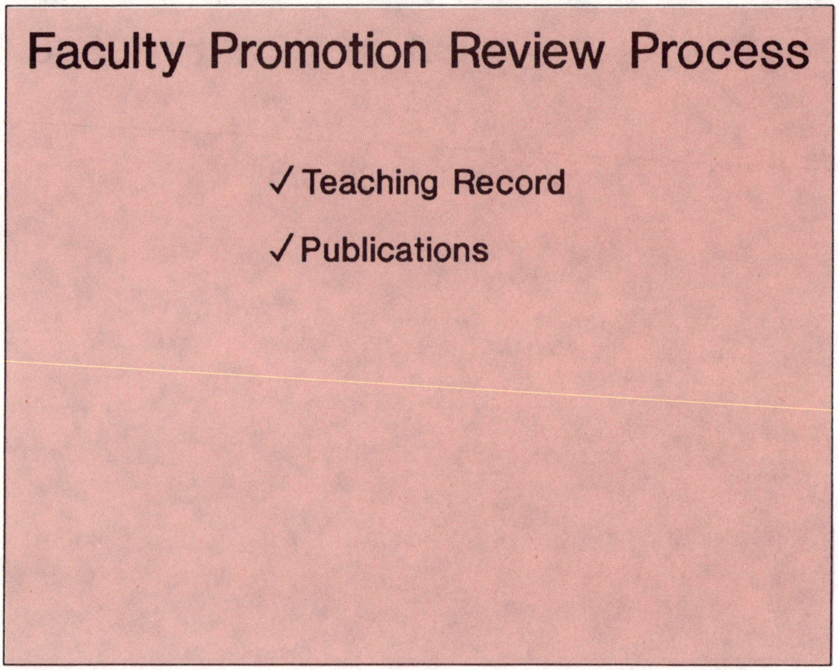

*Figure 6-13.   The second chart in a presentation;
each new chart adds one item at a time*

Creating a Two-Column Chart

To create a two-column chart, select Create new chart (1) from the
HG Main Menu, and then select Text (1) from the Create New
Chart menu. Finally, select the Two columns option (4) from the
Text Chart Styles menu (see Figure 6-1).

We will be creating an entirely new chart, so you can delete
(or save) the previous chart data. When HG displays the Two
Columns input screen, enter the sample data shown in Figure
6-14, and press F7 to activate the Size/Place menu.

Title, Subtitle, and Footnote

You enter the title, subtitle, and footnote as you would with any
other type of chart. After you finish entering data in these fields,

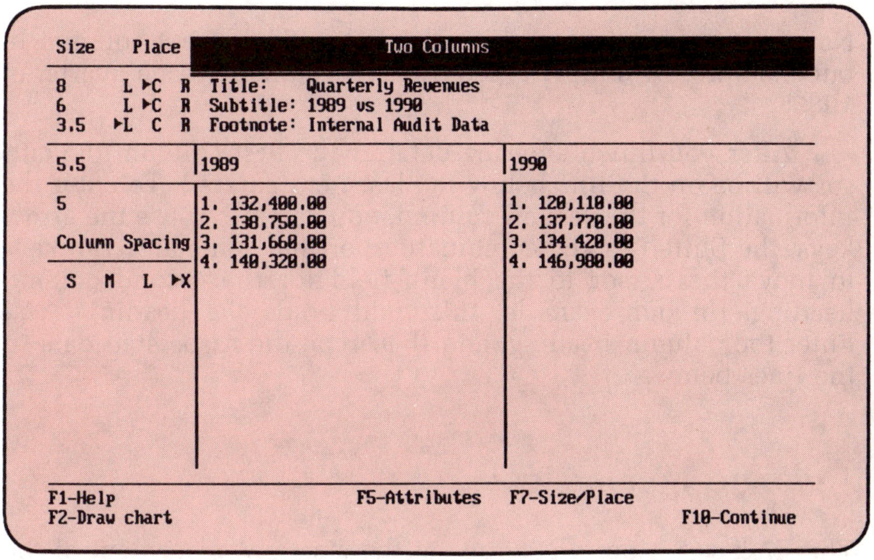

```
  Size    Place                      Two Columns
  ───────────────────────────────────────────────────────────────────────
  8       L ▸C  R   Title:    Quarterly Revenues
  6       L ▸C  R   Subtitle: 1989 vs 1990
  3.5    ▸L  C  R   Footnote: Internal Audit Data
  ───────────────────────────────────────────────────────────────────────
  5.5              │1989                      │1990
  ─────────────────┤                          │
  5                │1. 132,400.00             │1. 120,110.00
                   │2. 130,750.00             │2. 137,770.00
  Column Spacing   │3. 131,660.00             │3. 134,420.00
  ─────────────────│4. 140,320.00             │4. 146,900.00
  S   M   L ▸X     │                          │



  ───────────────────────────────────────────────────────────────────────
  F1-Help                        F5-Attributes   F7-Size/Place
  F2-Draw chart                                               F10-Continue
```

Figure 6-14.   The Two Columns input screen with sample data (after F7 has been pressed)

press F2 to be sure that the elements fit on the screen properly. If some text element is too long, press F7 and decrease the size of the text in that field. However, always remember to keep the size of the title text larger than the subtitle or footnote text size.

Column Headings

After you enter the footnote, HG advances the cursor to the space directly below the word Footnote. Use this field to insert the heading for the first column. After you type an appropriate column heading, press Enter. The cursor then moves to the first line in the large data-entry field below the column heading. (Note that column heads are right-justified when the chart is printed.)

Column Values

Now, enter the information associated with the first column. In our example, we simply typed dollar amounts for each quarter of 1989.

After you finish entering data for the first column, the cursor will be on the line below the last item entered. To enter the information for the second column, you can either use the arrow keys, the Shift-Tab key combination, or the Home and Tab keys to move the cursor to the blank field for the second column heading. (In our example, this field holds the heading 1990.) Enter the column heading, and then type the associated data in the lines below.

Column Spacing

190

The F7 key not only lets you set the size and placement of the text, it also lets you change the spacing between columns. If you look closely at the Size/Place menu in Figure 6-14, you will see the letters

S M L X

at the middle-left area of the screen. These options refer to Small, Medium, Large or eXtra large spacing between columns. You will need to experiment with these settings to determine which best suits your particular data. In our example, we selected the "extra large" spacing to split the information in the columns as far apart as possible. The finished chart is shown in Figure 6-15.

Actually, this chart is not very appealing. It seems unbalanced, with all of the data bunched together at the top and center portion of the screen. Let's see how a few simple changes can improve this first effort.

Refining the Two-Column Chart

To create a less crowded chart, move the cursor to the first line of column one, and press Ctrl-Ins. This inserts a blank line between the column heading and the first data value. Now press Enter twice to advance the cursor to the second quarter's entry,

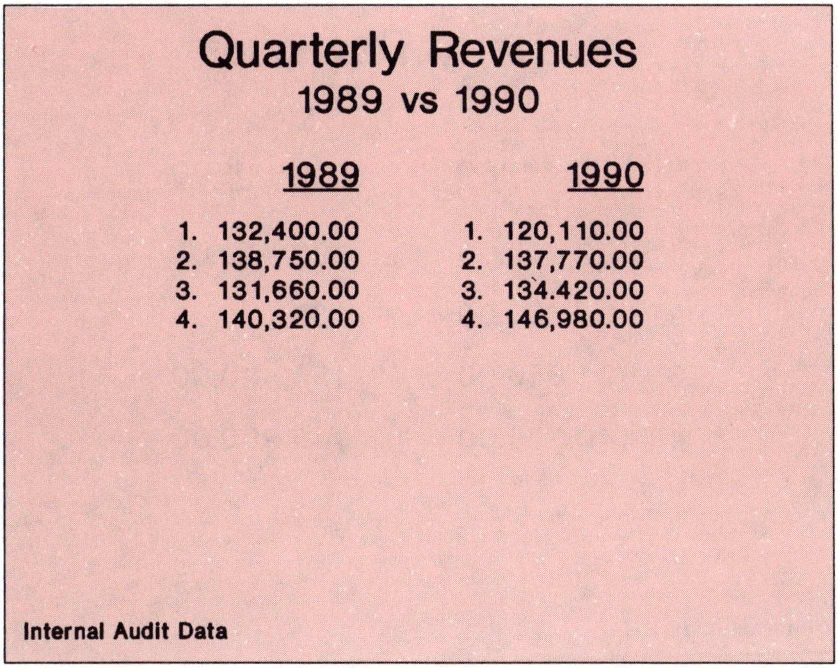

Quarterly Revenues
1989 vs 1990

<u>1989</u>	<u>1990</u>
1. 132,400.00	1. 120,110.00
2. 138,750.00	2. 137,770.00
3. 131,660.00	3. 134.420.00
4. 140,320.00	4. 146,980.00

Internal Audit Data

Figure 6-15. A first attempt at creating a two-column chart

and press Ctrl-Ins to add a blank line between the first and second quarters. Note that HG moves the data in both columns downward. Repeat these steps to insert spaces between all of the entries in both columns.

Now, move the cursor to the first data item in the second column and delete the quarter number (that is, 1.) from the entry. These quarter numbers are redundant because they correspond to the numbers in the first column. After you delete the rest of the quarter numbers in column two, press F2. The results of these two minor changes are shown in Figure 6-16.

Note that this chart is much easier to read than our first effort.

A Three-Column Chart

Creating a three-column chart involves the same steps as creating a two-column chart. Assuming that you still have the sample

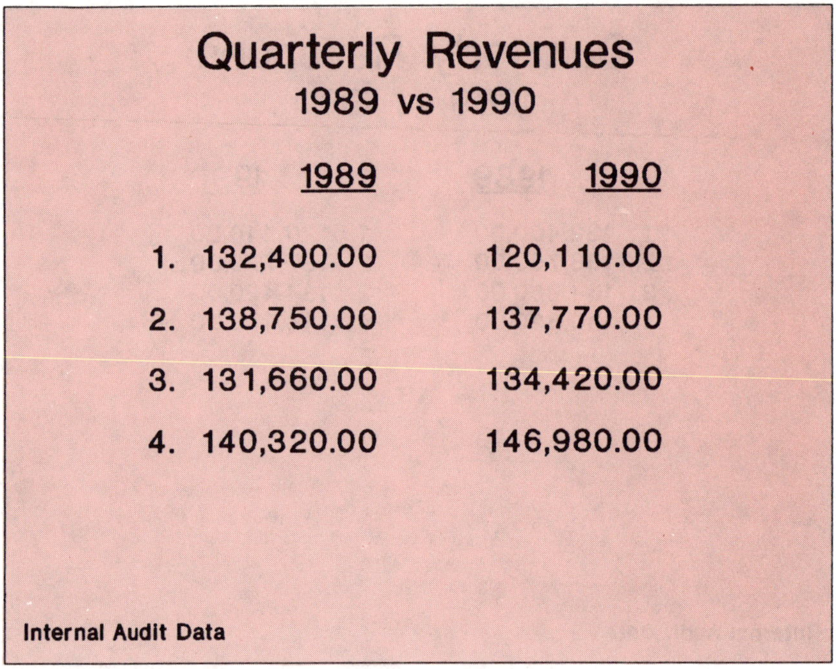

Quarterly Revenues
1989 vs 1990

	1989	1990
1.	132,400.00	120,110.00
2.	138,750.00	137,770.00
3.	131,660.00	134,420.00
4.	140,320.00	146,980.00

Internal Audit Data

Figure 6-16.   An improved two-column chart

192

two-column chart data in memory, select Create new chart (1) from the Main Menu, select Text from the Create New Chart menu, and then select the Three columns option (5) from the Text Chart Styles menu. When HG asks if you want to keep the current data, type Y. Let's simply add a third column to the previous "Quarterly Revenue" example chart.

You enter data in a three-column chart exactly as you did with a two-column chart. Press the Tab key to advance the cursor to the column heading field for the third column and type:

Gain(Loss)

After you finish, enter the numbers in the last column of Figure 6-17 into your own Three Columns input screen.

This figure also shows the (F7) Size/Place menu options. Notice that we decreased the column spacing option from X (extra large) to M (medium). We did this because the third column adds more data to a line and therefore lessens the amount of blank space that you have to work with. Pressing F2 displays the chart shown in Figure 6-18.

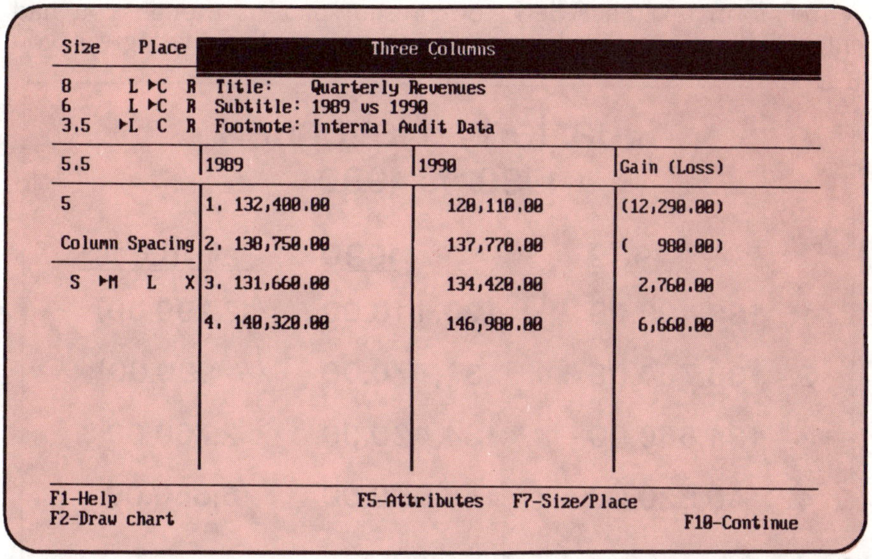

```
 Size    Place            ┌────────── Three Columns ──────────
 8       L ►C  R   Title:     Quarterly Revenues
 6       L ►C  R   Subtitle:  1989 vs 1990
 3.5    ►L  C  R   Footnote:  Internal Audit Data
 ─────────────────────────────────────────────────────────────
 5.5             │1989            │1990            │Gain (Loss)
                 │                │                │
 5               │1. 132,400.00   │128,110.00      │(12,290.00)
                 │                │                │
 Column Spacing  │2. 138,750.00   │137,770.00      │(  980.00)
                 │                │                │
 S  ►M   L   X   │3. 131,660.00   │134,420.00      │2,760.00
                 │                │                │
                 │4. 140,320.00   │146,980.00      │6,660.00
 ─────────────────────────────────────────────────────────────
 F1-Help                        F5-Attributes   F7-Size/Place
 F2-Draw chart                                          F10-Continue
```

193

Figure 6-17. The Three Columns input screen with sample data (after F7 has been pressed)

Although the chart is technically correct, it looks cramped and busy. You can use two quick methods to open more space between items: reduce the text size, or remove the decimal point and zeros from each entry. Figure 6-19 shows the beneficial impact of simply deleting the decimal points and zeros from your data.

You might want to experiment with this chart: Use the Size/Place menu (press F7) to reduce the size of the text in the columns to see if that creates a better looking chart. Remember, there really aren't "right" or "wrong" charts; some charts are merely more effective than others. A chart is "right" when it best appeals to your specific audience.

Free Form Text Charts

A free form text chart lets you present data as though you had entered it with a word processor; however, the chart gives you

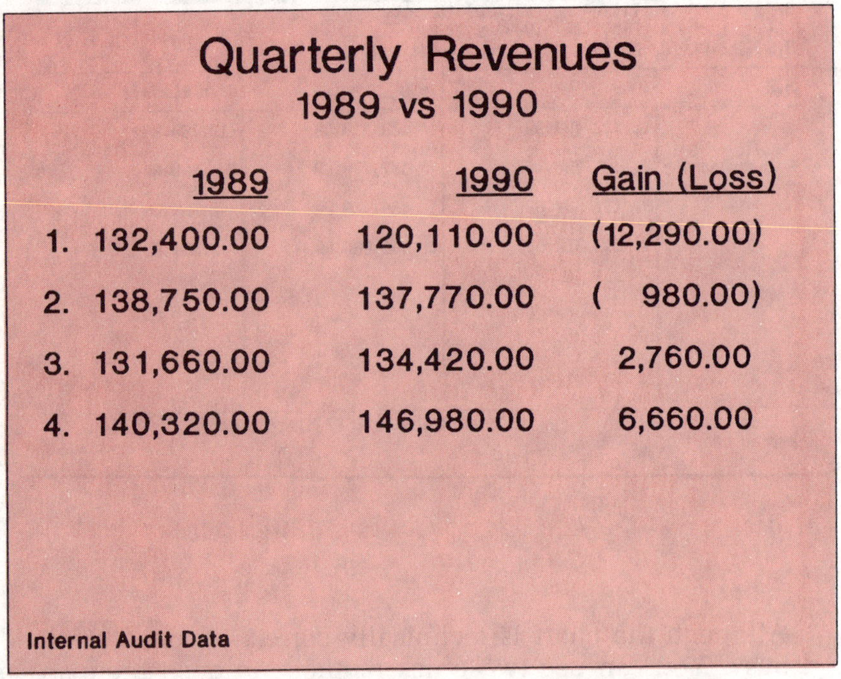

Quarterly Revenues
1989 vs 1990

	1989	1990	Gain (Loss)
1.	132,400.00	120,110.00	(12,290.00)
2.	138,750.00	137,770.00	(980.00)
3.	131,660.00	134,420.00	2,760.00
4.	140,320.00	146,980.00	6,660.00

Internal Audit Data

Figure 6-18.   An example three-column chart

more control over the text attributes that you can use. To create a free form chart, start at the Main Menu and select the Create new chart option. Then, select the Text chart option and finally the Free form option (6) from the Text Chart Styles menu. If you still have data in memory from a previous exercise, press N when HG asks if you want to keep the current data.

The example in Figure 6-20, uses the Free Form Text input screen to create a chart that shows a recipe for frying fish.

Entering Data into the Free Form Text Screen

The top of the input screen for a free form chart is similar to most other HG charts. Enter the title, subtitle, and footnote (if any) in the usual manner. The cursor then advances to the main section of the input screen. In this section you can type whatever you want to display in the free form chart. Enter data as you would with a word processor; note, however, that can enter only 60 characters on each line.

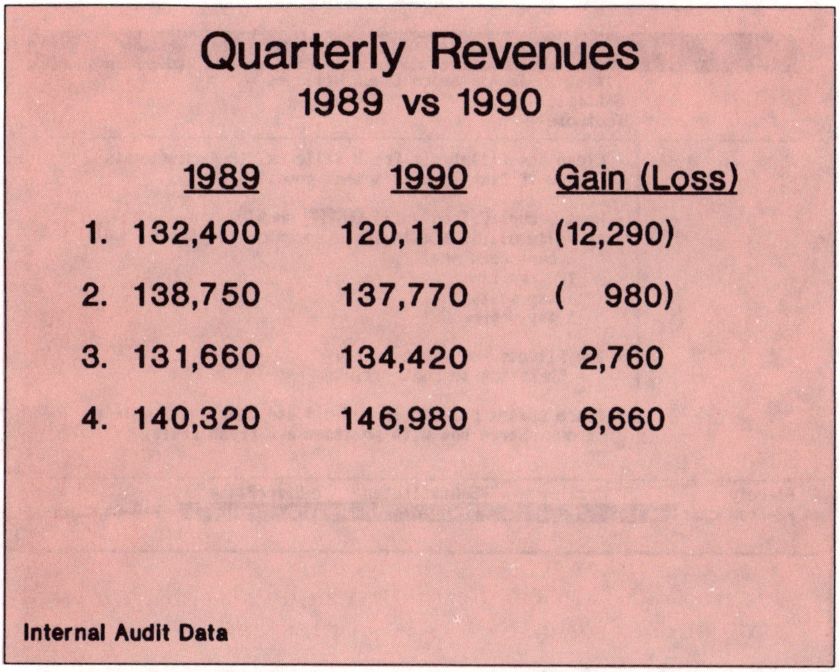

Quarterly Revenues
1989 vs 1990

	1989	1990	Gain (Loss)
1.	132,400	120,110	(12,290)
2.	138,750	137,770	(980)
3.	131,660	134,420	2,760
4.	140,320	146,980	6,660

Internal Audit Data

Figure 6-19.   An improved three-column chart

195

⊘ **Caution:** Often, chart makers set the Color attribute to red whenever they depict a negative value (or loss) in a chart. (They do this because the "red ink" metaphor for "loss" is so universal.) Although you can easily change this attribute using the F5 key, keep in mind that many people, especially men, are color blind with respect to red and green. If you decide to use red to represent negative numbers, consider adding a minus sign or parentheses to also signal the negative value.

Special Effects and Attributes

We inserted bullets in front of the major text headings in Figure 6-20 to emphasize the recipe steps. To do so, press the Ctrl-B key combination, and select the bullet you want to display

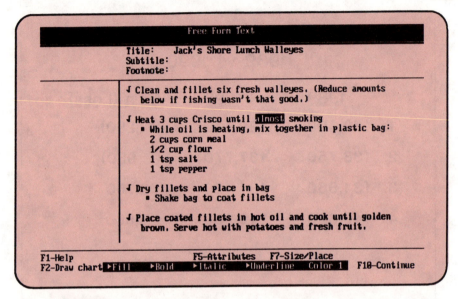

Figure 6-20.   A Free Form Text input screen with sample data (after F5 has been pressed)

before you type the text line. We also entered the secondary bullet beneath the second step by pressing Ctrl-B and selecting a bullet shape prior to typing the text in that line.

> ▶ **Tip:** You can enter more lines of text than are displayed on the input screen: Simply continue to type when you reach the bottom of the screen. HG will automatically scroll the screen to let you enter another line. Keep in mind, however, that you want all of your text to fit on one output screen. If you enter too many lines, the bottom lines will not be displayed in the final chart. Remember that you can always create additional charts to hold more information.

After entering all of the text, we used the F5 key to activate the Attributes menu. Note in Figure 6-20 that we positioned the cursor on the first letter of the word "almost" and pressed F5 until the word was completely highlighted. That action let us assign special attributes to the word. As you will recall from Chapter 2, you use the Tab key to advance from one attribute option to the next, and you press the spacebar to toggle an attribute on or off.

The default settings for all text are Fill and Bold. These attributes produce printed letters that are solid and heavy. In addition, we turned on the Underline and Italic attributes for the word "almost." The result of the text entry, bullet insertions, and attribute changes is shown in Figure 6-21.

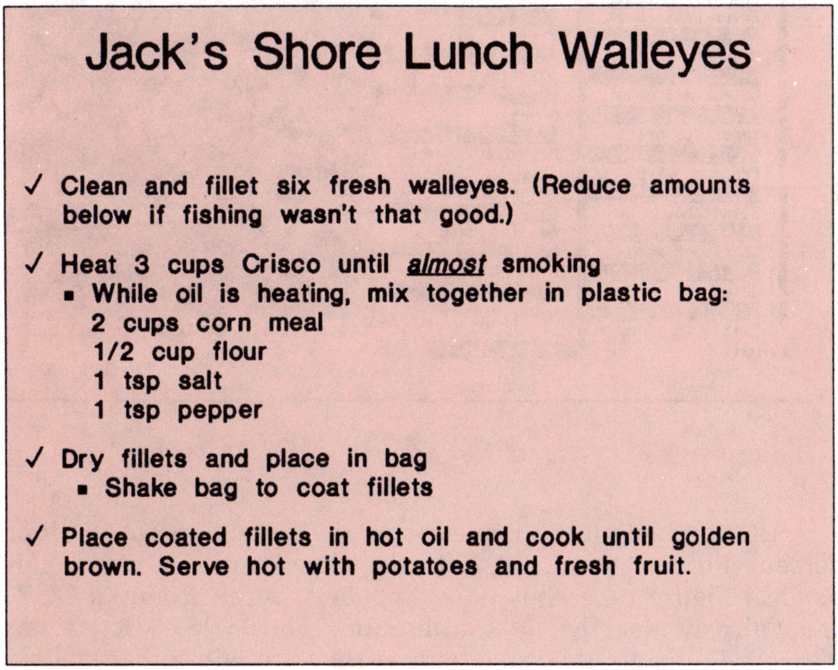

197

Jack's Shore Lunch Walleyes

✓ Clean and fillet six fresh walleyes. (Reduce amounts below if fishing wasn't that good.)

✓ Heat 3 cups Crisco until *almost* smoking
  ▪ While oil is heating, mix together in plastic bag:
    2 cups corn meal
    1/2 cup flour
    1 tsp salt
    1 tsp pepper

✓ Dry fillets and place in bag
  ▪ Shake bag to coat fillets

✓ Place coated fillets in hot oil and cook until golden brown. Serve hot with potatoes and fresh fruit.

Figure 6-21.   An example free form chart that uses bullets

If you will be displaying the chart on a color output device, you should also experiment with the Color attribute setting. Different colors can really spice up a recipe like this.

Organizational Charts

Organizational charts are used to show the structure of a business, a group, or any other collection of related elements. HG makes it easy for you to construct an organizational chart. Start by selecting the Create new chart option (1) from the Main Menu, and then select the Organization option (6) from the Create New Chart menu (see Figure 6-22).

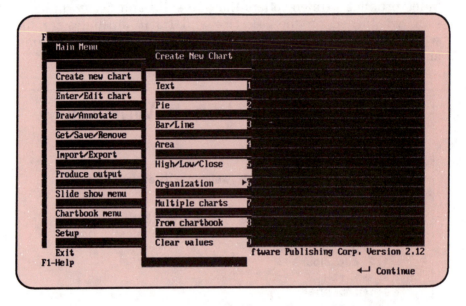

Figure 6-22. Selecting the Organization chart type

HG immediately displays the Organization Chart input screen. (From now on, we will abbreviate "organizational chart" as OC.) Figure 6-23 shows the first level of an example OC for the Fairway Real Estate Corporation. The Title, Subtitle, and Footnote fields are the same here as they are with other charts.

You will find it much easier to understand how HG constructs an OC if you enter the sample data shown in the figures of this section. We will discuss each of the fields that we fill on the OC input screen.

> ► **Tip:** OC's rarely use footnotes. However, if your business has a high turnover rate or you expect your organization to change in the near future, the `Footnote` field is a convenient place to enter the date of the structure represented by the chart.

Manager

OC's are usually constructed with the president of the organization at the top of the chart, followed by the management or group levels under the president's control. HG refers to each layer of the organization as a *level*. In our example, I made myself president, and we will assume that the only person that answers directly to me is Paul Pfeiffer. Likewise, Paul is the only person I directly "communicate" with (formally) regarding corporate policy decisions.

199

HG provides three fields that you can fill in for each manager: `Name`, `Title`, and `Comment`. Each of these fields can contain as many as 22 characters.

By default, the first Organization Chart input screen (*Level 1*) represents the top level of the organization; therefore, in our example, the first manager to be entered is myself. After you enter `Jack Purdum` in the `Name` field, the cursor will advance to the `Title` field.

Manager's Title

The `Title` field identifies the organization's title for the person in the above `Name` field. In our example, my title is `President`, as shown in Figure 6-23.

Comment

After you enter the manager's title, the cursor moves to the `Comment` field. You can use this field to personal data or other pertinent information. In this example, we chose to leave it blank.

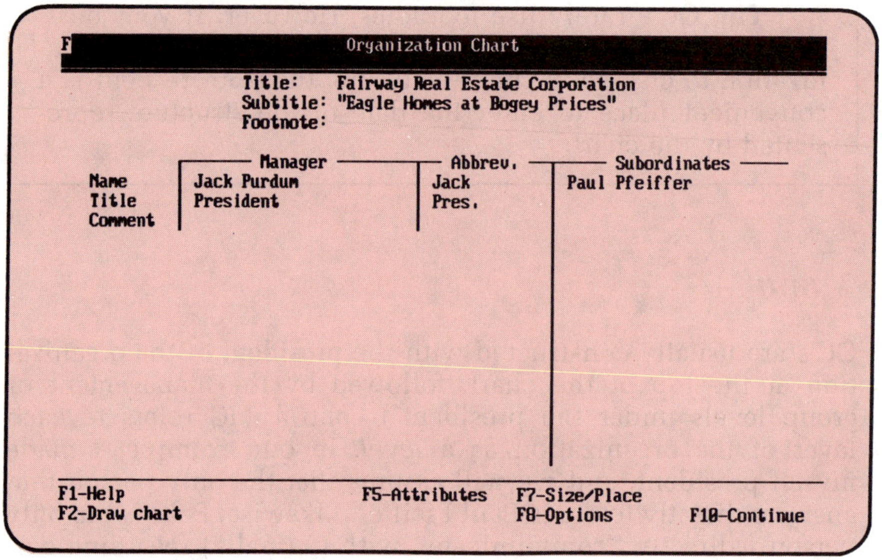

Figure 6-23.   Level 1 of an example Organization Chart input screen

> ▶ **Tip:** You can use the Comment field for a variety of pur-
> poses, depending upon the purpose of your OC. For
> example, if you are interested in showing length of service,
> you could enter the date the person began with the firm. If
> you are worried about retirement vacancies in middle and
> upper management, you might enter the earliest date that
> person could retire. If you choose to display the comment,
> it will appear directly below the manager's title when HG
> draws the OC.

If you want to experiment and enter a comment, do so now.
You can display the chart with or without your comment by
selecting the appropriate setting on the Org Chart Options menu,
which we will discuss later.

Abbreviations

HG lets you use abbreviations for each of the fields you just
entered. When you use abbreviations, HG can create the OC with

more levels and more information than it can when you use the full information input format. The `Abbrev.` entries include the same fields (`Name`, `Title`, and `Comment`) as before; however, these fields are now limited to a maximum length of 11 characters.

Even if you don't plan to use the abbreviations, you might want to enter them anyway. The Org Chart Options menu (discussed later) lets you turn abbreviations on or off at will.

⊘ **Caution:** When you are editing entries in the `Name`, `Title`, and `Comment` fields, the Ctrl-Del key combination does not clear the field. You must use either the Backspace or Del key to remove an entry. Ctrl-Del and Ctrl-Ins work only in the `Subordinates` field.

Subordinates

In the `Subordinates` field, you list all those people on the next level (that is, immediately below the current manager). In our example, the only subordinate is Paul Pfeiffer, so that is the only entry in the `Subordinate` field in Figure 6-23. That completes the top level of the example OC.

Level 2 of the OC

To proceed to the next level of the OC, press the Ctrl-PgDn key combination. HG then displays a new Organization Chart input screen in which Paul Pfeiffer's name appears in the `Manager` field. You can now fill in the information about Mr. Pfeiffer and his subordinates.

The interpretation of the `Name`, `Title`, and `Comment` fields is always the same, regardless of the OC level being displayed. Our only real concern is with the `Subordinates` field.

Subordinates

Figure 6-24 shows that four people in the corporation report directly to Paul. The names shown in the `Subordinates` field are those individuals that are on the next level below Paul in the OC. Enter the names shown in Figure 6-24.

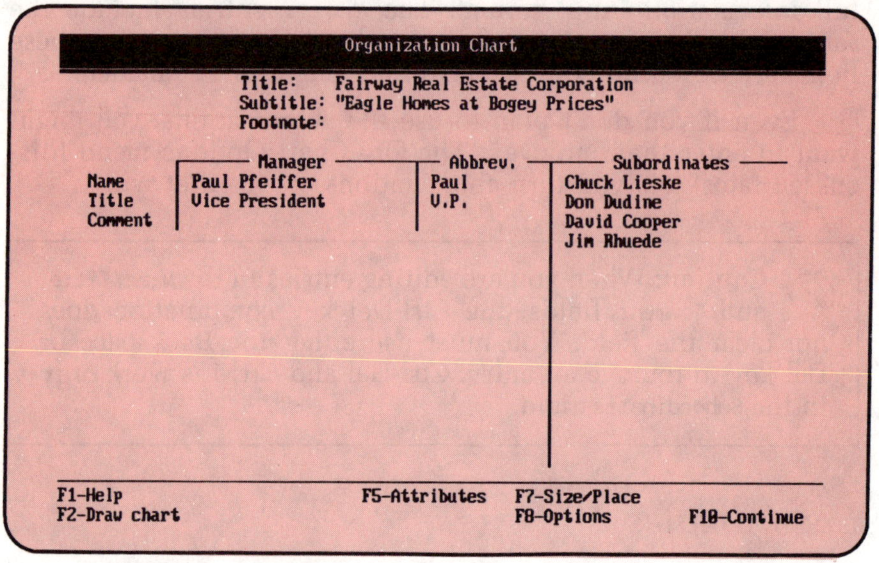

```
                        Organization Chart
            Title:    Fairway Real Estate Corporation
            Subtitle: "Eagle Homes at Bogey Prices"
            Footnote:

                ┌── Manager ──   ┌── Abbrev, ──   ┌── Subordinates ──
    Name        │ Paul Pfeiffer  │ Paul           │ Chuck Lieske
    Title       │ Vice President │ V.P,           │ Don Dudine
    Comment     │                │                │ David Cooper
                │                │                │ Jim Rhuede



    F1-Help                  F5-Attributes  F7-Size/Place
    F2-Draw chart                           F8-Options        F10-Continue
```

Figure 6-24. Level 2 of an example Organization Chart input screen

> ▶ **Tip:** You can use the Ctrl-↑ and Ctrl-↓ key combination to change the order of names in the Subordinates field. You can also use the Ctrl-Ins and Ctrl-Del keys to add or delete a line in the Subordinate field. (See the "Editing Information in HG" section in Chapter 1 for details.)

After you have entered Paul's subordinates, you can proceed to the next level in the OC.

Level 3 of the OC, with Multiple Subordinates

When we were at the top of the OC, Paul was the only name in the Subordinates field, so the Ctrl-PgDn command automatically selected Paul as the subject of the next OC input screen. In Figure 6-24, however, four people occupy the level below Paul. Who do you enter next?

Fortunately, it doesn't matter. If you press Ctrl-PgDn, HG automatically selects the first person in the Subordinate field list (in this example, Chuck Lieske). Figure 6-25 shows Level 3 of the OC from Chuck's perspective.

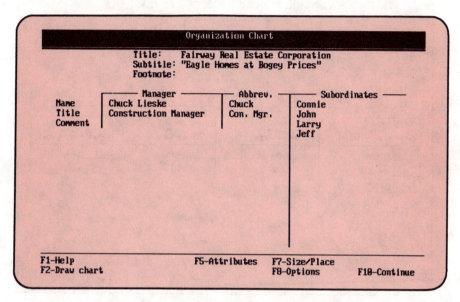

Figure 6-25. Level 3 of an example Organization Chart input screen

When you fill in the information for Chuck, press Ctrl-PgUp to return to the previous level (Paul), use the Tab key to move the highlight to the next person in the Subordinate field (Don Dudine), press Ctrl-PgDn, and that person becomes the current manager.

Obviously, we could continue to show deeper and deeper levels in the OC, but you probably understand the mechanics by now. Figure 6-26 shows the entire organization after we completed all of the levels for all of the employees and pressed F2 to display the chart.

You might want to experiment filling in some of the names for the third-level management people and their subordinates. When you finish, press F2 to view your work.

Remember, if you need to return to a previous level in the OC, press Ctrl-PgUp. By using the Ctrl-PgDn and Ctrl-PgUp key combinations, you can move to any location within the OC.

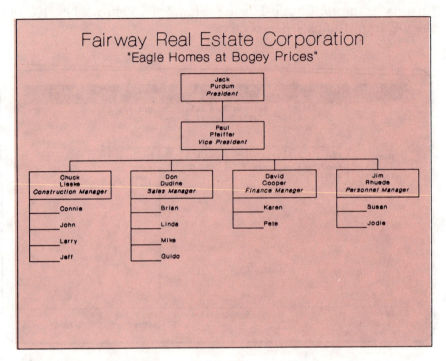

Figure 6-26. The completed example organization chart

OC Limits

Obviously there are limits to the size of an organization chart. Although HG will let you enter more than six subordinates, six is, in fact, the maximum number that you can use. If you enter more, when you press F2 to view the chart, HG displays a message that the chart is "too wide."

HG also sets the maximum depth of an OC to eight levels, but you will rarely need this depth. If you find that your organization requires more levels than HG can provide, chances are the OC is too complicated to be viewed on one chart anyway. In this case, you should consider creating separate OC's for each major division of the organization. The result will be a usable set of OC's that is also much easier to understand.

204

F8 Key: Org Chart Options Menu

Although the OC shown in Figure 6-26 is acceptable, it could be better. Press F8 to activate the Org Chart Options menu, as shown in Figure 6-27.

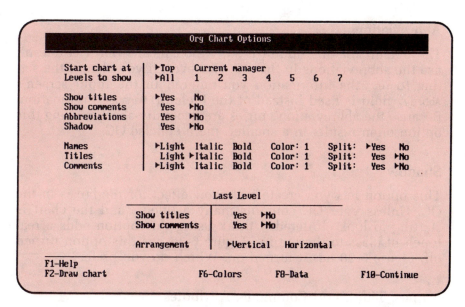

Figure 6-27.   The Org Chart Options menu

The Start and Depth of Chart

The Start chart at option determines where HG starts displaying the OC. (Top is the default starting place). The Levels to show option lets you specify how many levels of the OC that HG will display. Manipulating these settings gives you control over the final presentation of the chart. These options are especially useful when you have created a large chart and you need to display it in sections.

Show Titles and Comments

These two options determine whether HG will display the titles and comments in the chart output. Most charts show titles; fewer show comments. For example, if your comments include birthdates or personal information that you don't want others to see, set the Show comments option to No. Some people even use the

Comment field to make notes about the chart itself, and then they turn off the comments before printing the OC.

If you didn't make any entries in the Comment fields in the chart, but you set Show comments to Yes, HG will insert a blank line in the OC. This has the effect of adding depth to the boxes in the OC.

Abbreviations

The default for this option is No, which means that HG doesn't use the abbreviations in the OC. However, if you change the setting to Yes, the information you entered in the input screen's Abbrev. field is used instead of the (default) Manager information. Because the abbreviation entries are generally shorter, using this option often results in a smaller, more concise OC.

Shadow

206

This option lets you create a *shadow* effect for the boxes in the OC. Unless your OC contains many elements and the chart is starting to look cluttered, I think using this option adds a real touch of class to the output. Figure 6-26 has this option turned off; Figure 6-28 has it turned on. Which do you prefer?

Names, Titles, and Comments Attributes

The next three lines let you specify a variety of attributes for the entries in the Name, Title, and Comment fields. The Light, Italic, and Bold options refer to the font that HG uses when it displays the text.

The Color option lets you change the color of the text in each of these three fields in the OC. Press F6 to change the colors to a setting other than the defaults.

The Split option is a little more interesting. Let's examine its actions with a brief example. Consider the vice president's entry:

Paul Pfeiffer
Vice President

If the Names and Titles fields both have Split set to No, then Paul's name and title would each appear on a single line as shown above. If the Split option is set to Yes for both fields, the entry would be:

Paul
Pfeiffer
Vice
President

If the Split option is set to Yes, the width of the box decreases to fit the longest entry in the box. If the Names Split is set to Yes, but the Titles Split is set to No, the entry would appear as follows:

Paul
Pfeiffer
Vice President

Therefore, specifying Yes for the Split option will add depth to the box in any field that has two or more words in it. Specifying No for Split produces a wider box with less depth. (In Figure 6-28, the Names Split is Yes, and the Titles Split is No.)

207

Last Level

Organizations are shaped like a pyramid, with more people at the bottom of the chart than at the top. As you move toward the bottom of the OC, information tends to get more crowded. The Last Level options let you omit the titles and comments for those people that are displayed in the last level of the chart.

You might want to experiment with these settings to see which you prefer. With large, complex OC's, you probably will have no choice but to specify No for both of these options.

Arrangement

This option determines whether the last level of the chart is shown with the names in vertical or horizontal orientation. Figure 6-26 shows the Arrangement option with a Vertical setting, and Figure 6-28 shows Arrangement with a Horizontal setting. If space permits, the horizontal arrangement looks best.

 Creating an Organizational Chart

1. At the Main Menu, press 1.   Selects the Create new chart option.

2. Press 6   Selects the Organization option.

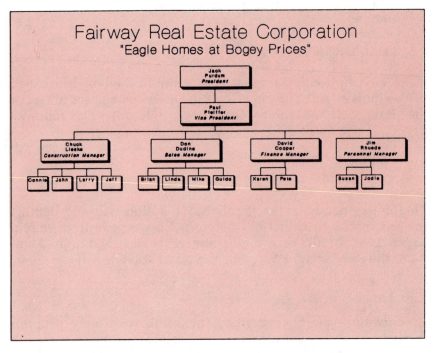

Figure 6-28. The finished example organization chart

208

3. Enter data in the Title, Subtitle, and Footnote fields.

   You must enter a title; the others are optional.

4. Enter the manager's name in Name field of the Manager column.

   Do this at every level.

5. Enter the manager's title in the Title field of the Manager column.

   This is optional.

6. Enter a comment in the Comment field of the Manager column.

   This is optional.

7. Repeat Steps 4, 5, and 6 for the Abbrev. column.

   This is optional; if you fill in this field, shorten the text you used in the Manager column.

8. In the Subordinates field, enter the names of the people under this manager.

   You can only specify six subordinates in this field.

9. Press F2.   Displays the OC so that
                                 you can check on your
                                 progress.

10. Move the highlight to the   Selects the next person on
    next manager.   the chart.

11. Press Ctrl-PgDn.   Advances to the next level;
                                 makes the highlighted
                                 name the current manager.

12. Repeat Steps 4 through 11.   Fill out the OC for all of
                                 the people in the
                                 organization.   ☐

The exact settings for your OC vary according to the structure of the organization you are depicting. The best approach is to enter the entire structure first, and then use the F8 options to refine the OC until you think it looks best.

209

What You Have Learned

This chapter showed you how to create all types of text charts, including organizational charts. You learned how to create title charts, simple list and bullet list charts, two- and three-column charts, and free form charts. You saw how easy it is to transfer data between these types of charts and how small changes of attributes, line spacing, and data organization help you refine and improve your text charts. You also learned how to create effective organizational charts and how to use all of the many HG options that let you enhance the final output of these important business tools.

Chapter 7
Drawing Custom Charts

In This Chapter

▶ *Drawing a custom chart*
▶ *Drawing a map*
▶ *Creating and moving elements in a chart*
▶ *Creating custom symbols*
▶ *Adding new elements to an existing chart*

HG provides a rich set of options and tools that let you create almost any type of custom chart you will need. The Main Menu Draw/Annotate option (3) lets you create a custom chart in one of two ways: you can start from scratch and draw just about anything you want, or you can take a chart you've already created with HG and annotate (add to) it.

In this chapter, we will use both the draw and annotate features of HG. Our first example will show you how to create the chart shown in Figure 7-1. This exercise not only will introduce you the drawing features of HG's Draw/Annotate option, it will show you how to use the cursor keys while you are drawing.

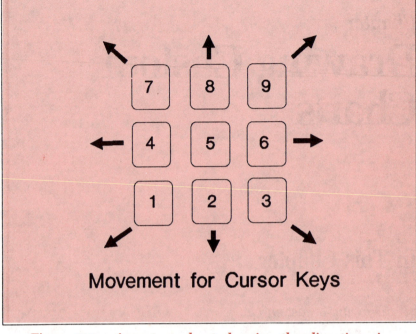

Movement for Cursor Keys

Figure 7-1.   A custom chart showing the directions in which various keys move the cursor

Changing the Default

Draw/Annotate Settings

Most of HG's default settings for the Draw/Annotate option are correct for our drawing session. However, let's change some of the settings now, so that you will know the procedure when you need to change the settings for one of your own projects.

To change the default settings, first select the `Draw/Annotate` option (3) from the Main Menu. Note that the drawing screen is unlike any of the other data entry screens you've seen so far; that's because HG is now letting us manipulate graphics as well as text and numbers. Now, press F8 to display the Default Options menu. As you can see in Figure 7-2, the Default Options menu replaces the Draw menu at the left side of the screen.

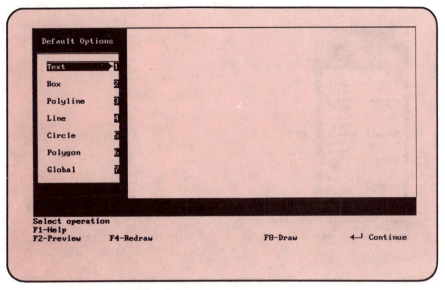

Figure 7-2. *The Default options menu*

213

Selecting one of the first six options in this menu displays a screen of default settings for that particular drawing element. You don't need to change any of these settings now, but after you finish this chapter, feel free to experiment so that you can see the results of using different settings. Next, select the Global option (7), which displays the Global Options menu as shown in Figure 7-3.

Let's look at each of these options and settings in detail. You might also want to change some or all of the defaults to suit your own preferences.

Display

Set the Display option to Final. This gives you a more precise view of what the final chart will look like. Many of the drawing operations will be slightly slower than they would be if you used the Quick option; however, it's worth a few seconds wait to have HG use its most accurate representation of your chart.

Redraw

If you set the Redraw option to Yes, HG redraws a chart every time you make a change. If you set it to No, you will have to press F4

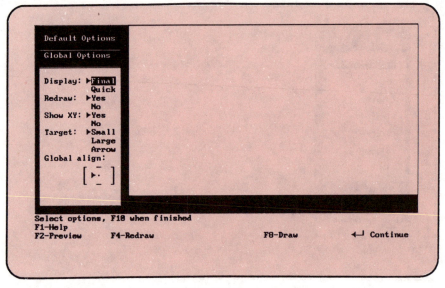

Figure 7-3.   The Global Options menu

after each change to see its effect on the chart. I always set this option to Yes.

Show XY

If you set the Show XY option to Yes, the X and Y coordinates of the *target* (the drawing cursor) are displayed directly below the lower-right corner of the drawing box. These coordinates are most useful when you need to draw an element at an exact location within the chart. Because this option does not affect performance and because the information might come in handy, set the option to Yes.

Target

The Target option refers to the size and type of cursor that you see in the drawing box. I prefer a small cross-hair cursor, so I set the default to Small. If you prefer a large cursor in which the cross hairs extend the entire length of the vertical and horizontal axes, set the option to Large. If you prefer an arrow-style cursor, set the option to Arrow.

Global align

This sets the *alignment point* for the cursor. This is the point within the target that HG uses when it calculates the position of the target as X and Y coordinates. I prefer the intersection of the cross-hairs as my alignment point so I set the dot directly at the center of the box. To set the point, tab to the `Global align` option, press the spacebar or arrow keys to move the highlight to the appropriate location within the box, and then press Enter to select that point.

After you have set these options to your liking, press Esc until the screen once again displays the Draw menu.

Drawing a Custom Chart

The Draw menu and the drawing box (which you display from the Main Menu by selecting the `Draw/Annotate` option) are shown in Figure 7-4. The large open area near the right side of the screen is the *drawing box*, and that is where you will do your actual drawing. HG uses the left portion of the screen to present various menus and list the different options that you will use to draw your charts.

Using a Grid

We want the cursor key layout in the example chart to be perfectly symmetrical. Therefore, let's use a grid to enable us to align the elements in the chart as precisely as possible.

First, select the `Grid` option (5) from the Draw menu. Change the `Size` to 3 and press Enter. This number is smaller than the default value; therefore, HG displays more grid points and we can place our elements in the drawing box more accurately.

Set the `Show` option to `Yes` and press Enter. This tells HG to display the grid in the drawing box. Leave the `Snap` option at its default setting. (The completed Grid menu settings are shown in Figure 7-5.) When you press Esc to return to the Draw menu, you will see a grid drawn on the screen as a series of dots, as shown in the drawing box portion of Figure 7-5.

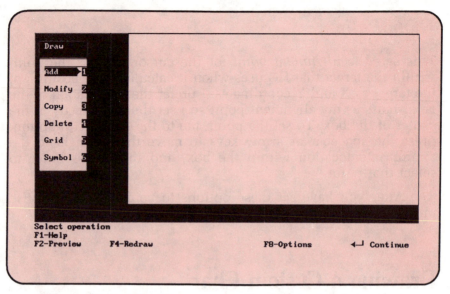

Figure 7-4. The Draw menu and drawing box

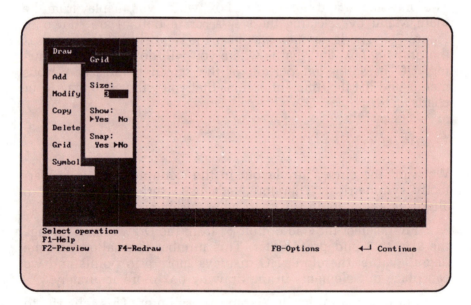

Figure 7-5. Using the Grid option

Adding a Box

Our next task is to draw a box that looks like a cursor key. To add an element to the drawing box, select the Add option from the Draw menu. Now, select Box from the Add menu. A crosshair cursor will appear in the drawing box. (You might see an arrow if you set your Target global option differently.)

Move the target cursor to the approximate position of key number 7 in Figure 7-1. Don't worry about its exact location; you can always move it later. Press Enter to *anchor* the top-left corner of the box. (The alignment point you selected in the Global Options menu determines the exact spot where the upper-left corner of the box is anchored.)

Now we have to draw the actual box. HG offers no less than 21 different box styles from which you can choose. These box styles are shown in Figure 7-6.

217

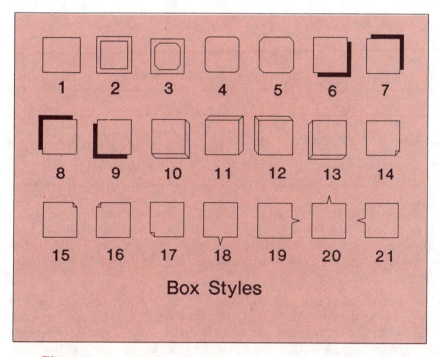

Figure 7-6. *HG box styles*

Press F8 to activate the Box Options menu so that you can select one of these styles. (The Box Options menu is shown in Figure 7-7.)

When HG draws a box, the Style option determines which type of box HG uses. The Size field for a box probably isn't what you think it is. The meaning of the value in the Size field varies with different box styles. Table 7-1 shows the impact that the Size field has on each box style.

Table 7-1. Relationship Between Size and Box Style

Box Style	Size Field Specifies...
1	No effect
2, 3	Gap between inner and outer box
4	Roundness of corners (radius)
5	Distance diagonals cut corners
6-9	Depth of shadow
10-13	Depth of box
14-17	Width of folded corner
18-21	Half distance from box edge to point.

218

▶ **Tip:** Note that the Size value never controls the actual size of the box. Instead, the magnitude of the Size setting determines the size of specific box attributes.

Examine the box style choices in Figure 7-6. We want the box to look like the top of a key, so style 4 seems like the best choice. Now that we've decided on a style, let's set some of the options in the Box Options menu so that our box will look more like a "cursor key.".

Press Y to set the Square field to Yes; then press Enter or Tab to move to the next field. Set Style to 4 and press Enter. According to Table 7-1, the Size setting affects the roundness of the corners of the box, *not* the size of the box. Type 7.5 and press Enter. We want the box to have an outline, so set Draw to Yes. Tab to Color, type 1, and press Enter. Finally, because we want a "hollow" box, type N for Fill and press Enter.

If you've made the proper selections for these options your Box Options menu will look like the one in Figure 7-7. Although Figure 7-7 also shows a completed box, your screen will not have the box drawn...yet. Press the F8 key to return to the drawing box portion of the screen.

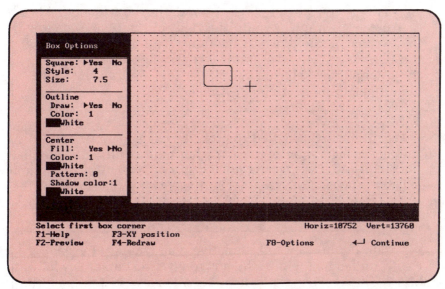

Figure 7-7. Using the Box Options menu to create a custom box

219

(Note that the square shown in Figure 7-7 is not a perfect square only because my screen-capture program doesn't match the HG aspect ratio perfectly. When you draw the box, be sure it looks square on your screen.)

Drawing the Box

The program is now waiting for you to move the target cursor to set the actual size of the box. To move the target cursor, you can either use the cursor keys shown in Figure 7-1 or you can slide the mouse in the appropriate direction. Because HG always starts drawing from the upper-left corner of the box, press the PgDn key to expand the box. If you are using a mouse, merely slide it towards the lower-right corner of the box. (This type of work makes a mouse a wonderful device to have!)

You can also use the other cursor movement keys shown in Figure 7-1 to adjust the box so it comes out square. Use the grid lines to help you determine when you have the box square. Note that our box is four squares by four squares on the grid.

> **Tip:** If the cursor keys expand the box too quickly, press the minus key (to the right of the 6 key) to slow the expansion rate down. If the movement is too slow, press the plus key (below the minus key) a few times. Pressing the asterisk key (above the minus key) returns the movement rates to their original settings.

When you are satisfied that the box is square, press Enter. (If you are using a mouse, press the left mouse button.) Note that the attributes that you gave the box do *not* take affect until after you have pressed Enter to anchor the lower-right corner of the box. You should now see a box that resembles a cursor key.

220

> **Tip:** If you want to be creative, you could put a smaller rounded box within the box to give the cursor key a 3D effect. This looks more realistic than box styles 2 or 3, but it adds clutter to the chart and might not be worth the effort.

Press Esc twice to return to the Draw menu.

Copying an Object

You could continue drawing boxes exactly as you drew this one, but that's more work than you need to do. After you are satisfied that the shape of the box is correct, you can use HG's Copy option to reproduce the box eight more times.

First, select the Copy option (3) from the Draw menu. Then, move the target cursor to the center of the box that you just drew. When you press Enter, HG will draw four "dots" around the box, as shown in Figure 7-8.

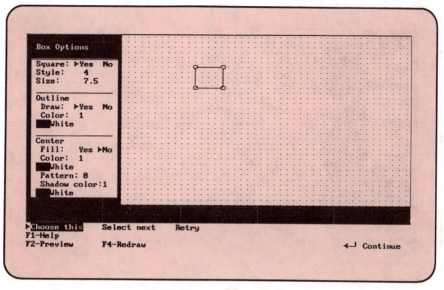

Figure 7-8.   Using HG's Copy option

221

Notice the one-line menu near the bottom of the screen. The first option in the menu is `Choose this`. If you press Enter with this option highlighted, you are telling HG that the dots outline the object you want to copy. (In a more complex figure, the dots might surround an object near the one you really want. In that case, you should specify `Select next` or `Retry` to try to reposition the cursor on the correct object.) If the dots indeed surround your box, highlight `Choose this` and press Enter. HG then displays another box on the screen.

Use the cursor keys to move the new box to the location at which you want to place the copy. In this example, you might want to slide it to the area that the "8" key will occupy. When you have the box positioned, press Enter to anchor it at the new location.

Continue moving the box to new locations and pressing Enter to create the remaining keys in the figure. When you finish, your screen should have a series of boxes that resemble a numeric keypad, as shown in Figure 7-9.

 Copy an Object in a Draw/Annotate Chart

1. Press 3.   Selects `Copy` from the Draw menu.

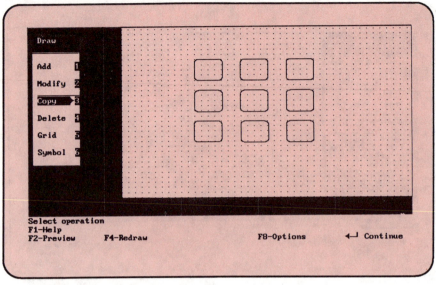

222

Figure 7-9.   The screen after you have made eight copies

2. Use the arrow keys (or mouse) to move the target (cursor) to the object you want to copy.

Specifies the object to be copied.

3. Press Enter.

Four dots surround the object; HG lets you know it will copy "this" object.

4. If the object is correct, highlight Choose this, and press Enter.

Duplicates the object on the screen. (If the dots are in the wrong location, select Retry and repeat steps 2, 3, and 4.)

5. Move the cursor to the location at which you want to place the copy.

6. Press Enter.

Anchors the copy at the new location.

Adding Text to a Drawing

Let's continue creating the example figure. We now need to fill in the numbers for each of the keys. Press Esc to return to the Draw menu. To add an object to a chart, select the Add option (1) from the Draw menu. In this case, we'll be adding a few numbers, so select the Text option (1) from the Add menu.

Notice that the cursor moves to a one-line field (labeled Text) near the bottom of the screen. This is the line in which you will type the text to be added to the drawing. However, before you type the text, press F8 to activate the Text Options menu. Let's change a few of these options:

Set the text Size field to 4, and press Enter. If your output will go to a color device, enter the color that you want the text to be. (Press F6 to display the available colors.)

The next five options determine the attributes that your text will have. For non-color output, use the following settings:

223

```
Fill: Yes
Bold: Yes
Italic: No
Underline: No
Shadow: No
Shadow color: 1
```

The Align option determines where the text is placed within the target cursor that you move around in the drawing box. Press the Tab key to highlight Base with center alignment. The Text Options menu in Figure 7-10 shows the correct settings for all of the text attributes in our example.

When your menu is identical to that in the figure, press F8 to deactivate the Text Options menu.

Now, type a 1 in the Text field at the bottom of the screen, and press Enter. HG immediately displays a small white box on the screen. This "box" actually holds the text that you just typed in the Text field. You must now move the box to the place where you want to display the text in the chart.

Use the arrow keys (or mouse) to move the box to the center of the "1" key in the drawing. When you press Enter, HG dis-

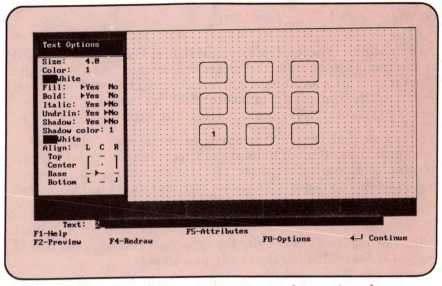

224

Figure 7-10. Setting text options when using the
Add text option

plays the character inside the cursor key. Your drawing box should now look similar to the one in Figure 7-10.

Repeat the previous text-entry and box-positioning procedures for all of the numbers on the keypad (that is, keys 2 through 9). By the time you finish, you'll be a pro at adding text to a drawing.

If you want, you can add the title of the drawing — Movement of Cursor Keys — near the bottom of screen as we did in Figure 7-1. Before you enter this text, however, you will need to increase the value in the Size field in the Text Options menu. When you finish, press Esc twice to return to the Draw menu.

Adding Arrows to the Chart

Our example chart is almost complete. The only elements we need to add are the arrows that point outward from each of the keys (see Figure 7-1). To add the arrows, first select the Add option (1) from the Draw menu; then, select the Line option (4) from the Add menu. Next, move the target cursor to a point just below and to the left of the 1 key. This will be the point where you want the arrow to begin (see Figure 7-11).

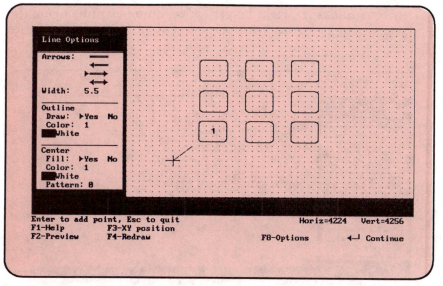

Figure 7-11. Using the Line option to draw an arrow

Before you can draw the arrow, you have to change some Line settings. Press F8 to activate the Line Options menu. Now, look at the options in the Arrow field. Because you want to draw an "outward-pointing" arrow, press the spacebar twice to select the third arrow, and then press Enter to advance to the next field.

The value in the Width field sets the thickness of the arrow. Enter 5.5. Set the Draw option to Yes, and if you have a color output device, press F6 to select a color for the arrow's outline.

The Center field options refer to the attributes of the "inside" of the arrow. Because you want a "solid" arrow, set Fill to Yes. To specify a value at the Color field, press F6 and select an available color. At the Pattern option, press F6 to see the patterns you can use. The figure you are creating calls for a solid arrow, so select 1.

When you finish making these selections, press F8 to close the Line Options menu and return control to the target cursor in the drawing box.

Press Enter to anchor the arrow. Then, press the End (1) key to draw a line down and to the left, as shown in Figure 7-11.

When your line is the right length, press Enter again to signal the endpoint of the arrow. Your screen will now resemble Figure 7-12.

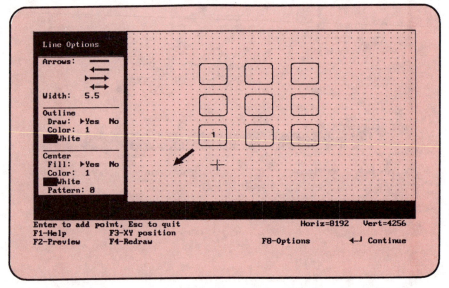

Figure 7-12. Using the Line option to draw an arrow

Repeat the procedure described in the previous paragraph for the rest of the arrows. Note that you do *not* have to reset the line options for each arrow. After you draw an arrow, move the target cursor to a new starting point, press Enter to anchor the line, use the cursor control keys to draw the line in the appropriate direction, and then press Enter again to set the endpoint. That's all there is to it.

When you finish drawing all the arrows, your chart should look like Figure 7-1. You might want to experiment with different settings in the Line Option menu to see what impact they have on the chart. When you are finally satisfied with the drawing, press Esc three times to return to the Main Menu; then, save the chart.

Drawing a Map

In this section, we will use some other HG drawing features to draw a map that will show you how to get to the Indianapolis Colts' training camp. Select Draw/Annotate (3) from the Main Menu. When you draw a map, a good place to start is with a distinctive landmark. Directly in front of the training camp is a small pond. Let's make this the first feature we put in our map.

Using the Polyline Option

If you still have the keypad drawing on your screen, select the Delete option (4) from the Draw menu; then, select the All option (3) from the Delete menu. To clear the screen, answer Yes to the Delete all drawings? prompt.

227

> ▶ **Tip:** If the grid is still on from the last exercise, you can turn it off by selecting Grid from the Draw menu and then selecting No for the Show option. Grids are most helpful when you need to position elements precisely. However, when you are drawing free form figures, the grid dots tend to clutter the screen and serve as a distraction.

Now you are ready to begin drawing the map. Select the Add option (1) from the Draw menu. Then, select the Polyline option (3) from the Add menu to display a screen that looks like Figure 7-13.

Press F8 to activate the Polyline Options menu. The default settings for the first two options are fine for our purpose, but let's change the last two options. Press the Tab key twice to advance the cursor to the Shape field.

The Shape Option

A *polyline* can have two basic shapes: sharp or curved. You construct a polyline by pressing Enter (or the left mouse button) for each point you want to draw on the line. A *sharp* polyline connects all of the points with a series of straight lines. A *curved*

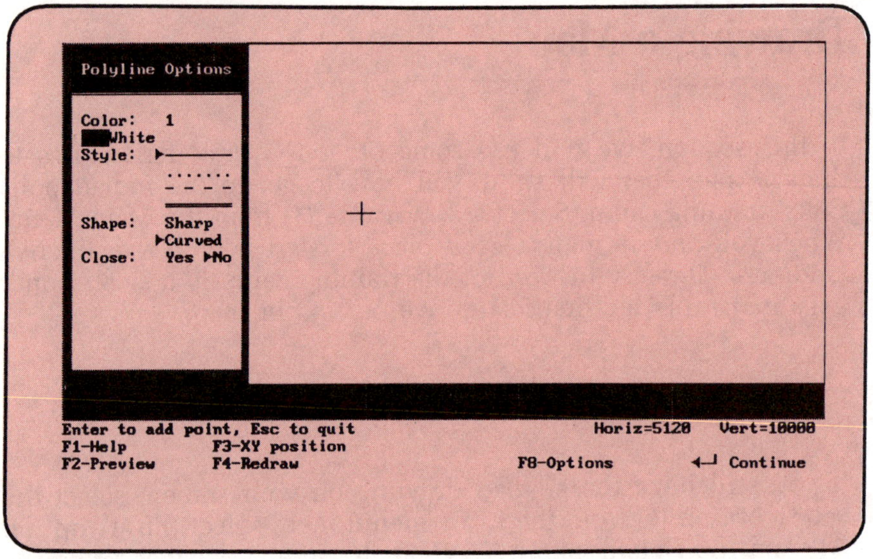

```
Polyline Options

Color:    1
    ■White
Style:  ▶─────

        .......
        ─ ─ ─ ─
        ─────

Shape:   Sharp
        ▶Curved
Close:   Yes ▶No
```

```
Enter to add point, Esc to quit          Horiz=5128   Vert=10000
F1-Help              F3-XY position
F2-Preview           F4-Redraw                F8-Options     ←┘ Continue
```

228

Figure 7-13.   Using the Polyline Options menu

polyline uses a spline algorithm to average the distance between points and produce a smooth line. Note that a curved polyline will rarely pass through each of the points you specify.

Figure 7-14 shows two polylines. Each polyline uses the same points, but the top line used the Sharp polyline setting, and the bottom line used the Curved setting.

Remember, you need to draw a pond. The figure will obviously look more realistic if you set the Shape field to the Curved option. Press C.

> ▶ **Tip:** Whenever you want to draw a smooth, non-linear line, set the Shape field to the Curved setting. The result is almost always more pleasing to the eye than a line drawn with the Shape field set to Sharp.

The Close Option

Any line can have two states: *open* or *closed*. The lines shown in Figure 7-14 are called open lines because the endpoints of the line do not meet. If the endpoints of the line meet to form an enclosed figure, it is said to be a closed polyline. Because you want to draw a pond, you must specify a closed polyline. There-

```
 Polyline Options

 Color:    1
 ███White
 Style:  ▶─────────
         ...........
         ─ ─ ─ ─
         ──────────

 Shape:  ▶Sharp
          Curved
 Close:   Yes ▶No


 Enter to add point, Esc to quit        Horiz=16896  Vert=15360
 F1-Help          F3-XY position
 F2-Preview       F4-Redraw           F8-Options      ◄┘ Continue
```

Figure 7-14.   A sharp polyline (top) and a curved polyline

fore, press the Tab key once, and press Y to set the Close option to Yes. Finally, press F8 to exit from the Polyline Options menu and return to the drawing box.

Drawing the Polyline

Now that you've set the options properly, move the target cursor to the middle of the drawing box and press Enter (or the left mouse button) to set the first point of the polyline. Next, move the cursor slightly down and to the left; then, press Enter to set another point of the polyline. (Notice that HG draws a *straight* line to connect the points. Don't worry; if you specified Curved for the Close option, HG will round the lines when you finish.) Gradually trace a circular shape similar to the one shown in Figure 7-15. Be sure that you set the last point on or near the first point you used to start the polyline. Now press Esc.

HG smooths the lines connecting all of the points along the polyline to produce a shape similar to the one shown in Figure 7-15. Your shape doesn't need to match mine exactly: As long as the figure looks something like a pond, the map will look fine.

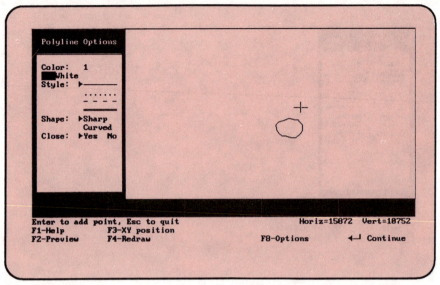

230

*Figure 7-15. The completed pond, drawn using the
Polyline option*

Also, don't worry if your shape is too large or too small; you will
soon find out how reduce or enlarge any object you want.

Press Esc twice to return to the Draw menu.

Drawing the Roads

Now let's draw some of the major roads that the map will depict.
First, select the Add option (1) from the Draw menu. Then, select
the Line option (4) from the Add menu. Because you will be
using the default settings for the line style, you don't need to
press F8 to display the Line Options menu. Simply move the target cursor to the left edge of the drawing box about a third of the
way from the top, and press Enter to anchor that end of the line.
Now move the cursor to the right edge of the drawing box and
press Enter to mark the other endpoint of the line.

HG immediately draws the line you just set. Look at Figure
7-16. Repeat the previous line-drawing steps to enter all of the
vertical "roads" in the map.

The precise placement of the roads isn't that important right
now. You can always redraw or move the lines at a later time.
Press Esc twice to return to the Draw menu.

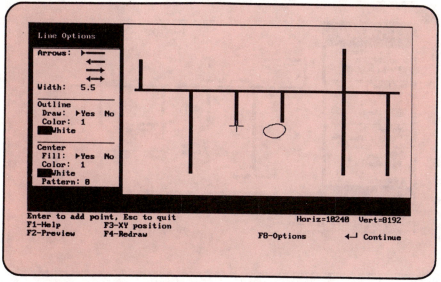

Figure 7-16. Adding lines to the example map

231

> ▶ **Tip:** Horizontal and vertical lines are easy to draw parallel to either axis. Just be sure the line has no jagged "steps" in it before you anchor it at the endpoint.

Adding Text to the Map

You already used the Text option of the Add menu when you drew the earlier cursor-key example chart. In this example, you will use the Text option to label the roads and other key points on the map.

To add text to the map, first select the Add option (1) from the Draw menu; then, select the Text option (1) from the Add menu. In the Text field at the bottom of the screen, type the name of a road or other landmark shown in Figure 7-17 and press Enter. Next, move the text box to the appropriate place on the map, and press Enter to set the text.

The Text field is still active. Therefore, type another block of text, press Enter, position the box in the map, and press Enter again. It's that simple. Repeat the procedure until you have labeled all of the roads and landmarks that appear on the map

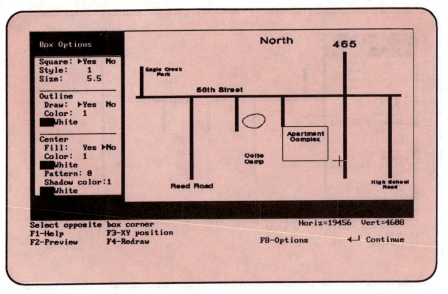

232

Figure 7-17.   The example map with text added

(see Figure 7-17). Note that you might have to change the size of the text in some cases (merely press F8 and change the Size option). For example, we used a smaller text size to write Apartment complex inside the box. (We drew the box here so you could see why the text must be smaller; you will draw these boxes in the next section.) Also note that we had to insert the words Apartment and complex as two separate entries so that they would appear on different lines in the map.

Press Esc twice to return to the Draw menu.

Adding Boxes to the Map

Now let's add two boxes to the map. One box will represent the training camp and the other a nearby apartment complex. This procedure is a familiar one and we've already discussed all the options involved; therefore, just quickly follow this brief list of instructions:

1. Select the Add option (1) from the Draw menu.
2. Select the Box option (2) from the Add menu.
3. Press F8 to activate the Box Options menu.

4. Set the Square option to Yes.

5. Set the Style option to 1.

6. Press the Tab key to advance the cursor to the Center field.

7. Set Fill to No.

8. Press F8 to return to the drawing box.

9. Use the arrow key to move the target cursor to the top-left edge of the box you want to draw, and then press Enter to anchor the box. (See Figure 7-19 for the position of these two boxes.)

10. Press the PgDn key to expand the box.

11. When the box is the proper size, press Enter to draw the box.

12. Repeat steps 9 through 11 to draw the second box. (See Figure 7-19 for the proper location.)

233

Adding Symbols to the Map

Press Esc twice to return to the Draw menu. Now let's add a little class to the map. To do this, we will use some predrawn symbols that HG supplies as part of its software package.

First, select the Symbol option (6) from the Draw menu. Next, select the Get option (1) from the Symbol menu. HG includes a file of drawings that are all related to the topic of transportation. Highlight the TRANSPT.SYM symbol file in the list of files and press Enter (or type TRANSPT.SYM at the Filename field and press Enter). After HG displays the drawings, move the target cursor to the traffic light symbol and press Enter (see Figure 7-18).

HG will retrieve the traffic light symbol and create a box on the screen. At this point, *do not* press Enter. HG provides a shortcut method by which you can move and resize the symbol.

 Get a Symbol from a Symbol File

1. Press 6. Selects the Symbol option from the Draw menu.

2. Press 1. Selects the Get option from the Symbol menu.

3. Enter a symbol filename, or highlight the file and press Enter.

Selects the named symbol file.

4. Position the target cursor on the symbol you want.

Selects a symbol.

5. Press Enter.

Loads the symbol from disk.

6. Press the Backspace key.

Replaces the symbol box with your target cursor.

7. Move the cursor to the appropriate location, and press Enter.

Anchors the corner of the symbol.

8. Use the mouse or cursor keys to expand the box that holds the symbol.

Sets the size of the symbol.

234

9. Press Enter.

Draws the symbol in the chart.

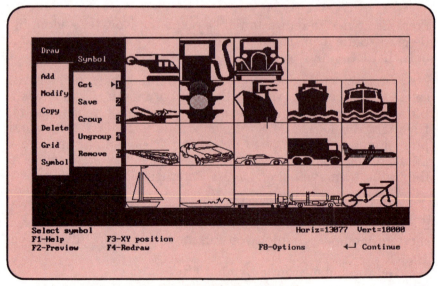

Figure 7-18.   Available symbols in the TRANSPT.SYM file

Moving and Sizing a Symbol

When HG draws the symbol box on your map, it's likely that the symbol is not in the right location. However, you can easily re-size it and move it to a new position before HG actually draws it on your map.

First, press the Backspace key to replace the symbol box with the target cursor. Then, move the cursor to the upper-left corner of the position you want to place the symbol. (Note that you are really positioning the *alignment point* of the cursor. Usually the alignment point is the center of the cross-hair cursor or the tip of the arrow cursor. For a detailed discussion of the alignment point, see the "Global Align" section earlier in this chapter.)

When the cursor is at the proper location, press Enter to anchor the upper-left corner of the symbol. Use the arrow keys or mouse to expand the symbol's box outline to the desired size. As soon as you press Enter again (to anchor the lower-right corner of the symbol), HG will move the symbol to the new location and adjust its size to fill the box you just drew. Your map should now look similar to Figure 7-19.

235

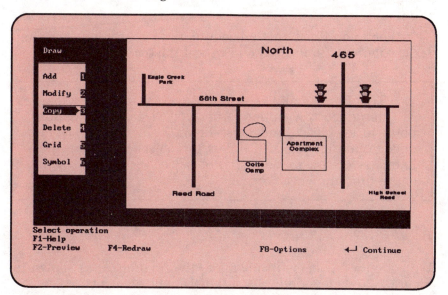

Figure 7-19. The map after moving, sizing, and copying traffic-light symbols

If you look closely at this figure, you will see two traffic lights in Figure 7-19. Let's discuss how you create the second symbol.

Copying a Symbol

Because the map requires two traffic-light symbols, let's use the Copy option to duplicate the symbol you just placed in the map. Press Esc to the return to the Draw menu.

First, select the Copy option (3) from the Draw menu. Then, place the target cursor on the traffic light and press Enter. Four "dots" should appear around the symbol. If the dots surround the traffic light, press Enter to select the Choose this option in the one-line menu near the bottom of the screen. If the dots outline some other object, select the Retry option; then, reposition the cursor on the traffic light, and press Enter twice.

236

HG now creates the familiar box around the traffic light. Move the box (which holds an exact copy of the traffic light) to its proper location, and press Enter to place the copy on the screen.

When you finish this procedure, the map should look similar to Figure 7-19. Press Esc to cancel the Copy option.

> ▶ **Tip:** The Move and Size options work like the previously described Copy option. After you select these options, point to an object, and press Enter, HG will display four dots around an object. If this is the object you want, press Enter (select Choose this); if not select Retry, and try the entire procedure again.

Finishing Touches

We added a few embellishments to the final chart, as shown in Figure 7-20. Let's briefly discuss these new elements.

First, we copied the tree symbol from the MISC.SYM file and placed it near the road to Eagle Creek Park. We then used the Copy option to make two duplicates of the symbol. Next, we used the Polyline option to draw the on- and off-ramps to Inter-

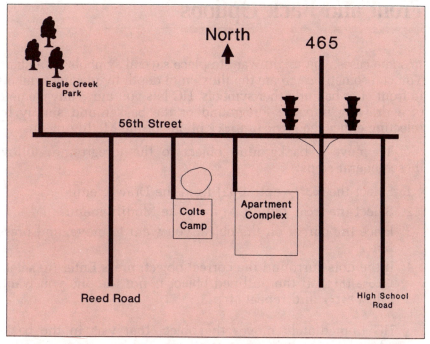

Figure 7-20. The final example map

237

state 465. (These ramps are near the traffic lights.) Finally, we used the Line option to draw an arrow pointing north and used the Text option to write the word "North" on the map. If you want, you might even add the word "pond" over the pond in front of the training camp. (If you've looked at the map closely, you're probably wondering where the other on- and off-ramps for 465 are. I've been wondering the same thing for the past eight years!)

To test what you've learned so far, try adding the missing elements to the map. Use Figure 7-20 and the discussion in the preceding paragraph as your guide. You'll probably be amazed at how easy the entire process is.

When you finish, return to the Main Menu and save the chart.

Front and Back Options

In some cases, you might want to place several symbols on a chart. You can sometimes create the illusion of depth by placing symbols in front of or behind other symbols. HG lets you move any element of a drawing into the foreground or the background simply by selecting either the Front or Back options of the Modify menu.

To move a background object to the foreground, follow these general steps:

1. Select the Modify option (2) from the Draw menu.
2. Select the Front option (4) from the Modify menu.
3. Place the cursor on the object you want to move, and press Enter.
4. If the dots surround the correct object, press Enter (to select Choose this). If the outlined object is not the one you want, select Retry and repeat step 3.

238

HG immediately moves the object that was in the background and places it in front of all other objects occupying the same space in the drawing (see Figure 7-21). To move a foreground object to the background, repeat the previous steps, except use the Back option (5) in Step 2.

> ▶ **Tip:** The Front and Back options have a visible effect only when the objects you are moving are solid or have been filled in. HG views "wire frame" objects as though they were transparent, so the Front and Back options have no effect on them.

Circles and Ellipses

Let's examine how to use another drawing option. If you still have the map on your screen, select the Delete option (4) from the Draw menu; then, select ALL (3)from the Delete menu. To clear the screen, answer Yes to the Delete all drawings? prompt.

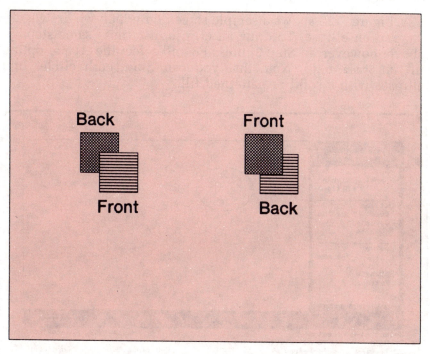

Figure 7-21   *The result of moving a background object into the foreground.*

239

HG offers a simple method for creating circles and ellipses. Because using the Circle option is so similar to the procedure you used to draw boxes, you need only the following brief steps to be able to use the option proficiently:

1. Select the Add option (1) from the Draw menu.

2. Select the Circle option (5) from the Add menu.

3. If you want to change the options in the Shape, Outline, or Center fields, press F8. Tab to the appropriate fields and make your changes. Press F8 when you finish.

4. Move the target cursor to the spot where you want to draw the circle. Press Enter to anchor the top-left portion of the circle.

5. Use the mouse or the arrow keys to expand the circle. (Note that HG displays a square box as you size the circle; it doesn't display the circle itself until you later press Enter.)

6. When the box is the size of the circle you want to draw, press Enter.

Figure 7-22 shows a sample screen on which we drew a circle and an ellipse. To draw an ellipse, use these same steps as above; however, in Step 3, press F8 and select the Ellipse option in the Shape field. Note that you can draw both circles and ellipses with a solid or patterned fill.

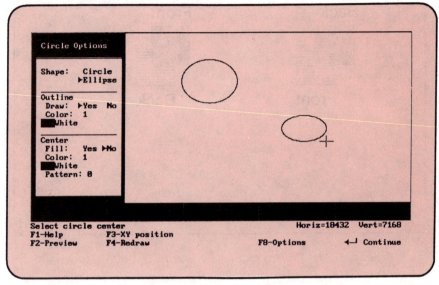

240

Figure 7-22. *Using the Circle option to draw a circle and an ellipse*

Creating Custom Symbols

Appendix B includes a series of figures that show the complete collection of HG's predrawn symbols. You can use any of these symbols in your charts as easily as pressing a few keys. However, your charts are not limited to these drawings; you can create your own custom symbols. To do this, merely use the Draw menu options to create whatever symbol you need. You can even start with an existing symbol and use the various Draw menu options to transform it into a new symbol that fulfills some specialized need.

When you finish creating the drawing, press Esc until you display the HG Main Menu. Select the Get/Save/Remove option (4) from the menu; then, select the Save as symbol option (6). When

HG displays the Save Chart As Symbol menu, specify a new directory (optional), a name for the symbol, and whether the symbol will be used on a printer or a plotter. A New Symbol File menu follows in which you enter a brief description of the symbol. After you enter this information, HG saves your drawing as a symbol in a disk file that has the SYM extension.

You can now include the drawing in other charts. Simply access it as you would any other symbol (that is, through the Symbol option in the Draw menu).

▶ **Tip:** When you save a drawing on disk as a new symbol, HG stores the image in the form that it was drawn. Therefore, when you incorporate the new symbol into another chart, the new symbol will seem to occupy the entire drawing box. Use the arrow keys to reduce the size of the symbol before you press the Enter key to anchor the symbol in the chart (for details, see the "Moving and Sizing a Symbol" section earlier in this chapter). Also, you can always use the Move and Size options to further refine its placement and size.

241

Annotate

You use the "annotate" aspect of the Draw/Annotate option when you want to add something to an existing chart. An *annotation* is merely any additional information, element, or emphasis that you want to add to a chart. Therefore, annotation involves two basic steps: 1) preparing the original chart for changes and 2) using the Draw menu options to add the annotations. Because you are now familiar with the Draw menu options, the following Quick Steps will show you how to prepare the original chart for annotation.

 Annotate an Existing Chart

1. From the HG Main Menu, press 4.

   Selects the Get/Save/Remove option to get the original chart to be annotated.

2. Press 1.

   Selects the Get Chart option.

3. Highlight a file and press Enter, or type a file name and press Enter.	Selects the file to be annotated.
4. Press Esc twice.	Returns control to the HG Main Menu.
5. Press F7.	Selects the Size option.
6. Place target cursor at upper-left corner where chart is to be drawn.	Positions the chart.
7. Press Enter.	Anchors the upper-left corner of the chart.
8. Press PgDn.	Expands the box.
9. Repeat Step 6 until the box is the correct size.	Establishes the size of the chart.
10. Press Enter.	Anchors the lower-right corner of the box and draws the chart to size.
11. Press Esc.	Returns control to the HG Main Menu.
12. Press 3.	Selects the Draw/Annotate option and displays the Draw menu.
13. Use the Draw menu options to make the appropriate additions or changes.	Annotates the chart.

242

The previous Quick Steps will resize an existing chart so that you can add text, lines, symbols, or additional features to the selected chart. You can use any of the features that we discussed earlier in this chapter. Be sure to press F2 often to review your progress and make sure that the chart is not getting too cluttered.

When you finish making your changes, be sure to save the annotated chart with a different file name than the original chart. This lets you preserve both the old and the annotated versions of the chart.

What You Have Learned

In this chapter, you learned how to use one of HG's most powerful features—the Draw/Annotate option. This set of drawing tools gives you the ability to construct complex charts, enhance written reports, or generate company logos. It elevates visual communication to a higher, more creative level than most other software packages, and it does so with surprisingly few restrictions.

You learned how to use the set of tools within the Draw/Annotate option by actually creating charts. By drawing a custom chart and a detailed map, you learned how to create boxes, arrows, lines, and free form figures; you saw how to add text and symbols to any chart; and you learned how to size, move, and copy elements within a chart.

243

Templates, Macros, and Other Advanced Features

In This Chapter

▶ *Creating a template*
▶ *Creating a chartbook*
▶ *Using macros*
▶ *Creating multiple charts*
▶ *Creating a slide show*

Most of the topics in this chapter show you how to work "smarter" rather than "harder." For example, templates, chartbooks, and macros let you quickly perform often-used operations or procedures. You will also learn how to exploit some of HG's more useful advanced features, such as creating multiple charts and slide show presentations.

Templates

As you worked your way through this book, you probably noticed that almost all charts share common characteristics. For example, most of the charts use titles, subtitles, footnotes, and related elements. In your own work, you probably have found that most of the chart styles you use regularly share common attributes.

A *template* lets you create a "generic" chart with most of these chart attributes already defined. Then, when you need a new chart of that specific type, you can call up the template and most of the work of setting up attributes is already completed. In most cases, all you will need to do is add new data.

Because HG permits multiple templates, you can create a template for every basic chart type that you use on a regular basis. When it comes time to create the next company or departmental report, almost all of your chart work will already be saved on disk. A cup of coffee, some new data, and a template or two and the report's done!

Using templates saves you time (you don't have to set attributes, enter axis titles or series names, and so on), reduces chart errors (the less typing you do, the less chance of error), and adds consistency to your charts (because the basic elements of the generic chart are already set). If you plan to use HG regularly, you probably should create a library of templates.

Creating a Template

Creating a new template is not much different than creating a new chart. In the following example, we will create a line chart that graphs my 10 lowest golf scores and then draws a line that represents the average of those 10 scores. When the chart is complete, we will save it as a template.

Start by selecting Create new chart (1) from the Main Menu and Bar/Line (3) from the Create New Chart menu. At the X Data Type menu, select Name. In our example, the X axis will show the dates of each round of golf. Because the dates for my lowest 10 rounds are scattered throughout the summer months (I'm not a consistent golfer), leave the Starting with, Ending with, and Increment fields blank.

246

Next, you need to enter the data shown in Figure 8-1 into the Bar/Line Chart Data screen. Most of this should be old hat to you by now; however, there are a few elements that we should examine before you actually input the text and values into your own screen.

```
                      Bar/Line Chart Data                          ▼

   Title: Jack's Golf Scores
Subtitle: Lowest 10 of Last 20 Rounds
Footnote:


         X Axis          Scores   | ◆   Sum      Average      Series 4
Pt       Name
_____
1     May 31             80          80          77.3
2    |June 2             78          158
3     June 4             80          238
4    |June 25            72          310
5     June 29            79          389
6    |July 9             77          466
7     July 18            80          546
8    |July 30            75          621
9     August 20          75          696
10   |August 26          77          773          77.3
11
12

F1-Help         F3-Set X type                          F9-More series
F2-Draw chart   F4-Calculate            F8-Options     F10-Continue
```

Figure 8-1.   Sample data for bar/line chart

First, notice that we inserted a vertical bar before every other date in the X axis field. This causes HG to display the dates on alternate lines along the X axis, thus preventing the dates from running together. This makes it easier for the viewer to read the X axis information.

HG Keywords For Calculations

The second element that needs some explanation is the Sum column (that is, Series 2). In addition to charting my low scores, I want to find my average golf score for the 10 lowest rounds. Unfortunately, HG does not provide a direct method for calculating the average of a series (column) of data; the HG averaging function is row-oriented (see Table 8-1). However, HG does provide the @CUM function, which calculates the total of a column of values. The @CUM function provides a cumulative total for a column and writes the results as a new variable.

247

Table 8-1. HG Keywords for Calculations (F4)

Keyword	Description
@AVE	Find average across rows
@MAX	Find maximum value in a row
@MIN	Find minimum value in a row
@SUM	Find sum across rows
@CLR	Erase data in a series (column)
@COPY(#n)	Copy from series n to current cursor series
@CUM(#n)	Write cumulative totals from series n to the current cursor series
@DIFF(#n)	Write difference between n and (n - 1) to the current cursor series. If n is 3, then the difference between 3 and 2 is written into the current cursor column
@DUP(#n)	Duplicate series n in the current cursor series. Like @COPY, but you can duplicate series n by pressing F10 as often as needed
@EXCH(#n)	Exchange the current cursor series with series n
@MAVE(#X,Y,Z)	Calculate moving average of series X using Y points before and Z points after the value.
@MOVE(#n)	Move values from current cursor series to series n. Because this moves the data, the current cursor series is empty after the move
@PCT(#n)	For the current cursor series, calculate the percentage that each value at n is of the total of series n
@REDUC	Sort, reorder, and eliminate duplicate data for all series and X data in a Bar/Line chart
@RECALC	Recompute all calculated values in the chart
@REXP(#n)	Do exponential (non-linear) regression of series n
@RLIN(#n)	Do linear regression on series n
@RLOG(#n)	Do logarithmic regression on series n
@RPWR(#n)	Do power regression for series n

248

In Table 8-1, note that the first four keywords apply to operations across rows. The remainder of the keywords operate on series, or columns, of data. You can use any of these keywords by pressing F4.

After you enter the scores in Series 1, press the Tab key to move the cursor to the Series 2 column. Then press F4 to activate the HG Calculate option. Press Enter without making an entry in the Legend field of the Calculate menu to advance the cursor to the Calculation field. Then type:

@CUM(#1)

This tells HG to take the cumulative totals for the data in the Series 1 field (that is, my scores) and enter them into the Series 2 field. You can see the results of this in Figure 8-1. Because the value in row number 10 of the Series 2 column is the sum of all the scores in Series 1, that value divided by 10 is my average score. Enter this average score in rows 1 and 10 of Series 3 (the Average column), and leave the other Series columns blank (see Figure 8-1).

249

Bar/Line Chart Titles & Options: Page 1

Press F8 to display Page 1 of the Titles & Options menu. The following list shows the fields that we changed and the data that you should enter into the corresponding fields:

```
X axis title: Date Posted
Y1 axis title: Score
Series 1: Scores
Series 2: Sum
Series 3: Average
```

Also, set the first three series in the Type column to Line; set the Sum row (Series 2) in the Display column to No; and set the Scores and Average rows (Series 1 and 3) in the Display column to Yes. The completed Page 1 Titles & Options menu is shown in Figure 8-2.

Let's use all of the default values on Page 2. Press the PgDn key to display Page 3.

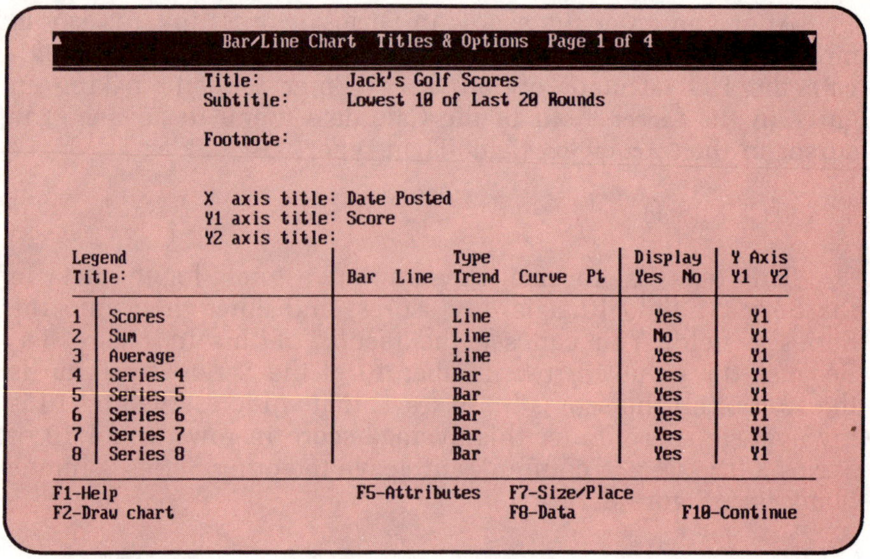

```
┌──────────────────────────────────────────────────────────────┐
│▲         Bar/Line Chart  Titles & Options  Page 1 of 4       ▼│
├──────────────────────────────────────────────────────────────┤
│            Title:        Jack's Golf Scores                   │
│            Subtitle:     Lowest 18 of Last 28 Rounds          │
│                                                                │
│            Footnote:                                           │
│                                                                │
│            X  axis title: Date Posted                          │
│            Y1 axis title: Score                                │
│            Y2 axis title:                                      │
│    Legend                        Type          Display  Y Axis │
│    Title:             Bar  Line Trend Curve Pt  Yes  No  Y1 Y2 │
│                                                                │
│    1  Scores                Line               Yes      Y1     │
│    2  Sum                   Line                    No   Y1     │
│    3  Average               Line               Yes      Y1     │
│    4  Series 4              Bar                 Yes      Y1     │
│    5  Series 5              Bar                 Yes      Y1     │
│    6  Series 6              Bar                 Yes      Y1     │
│    7  Series 7              Bar                 Yes      Y1     │
│    8  Series 8              Bar                 Yes      Y1     │
│    ──────────────────────────────────────────────────────     │
│    F1-Help              F5-Attributes   F7-Size/Place          │
│    F2-Draw chart                        F8-Data     F18-Continue│
└──────────────────────────────────────────────────────────────┘
```

Figure 8-2.   The completed Page 1 Titles & Options menu for the sample line chart

Bar/Line Chart Titles & Options: Page 3

Let's change a few of the default settings here. In the first field on the page, Data Table, select Normal. This tells HG to display the chart with the scores as part of the chart.

Next, advance the cursor to the Minimum Value field of the Y1 Axis column, and type 70. Then, press Enter, and type 85 in the Maximum Value field of the Y1 Axis column. We changed the minimum and maximum values for the Y1 Axis (Score) so that the line for the scores doesn't look "flat." If you use the default values, the Y axis of the chart starts at 0 (a *very* good golfer!) and ends with 100. Because my scores fall between 72 and 80, the line shows almost no change when using the default scaling. Using the values shown in Figure 8-3 makes the variations more dramatic and creates a more interesting chart.

You don't need to make any changes on Page 4 of the Titles & Options menu, so the chart is now complete. Press F2 to display the chart; Figure 8-4 shows the result.

```
▲              Bar/Line Chart  Titles & Options  Page 3 of 4              ▼

   Data Table          │▶Normal   Framed    None

   X  Axis Labels      │▶Normal   Vertical  %         None
   Y1 Axis Labels      │▶Value    $         %         None
   Y2 Axis Labels      │▶Value    $         %         None

   X  Grid Lines       │  ····      ——     ▶None
   Y1 Grid Lines       │▶ ····      ——      None
   Y2 Grid Lines       │▶ ····      ——      None

   X Tick Mark Style   │▶In       Out       Both      None
   Y Tick Mark Style   │▶In       Out       Both      None

                       │    X Axis          Y1 Axis          Y2 Axis

   Scale Type          │▶Linear   Log     ▶Linear   Log    ▶Linear   Log
   Format              │
   Minimum Value       │                     70
   Maximum Value       │                     85
   Increment           │
   ─────────────────────────────────────────────────────────────────────
   F1-Help
   F2-Draw chart                         F8-Data            F10-Continue
```

Figure 8-3. **The completed Page 3 Titles & Options menu for the sample line chart**

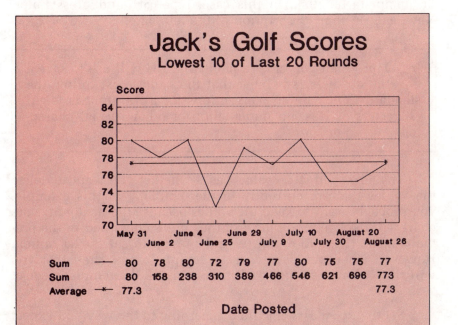

Figure 8-4. **The final line chart**

251

The chart is a little busy, but I prefer to have the scores shown on the chart. If you think the chart would look better with fewer elements, you might remove the scores; simply change the Data Table field on Page 1 of the Titles & Options menu to None.

Saving the Chart as a Template

Now that the chart is finished, let's save it as a template. Obviously, this is the type of chart that will need to be updated periodically, and that is an important reason for converting it into a template. Then, you can easily update the chart as often as you want. You can also use this template as the basis for creating other "sports" charts, so that they all have the same "look."

252 From the HG Main Menu, select the Get/Save/Remove option (1), and then select the Save template option (4). When HG displays the Save Template menu (see Figure 8-5), fill in the Template name field with a file name; HG uses this name to store the template on disk. In this case, type golf and press Enter. Now, enter a short description of the template.

> ▶ **Tip:** When you enter a name that HG will use to save a file on disk, remember that the name must follow the standard DOS naming conventions for a file (that is, eight characters or less, no punctuation or other special characters, and so on).

The next field (Clear values) asks whether you want to delete the values that are currently in the template. In this example, you probably want to keep the values because the next golf score chart will likely contain most of the values contained in the previous chart. Therefore, you would press N to set the No option. However, whenever you need an "empty" chart shell that you will fill with new values each time you use the template, select Yes.

Set the Import data link field according to the way you expect to be inputting data into the chart. For example, if you will be using the template to generate a weekly sales report from a Lotus spreadsheet file, you would select the Lotus option. Likewise, if you will be importing data from a database that produces ASCII files, you would select the ASCII option. In our example, the data will be entered manually, so you need to select None. Figure 8-5 shows the Save Template menu completed with the appropriate responses for our sample golf template.

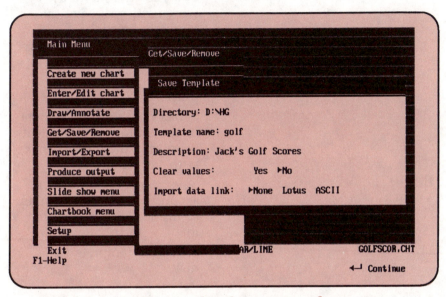

253

Figure 8-5. *The completed Save Template menu for the example template*

After you respond to the last field, HG saves the template to disk. Any time you need to create this type of chart, simply begin with this template; after all, most of the chart work is already finished.

 Creating and Saving a Template

1. From the Main Menu, press 1.	Selects the Create new chart option.
2. Select a chart type.	Your choice depends on your needs.
3. Fill in the fields of the chart.	Enter the data, types, titles, options, and other information needed to construct the chart.
4. Press Esc.	Returns control to the Main Menu.

5. Press 4. — Selects the Get/Save/Remove option.

6. Press 4. — Selects the Save template option.

7. Fill in the Template name field and press Enter. — Specifies the name by which HG will save the template on disk.

8. Fill in the Description field and press Enter. — A brief description of the template serves to remind you of the template's purpose.

9. Set the Clear values field. — Select Yes to erase the data in the current chart; select No to save the current data with the template.

254

10. Set the Import data link field. — Select None, Lotus, or ASCII, according to how you plan to input data into charts made with this template.

11. Press Enter. — Saves the template to disk. □

You can now recall the template any time you need to create this particular chart form. To retrieve the template, select the Get/Save/Remove option (4) from the Main Menu, select the Get Template option (3) from the Get/Save/Remove menu, and select the appropriate file from the list that HG displays.

Chartbooks

You might find that you need to use more than one template to prepare weekly or monthly reports. In that case, you should organize your related templates into a *chartbook*. A chartbook is HG's method of letting you organize templates into convenient chart categories. When you fully recognize the benefits of using templates, your list of files will grow rapidly; chartbooks make it easier for you to find the templates you need.

Most users organize a chartbook by one of two primary themes. First, you can organize a chartbook along project lines. For example, the chartbook might contain all of the templates you need to complete a specific project or report. The second theme is to organize templates by chart type. For example, you might create one chartbook that contains templates for line charts, a second chartbook for bar charts, and a third for text charts.

Chartbooks are merely a method by which you can organize a collection of templates in a meaningful way. Your own chart requirements determine what type of templates your chartbooks will contain.

Creating a Chartbook

To begin creating a new chartbook, select the Chartbook menu option (8) from the HG Main Menu. From the Chartbook Menu, select the Create chartbook option (1). When HG presents the Create Chartbook menu, enter a file name in the Chartbook name field. (The name must follow the standard DOS naming conventions for a file.) Note that HG assumes that all templates are located in the current working directory (see the top of the Create Chartbook menu shown in Figure 8-6). If your templates are stored in different directory, press the Shift-Tab key combination to move to the Directory field so that you can enter the correct directory name.

After you enter the directory and chartbook names, enter a description for the chartbook. This description should be a "memory jogger" that immediately lets you know what the chartbook contains. Press Enter after you type a description.

HG now presents the Create/Edit Chartbook screen. Yours will be similar to the one shown in Figure 8-7.

The Create/Edit Chartbook screen is divided into two parts. The top half lists all of the templates in the current directory, and the bottom half holds the template names(s) that you assign to this chartbook. By default, HG displays the first template name from the top listing in the new chartbook.

255

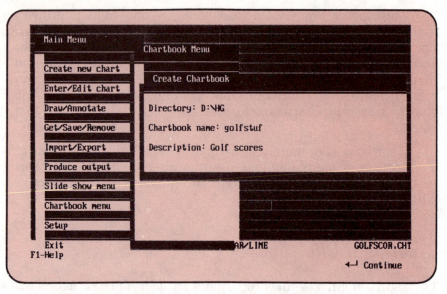

Figure 8-6.   The Create Chartbook menu

256

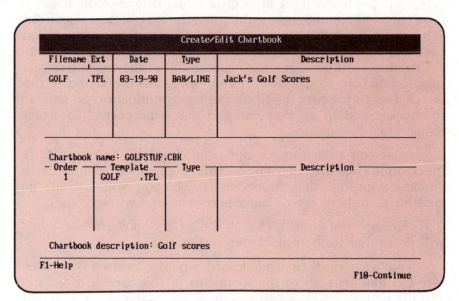

Figure 8-7.   The Create/Edit Chartbook screen

Adding Templates

You can add a template to the chartbook in either of two ways. First, you can use the arrow keys to highlight a template name in the top listing and press Enter. HG then writes the highlighted template into the new chartbook section in the lower half of the screen. Second, you can type in the name of the template to be added to the chartbook.

After you have added all of the templates to the chartbook, press F10 to save the chartbook.

 Creating a New Chartbook

1.	Press 8.	Selects the `Chartbook menu` option from the Main Menu.
2.	Press 1.	Selects the `Create new chartbook` option.
3.	Fill in the `Chartbook name` field and press Enter.	Specifies the name by which HG will save the new chartbook.
4.	Fill in the `Description` field and press Enter.	A brief description of the chartbook serves to remind you of the chartbook's purpose.
5.	Add template names to the chartbook.	Use arrow keys to highlight files or type in template name (and press Enter).
6.	Press F10.	Saves the new chartbook. □

257

Using a Chartbook

Using a chartbook is as easy as opening a folder and retrieving its contents. The following Quick Steps tell you how to create a new chart from a template in a chartbook.

 Using a Chartbook

1.	From the Main Menu, press 1.	Selects the `Create new chart` option.

2. Press 8.	Selects the From chartbook option.
3. Select a chartbook.	Highlight a file and or type a name (and press Enter).
4. Select a template.	Enter the name of template to be used to create the new chart. □

After you complete the preceding Quick Steps, HG immediately draws the template chart. You can now add or modify the chart's data or attributes to customize it for the new data you will add.

Macros

A *macro* is a record of the keystrokes that you used to perform a specific HG task. When you enable the macro feature, HG remembers every keystroke that you enter until you turn off the feature. When you have completed the task, HG writes the keystrokes to a disk file. You can then "replay" this disk file later, thereby repeating the exact sequence of keystrokes without your having to type them!

Macros are a great way to automate repetitive procedures in HG. By saving the keystrokes in disk file, HG will faithfully duplicate the task every time you replay the macro. This can add consistency to your work, relieve you of some of the repetitive tasks associated with updating charts, and even let a novice user initiate sophisticated HG operations.

Creating a Macro

When you installed HG, a program named MACRO.COM and a data file named MACRO.DAT were copied to your hard disk. Both files are needed to initiate the macro features of HG.

> **Caution:** The MACRO.COM program is a separate program that must be running in the background while HG is also running. (Such programs are called Terminate-and-Stay-Resident programs, or TSR's.) Because both programs must reside in memory at the same time, you need at least 500 KB of *free* RAM memory to use the HG macro features. Therefore, before you use the macro feature, use the DOS CHKDSK command to see if you have enough memory to run both programs at the same time.

To start the macro program from the HG directory, type:

MACRO

at the DOS prompt and press Enter. If the macro program runs properly, your screen will look similar to Figure 8-8.

259

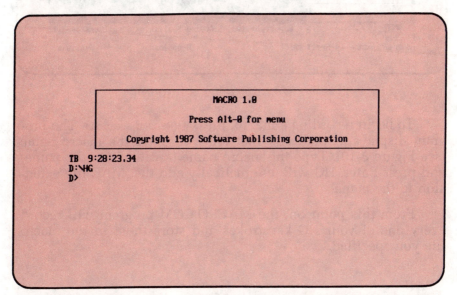

```
                        MACRO 1.0

                    Press Alt-0 for menu

        Copyright 1987 Software Publishing Corporation

TB  9:28:23.34
D:\HG
D>
```

Figure 8-8.   A sample DOS screen after running MACRO.COM

As you can see Figure 8-8 shows, you call the macro features from within HG by pressing the Alt and zero keys (Alt-0) simultaneously.

After you load the MACRO.COM program, run HG as you normally would. To begin recording a macro, press Alt-0. (Note that in most cases you probably will start recording a macro from the Main Menu.) After you press Alt-0, a small menu will appear at the upper-left corner of your screen, as shown in Figure 8-9.

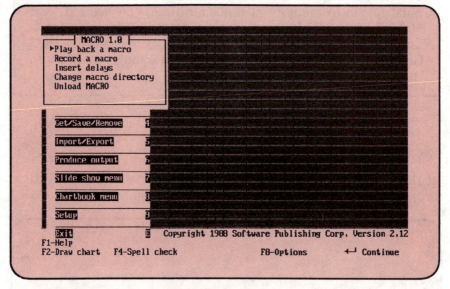

260

Figure 8-9.   The MACRO program menu

To begin recording a macro, press R (Record a macro). The program displays a small box that lets you enter the macro name (see Figure 8-10). Type the macro name (a valid DOS file name) and press Enter. HG will automatically add the .MAC file extension to the name.

From this point on, the MACRO.COM program will record every one of your HG keystrokes and store them in the macro file you specified.

Entering Data During a Macro

In our golf example, you will need to periodically delete the first score in the list and add the latest low score at the end of the list. You can use a macro to automatically update the chart, except for the entering of the new data itself.

Start the macro feature, get the chart, delete the first score with Ctrl-Del, and move to the field at which you will enter the

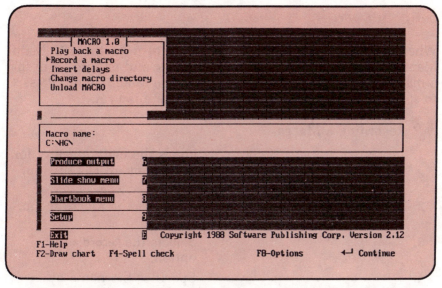

Figure 8-10.   Entering the name of a new macro

261

latest low score. Now, because you need to add new data, press the Ctrl-- (Ctrl and hyphen) key combination. This stops the macro from recording your keystrokes while you enter the latest score. (There is no visual evidence that the macro has stopped recording your keystrokes.)

After you enter the new score, press Alt-0 again and resume recording. To update the Sum data series, press the Tab key, and then press F4 to recalculate the column. Stop the macro recording (Ctrl--) again while you enter the new average scores manually. Then, press Alt-0 and resume recording.

F2 Key: Viewing the Chart

To display the chart after you have entered the new score, press F2. When you finish viewing the chart, press Esc twice to return to the HG Main Menu.

> ▶ **Tip:** When you replay the macro, HG automatically delays the macro for about 30 seconds after it reads an F2 keypress. You might think your system has locked up the first time the macro stops, but all is well. Merely wait 30 seconds, and the macro will resume operation.

Stop Recording a Macro

When you finish recording a macro, return to the HG Main Menu: The Main Menu is a logical starting and ending point for a macro session. Press Alt-0 to activate the Macro menu. Press S to stop recording the macro. That's all there is to it.

Q **Recording a Macro**

1. Before you run HG, type MACRO at the DOS prompt.	Loads the macro feature for use during an HG session.
2. At the HG Main Menu, press Alt-0.	Activates the Macro menu.
3. Press R.	Selects the Record a macro option.
4. Fill in the Macro name field and press Enter.	Specifies the name by which you can replay this macro.
5. Create or modify a chart.	Executes the keystrokes you want to record.
6. Return to the HG Main Menu.	The Main Menu is the logical starting and ending place for a macro.
7. Press Alt-0.	Activates the Macro menu.
8. Press S.	Stops the recording of a macro.

262

Play Back a Macro

When you want to use a recorded macro, run the MACRO.COM program before you start HG. At the Main Menu, press Alt-0 to activate the Macro menu. Then, press P to "play back" a macro. When the program displays the box with the Macro name field, enter the name of the macro you want to play.

If you used the Ctrl-- key combination at any point when you recorded the original macro, a small box will open near the top of the screen telling you that the macro is waiting for you to type some information. Before you start typing, press F10 to tell HG that you will begin typing the data. When you finish entering the new data, press Alt-0 to resume the macro.

Operations are performed quickly when a macro is in control of HG. By using templates to create new charts from existing designs and macros to fill in or update those charts, you can save hours of work at a time. Remember, macros and templates can greatly increase your efficiency; use them whenever you can.

Q Playing a Macro

1. Before you run HG, type MACRO at the DOS prompt.

   Loads the macro feature for use during an HG session.

2. At the HG Main Menu, press Alt-0.

   Activates the Macro menu.

3. Type P.

   Selects the Play back a macro option.

4. Fill in the Macro name field and press Enter.

   Specifies the name of the macro you want to replay.

5. Observe the automatic operations. Enter data if the program requires input.

   The macro will display a prompt (a box opens) when it needs you to enter information. Also, remember that an F2 keypress forces a 30-second delay in macro execution. □

263

Multiple Charts

Sometimes you may wish to create a chart that is comprised of several other charts. A multiple chart allows the viewer to see related sets of data or text at the same time. HG lets you create a single chart consisting of up to six other charts. As you will see, multiple charts are easy to construct.

> ► **Tip:** Although HG lets you create a six-level multiple chart, you should rarely use this many elements. Keep in mind that too many charts actually dilute the point you are trying to make.

Creating a Multiple Chart

HG's *multiple chart* feature let's you create a chart that consists of as many as six previously created charts. First, select the Create new chart option (1) from the Main Menu, and then select the Multiple charts option (7) from the Create New Chart menu. HG then displays the Multiple Charts Styles menu, as shown in Figure 8-11.

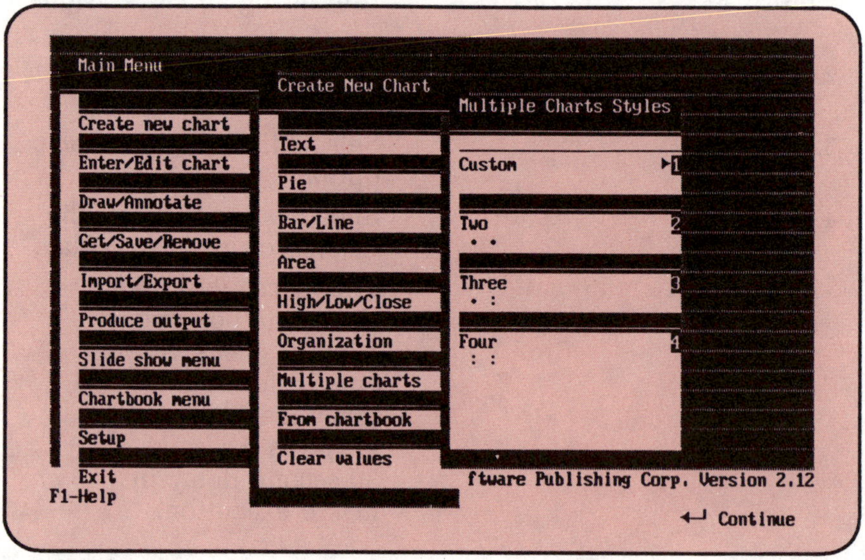

264

Figure 8-11.   The Multiple Charts Styles menu

To create a chart that contains two, three, or four separate charts, merely select the appropriate number from the menu (that is, select 2 to create a multiple chart consisting of two charts, and so on); if you want to include more than five or six charts, select the Custom option (1).

The following example creates a new chart from two other charts. Select the Two option (2) from the Multiple Charts Styles menu. HG then displays a screen similar to Figure 8-12.

The top half of this screen presents a file directory of your existing charts. The bottom half is where you enter the names of the two charts that you want to use. You can either type the file names in the bottom half, or you can use the arrow keys to highlight the appropriate charts in the file directory section and then press Enter to select them one at a time.

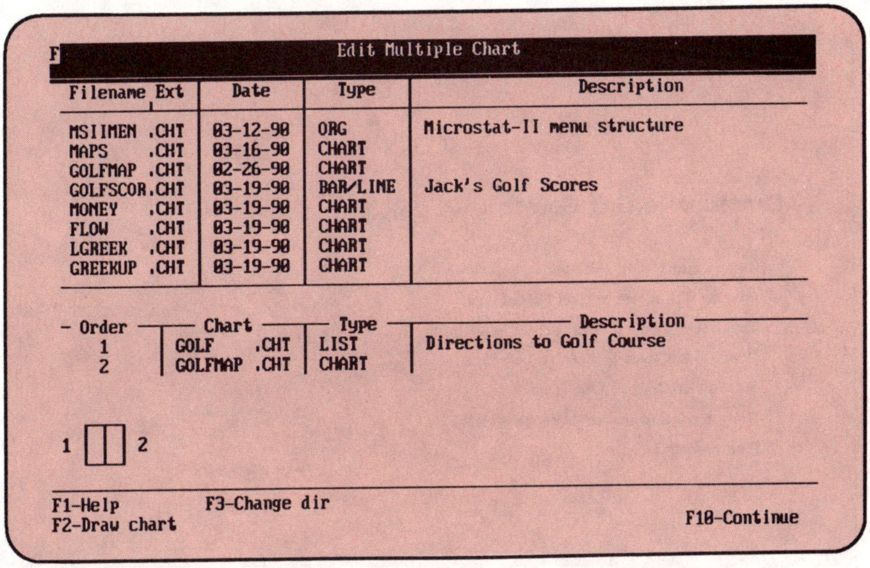

```
┌────────────────────────────────────────────────────────────────────┐
│ F                        Edit Multiple Chart                        │
│  ┌────────────┬──────────┬──────────┬──────────────────────────────┐│
│  │Filename Ext│   Date   │   Type   │          Description         ││
│  ├────────────┼──────────┼──────────┼──────────────────────────────┤│
│  │ MSIIMEN .CHT│ 03-12-90│ ORG      │ Microstat-II menu structure  ││
│  │ MAPS    .CHT│ 03-16-90│ CHART    │                              ││
│  │ GOLFMAP .CHT│ 02-26-90│ CHART    │                              ││
│  │ GOLFSCOR.CHT│ 03-19-90│ BAR/LINE │ Jack's Golf Scores           ││
│  │ MONEY   .CHT│ 03-19-90│ CHART    │                              ││
│  │ FLOW    .CHT│ 03-19-90│ CHART    │                              ││
│  │ LGREEK  .CHT│ 03-19-90│ CHART    │                              ││
│  │ GREEKUP .CHT│ 03-19-90│ CHART    │                              ││
│  └────────────┴──────────┴──────────┴──────────────────────────────┘│
│                                                                      │
│  ─ Order ──┬── Chart ───┬─ Type ─┬────────── Description ──────────  │
│      1     │ GOLF   .CHT│ LIST   │ Directions to Golf Course         │
│      2     │ GOLFMAP.CHT│ CHART  │                                   │
│                                                                      │
│    ┌──┬──┐                                                           │
│  1 │  │  │ 2                                                         │
│    └──┴──┘                                                           │
│                                                                      │
│  F1-Help        F3-Change dir                                        │
│  F2-Draw chart                                          F10-Continue │
└────────────────────────────────────────────────────────────────────┘
```

265

Figure 8-12.   The Edit Multiple Chart screen

Note the small box near the lower-left corner of the screen. This shows you where HG will place the two charts in the final new chart. The first chart you select occupies the left side of the new chart, and the second chart fills the right side. Always consider these positions before you decide the order in which you will select the charts.

Select any two charts in your directory, and press F2 to view the results. My example results are shown in Figure 8-13.

In this example, the final chart consists of a text chart that gives directions to a golf course, coupled with a map (created through the Draw/Annotate option) that graphically shows those directions. I selected these two charts because they complement each other well. You can, however, use any chart types you want. Note that after you create a multiple chart and save it, you can use the Draw/Annotate option to modify it as you would any other chart.

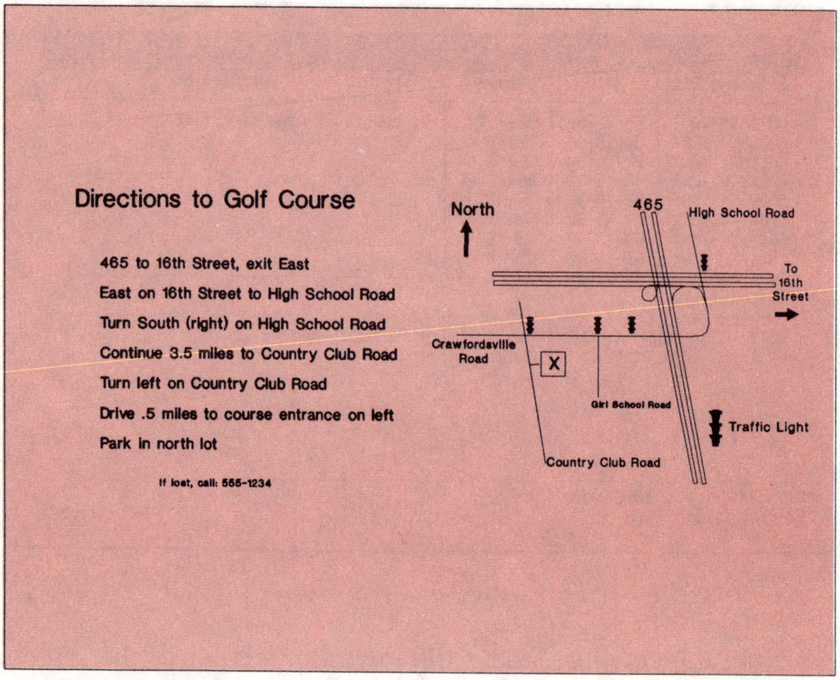

Directions to Golf Course

465 to 16th Street, exit East

East on 16th Street to High School Road

Turn South (right) on High School Road

Continue 3.5 miles to Country Club Road

Turn left on Country Club Road

Drive .5 miles to course entrance on left

Park in north lot

If lost, call: 555-1234

North   465   High School Road
To 16th Street
Crawfordsville Road
X
Girl School Road
Traffic Light
Country Club Road

Figure 8-13. An example of a two-chart multiple chart

266

Q Creating a Multiple Chart

1. From the Main Menu, press 1.	Selects the Create new chart option.
2. Press 7.	Selects the Multiple charts option and displays the Multiple Charts Styles menu.
3. Enter a chart style.	Selects a chart that will contain from two to six other charts.
4. Highlight chart names in the file directory and press Enter, or type the names and press Enter.	Selects the charts that HG will use to create the final multiple chart.

5. Press F2.   Displays the chart. You can
                                now use the Draw/Annotate
                                option to modify it, or you
                                can return to the Main
                                Menu and save the
                                multiple chart.   □

Slide Shows

This section presents information that you can use to set your presentation apart from the rest. Although this section refers to a *slide
show*, the more precise term for this feature is a *screen show*. We
will assume that your presentation, or *show*, will be viewed on a
computer screen. However, if you are using hardware that can project a full-color computer screen the same way as a slide is projected, some of HG's special effects are quite impressive.

267

Creating a Slide Show

To create a slide show, you must first decide which charts
should be used and the order in which they should be presented. After you make your list and plan your strategy, be sure
that all of the charts you will be using are available from within
the same directory. Now, you are ready to create the actual
show.

Select the Slide show menu option (7) from the Main Menu.
Now select the Create slide show option (1) from the Slide Show
Menu. When HG displays the Create Slide Show menu (see Figure 8-14), be sure that the Directory field lists the directory that
contains all of your files; if it does not, type the correct directory
name and press Enter. Next, enter the name of the new slide
show (a valid DOS file name of eight characters or less) and a
brief description of the contents or purpose of the show.

After you type a description and press Enter, HG displays
the Create/Edit Slide Show screen. Although your screen will
show different file names, it will be similar to the one shown in
Figure 8-15.

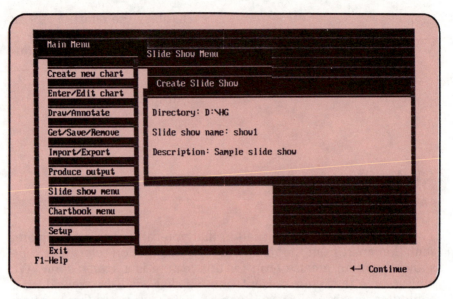

Figure 8-14. *The Create Slide Show menu*

```
                        Create/Edit Slide Show

 Filename Ext    Date      Type           Description

 POLLUTE .CHT    02-19-90  AREA     Polution Abatement Expenditures
 DEFECTS .CHT    02-13-90  H/L/C    Average Defects Per Hour
 PERT    .CHT    02-13-90  H/L/C    New Home Construction Plan
 MEETING .CHT    02-15-90  TITLE    Divisional Managers Meeting
 GOLF    .CHT    02-16-90  LIST     Directions to Golf Course
 MEETING2.CHT    02-18-90  CHART

 Show name: SHOW1    .SHW
 — Order ——— File ———— Type ———————— Description ——————
    1        POLLUTE .CHT  AREA     Polution Abatement Expenditures
    2        DEFECTS .CHT  H/L/C    Average Defects Per Hour
    3        GOLF    .CHT

 Show description: Sample slide show

 F1-Help                                              F10-Continue
```

Figure 8-15. *The Create/Edit Slide Show screen*

This screen looks similar to the Create/Edit Chartbook
screen shown in Figure 8-7, and, in fact, you use it in the same
way. The top half lists all of the available charts in the current
directory, and the bottom half holds the chart names that you

assign to this slide show. By default, HG displays the first chart name from the top listing in the new slide show. Use the Tab and arrow keys to highlight a chart file in the top half, and then press Enter to add it to the slide show list at the bottom of the screen. You can also simply type the names of charts into the listing at the bottom half of the screen.

> ▶ **Tip:** Note that you are not limited to "pure" charts. The files shown in the upper half of the screen can be charts, templates, other slide show files, and even bit-mapped files from other programs.

As shown in Figure 8-15, the `Type` field lets you know the chart type of the file, and the `Description` field contains the brief "memory-jogging" text you added when you created the chart.

269

Add all of the charts that you want to use in your slide show. Don't forget that HG presents them in the order in which you enter them. If you need to change the order of charts, press the Tab key to move to the appropriate location, and use the Ctrl-↑ or Ctrl-↓ key combinations to move a file up or down in the list. When you are satisfied that the list of files is in the proper order, press F10 to save the list as a slide show file with the SHW file extension. That's all there is to it!

A Slide Show Trial Run

Now that you've put together a show, select the `Display Screenshow` option (4) from the Slide Show Menu. HG will automatically load and display the first chart of your slide show. After you have viewed the chart, press any key to display the next chart.

> ▶ **Tip:** If you press the spacebar to continue to the next chart, nothing appears to happen. Don't worry. When you press it a second time, the next chart will appear. The spacebar has a special use during a slide show, the explanation of which is discussed later in the chapter. For now, if you use the spacebar as a continuation key, you will have to press it twice to continue.

Edit a Slide Show Chart

If, while previewing a slide show, you see something in a chart that needs to be changed, press Ctrl-E. This immediately loads the chart data into the appropriate chart type so that you can make the correction. When you finish changing the chart, press F10 to return to the Main Menu so that you can save the changes with the Get/Save/Remove option (4). To view the slide show again, simply restart the show as described in the previous section.

Note that the Ctrl-E feature does not work with charts created with the Draw/Annotate option. To edit these charts, you must use the Draw/Annotate option (3) from the Main Menu.

Special Effects

270

As you ran your slide show, HG probably displayed your charts much as you expected. However, you can really add spice to a presentation by using the special effects that HG makes available to you. To add these effects, select the Add Screenshow effects option (3) from the Slide Show Menu. (Because you can make actual slides from HG charts, but you cannot integrate these special effects into a slide, HG refers to these special effects as *Screenshow effects.*)

If you are not currently working with a slide show, HG will display a screen that lets you select one. After you select a slide show, HG displays a Screenshow Effects screen similar to the one shown in Figure 8-16.

This screen consists of seven columns. The first two columns simply tell you the name of the charts that are in the slide show. The following list gives a brief description of the remaining five columns (detailed discussions are provided in later sections):

Draw	Lists the special effect used to draw the chart on the screen
Dir	Tells the direction from which the chart will be drawn
Time	Lets you specify a time delay in minutes and seconds; determines how long HG displays a chart on the screen

`Erase`	Lists the special effect used to remove the chart from the screen
`Dir`	Tells the direction from which the chart will be erased

The first two columns (`Draw` and `Dir`) determine how HG draws the chart, the middle column (`Time`) represents how long HG displays the chart during the slide show, and the last two columns (`Erase` and `Dir`) determine how HG removes the chart from the screen.

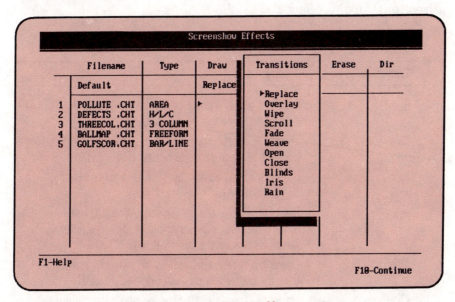

271

Figure 8-16. The Screenshow Effects screen

If the `Draw`, `Erase`, and `Dir` columns are left blank, the slide show does not use any special effects. If the `Time` column is left blank, the viewer must press a key to continue the show. If you enter a time value, using a *mm:ss* (*minutes:seconds*) format, the chart remains on the screen for the specified time interval.

> ► **Tip:** If you set a display time, the viewer can cancel the specified time delay by pressing the spacebar. This suspends the timer. Pressing the spacebar a second time restarts the timer. This procedure lets the viewer display a chart for a longer period than is set by the `Time` column setting.

Transition Types

Examine Figure 8-16 closely; notice the Transitions menu at the right-center portion of the screen. When you are in the Screenshow Effects screen, you can display this menu by pressing F6. The Transitions menu lists the different special effects that HG can use to draw and erase a chart. Although Table 8-2 describes these special effects, you really have to see them in action to appreciate their visual impact. (Note that the letters in parentheses at the end of each description in the table refer to valid directions for the effect.)

272

Table 8-2. Transition Effects

Transition Type	Description
Blinds	Draws or erases a chart as though it were on the slats of Venetian blinds. (L, R, U, D)
Close	Closes the screen horizontally or vertically, moving from the sides toward the center. (L, R, U, D)
Fade	Draws or erases a chart by turning random pixels on or off. (D, A)
Iris	Draws starting at the center and expanding outward in all directions; erases starting at the sides and shrinking toward the center. (I, O)
Open	Opens the screen horizontally or vertically moving from the center towards the sides. (L, R, U, D)
Overlay	Draws or erases a chart pixel by pixel; like painting the chart. (No Dir)
Rain	Draws or erases by gradually fading a chart in streaks from the top of the screen to the bottom. (No Dir)
Replace	Replaces the screen instantly; the default for a slide show. (No Dir)
Scroll	Smoothly scrolls a chart on or off the screen. (R, L, U, D)
Weave	Draws or erases a chart by sliding alternating lines of the chart in opposite horizontal directions. (No Dir)
Wipe	Slides the chart on or off the screen. (R, L, U, D)

For Table 8-2 to be meaningful, you will have to experiment with the effects in your own slide show. To specify an effect for a chart, you must first position the cursor in the Draw or Erase column of the appropriate chart. Then, you can either type the initial letter of the effect into the column and press Enter, or you can press F6 to display the Transitions menu, highlight the appropriate effect, and press Enter.

Direction

After you experiment with different combinations of the effects listed in Table 8-2, note that you can assert even greater control over your slide transitions. Except for the Overlay, Rain, Replace, and Weave options, you can control the direction used for a transition. Figure 8-17 shows the Directions menu, which lists the directions that you can specify.

273

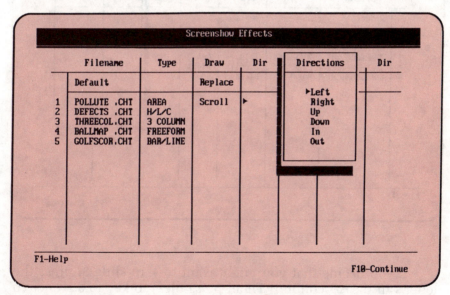

Figure 8-17.   The Directions submenu

Use the parenthetical references to directions in Table 8-2 as a guide to which directions you can use. To specify an direction for an effect, you must first position the cursor in the appropriate Dir column (draw or erase) of a chart. Then, you can either type the initial letter of the direction into the column and press

Enter, or you can press F6 to display the Directions menu, high-light the appropriate option, and press Enter.

Selective Slides

Let's assume that you've created a long slide show, and you want to vary the order in which the slides are shown and skip other slides that you think are unnecessary. For example, sup-pose you want to skip slide 3 depending upon the audience's reaction to slide 2. To do this, move the cursor to any column for slide 2, and then press F8 (User menu). The Key/Go To menu appears, as shown in Figure 8-18.

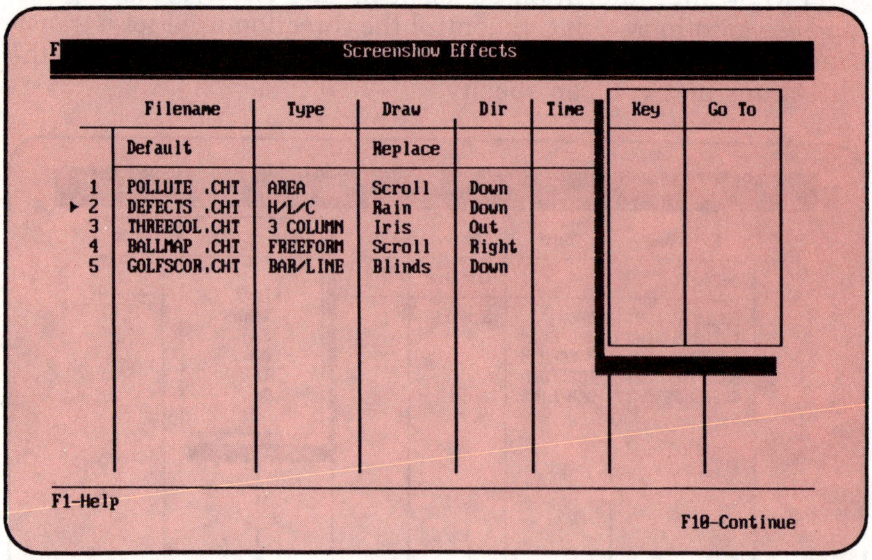

Figure 8-18. The Key/Go To submenu

If you decide that you might want to skip slide 3, press the letter s in the Key column. Then, press the Tab key to advance to the Go To column, and enter the number 4. These entries in the Key/Go To menu give HG the following directions: "If I press the letter s to end viewing slide 2, go directly to slide 4. If I press a letter other than s, show slide 3." This gives you a means by which you can use the same slide show for different audiences.

> ▶ **Tip:** Note in the previous example that HG marks the second slide with a diamond-shaped character next to the 2. This character is meant to remind you that you have specified a special instruction for slide 2.

The following Quick Steps show you how to create a repeating slide show, perhaps for use in a sales booth.

 Creating a Repeating Slide Show

1. Select or create a slide show.

2. From within the Screenshow Effects screen, press End.
   Moves the cursor to the last chart in the show.

3. Press F8.
   Displays the Key/Go To menu.

4. Press Tab.
   Leaves the Key column empty.

5. Press 1.
   Tells HG to go to the first chart. (Therefore, after the last chart is displayed, HG runs chart 1 again.)

275

Conclusion

If you entered the examples as you read through this text, you should now have a thorough knowledge of how to use Harvard Graphics. You should also have a better appreciation of its power and flexibility. HG not only lets you be as creative as you want to be, it lets you perform your creative work simply, quickly, and efficiently.

Throughout this text, you followed the examples that I chose to use. I selected most of these exercises because they were short and easily understood, while clearly demonstrating the concepts and options involved in the targeted HG operation.

Still, my preferences were bound to have slanted this presentation, so I might have failed to present some combination of features that suits your particular preferences or needs. For that reason, plus the fact that you now have a firm grasp of HG's operation, I encourage you to experiment with all of the features of HG. Chances are, you *will* find the perfect combination of features that fulfills your needs.

What You Have Learned

In this chapter, you learned how to use several of HG's advanced features. Some of these features let you perform operations more quickly, others let you create and use charts more efficiently, and still others let you produce professional charts and presentations with style and ease.

Using *templates*, you generate a chart type that includes specialized fields and settings so that you can quickly create a similar chart without having to type every field and select every option. *Chartbooks* let you organize and access groups of related templates. With *macros*, you can record and then replay long, complicated sequences of keystrokes to quickly create, update, or modify charts. Creating *multiple charts* is an effective method for combining text and graphics charts and for enabling the viewer to compare and contrast two or more charts in a presentation. The last advanced feature discussed in this chapter was the *slide show*, a visual *tour de force* that is so easy to create, yet so rich with options and special effects, that you can literally create professional-looking screen presentations in a matter of minutes.

Standard ASCII Character Set

This appendix presents the standard ASCII (American Standard Code for Information Interchange) character set. Although you might not need to use ASCII codes very often, this listing will come in handy when you need to figure out what delimiters an ASCII file is using before you import it into HG. This table includes the decimal, hexadecimal, and binary representations of each ASCII character.

The Standard ASCII Character Set

Decimal	Hex	Binary	ASCII
0	0	00000000	NUL
1	1	00000001	SOH
2	2	00000010	STX
3	3	00000011	ETX
4	4	00000100	EOT
5	5	00000101	ENQ
6	6	00000110	ACK
7	7	00000111	BEL
8	8	00001000	BS
9	9	00001001	HT

continued

Decimal	Hex	Binary	ASCII
10	a	00001010	LF
11	b	00001011	VT
12	c	00001100	FF
13	d	00001101	CR
14	e	00001110	SO
15	f	00001111	SI
16	10	00010000	DLE
17	11	00010001	DC1
18	12	00010010	DC2
19	13	00010011	DC3
20	14	00010100	DC4
21	15	00010101	NAK
22	16	00010110	SYN
23	17	00010111	ETB
24	18	00011000	CAN
25	19	00011001	EM
26	1a	00011010	SUB
27	1b	00011011	ESC
28	1c	00011100	FS
29	1d	00011101	GS
30	1e	00011110	RS
31	1f	00011111	US
32	20	00100000	(space)
33	21	00100001	!
34	22	00100010	"
35	23	00100011	#
36	24	00100100	$
37	25	00100101	%
38	26	00100110	&
39	27	00100111	'
40	28	00101000	(
41	29	00101001	)
42	2a	00101010	*

278

Decimal	Hex	Binary	ASCII
43	2b	00101011	+
44	2c	00101100	,
45	2d	00101101	-
46	2e	00101110	.
47	2f	00101111	/
48	30	00110000	0
49	31	00110001	1
50	32	00110010	2
51	33	00110011	3
52	34	00110100	4
53	35	00110101	5
54	36	00110110	6
55	37	00110111	7
56	38	00111000	8
57	39	00111001	9
58	3a	00111010	:
59	3b	00111011	;
60	3c	00111100	<
61	3d	00111101	=
62	3e	00111110	>
63	3f	00111111	?
64	40	01000000	@
65	41	01000001	A
66	42	01000010	B
67	43	01000011	C
68	44	01000100	D
69	45	01000101	E
70	46	01000110	F
71	47	01000111	G
72	48	01001000	H
73	49	01001001	I
74	4a	01001010	J
75	4b	01001011	K

279

continued

Decimal	Hex	Binary	ASCII
76	4c	01001100	L
77	4d	01001101	M
78	4e	01001110	N
79	4f	01001111	O
80	50	01010000	P
81	51	01010001	Q
82	52	01010010	R
83	53	01010011	S
84	54	01010100	T
85	55	01010101	U
86	56	01010110	V
87	57	01010111	W
88	58	01011000	X
89	59	01011001	Y
90	5a	01011010	Z
91	5b	01011011	[
92	5c	01011100	\
93	5d	01011101	]
94	5e	01011110	^
95	5f	01011111	_
96	60	01100000	'
97	61	01100001	a
98	62	01100010	b
99	63	01100011	c
100	64	01100100	d
101	65	01100101	e
102	66	01100110	f
103	67	01100111	g
104	68	01101000	h
105	69	01101001	i
106	6a	01101010	j
107	6b	01101011	k
108	6c	01101100	l

280

Decimal	Hex	Binary	ASCII
109	6d	01101101	m
110	6e	01101110	n
111	6f	01101111	o
112	70	01110000	p
113	71	01110001	q
114	72	01110010	r
115	73	01110011	s
116	74	01110100	t
117	75	01110101	u
118	76	01110110	v
119	77	01110111	w
120	78	01111000	x
121	79	01111001	y
122	7a	01111010	z
123	7b	01111011	{
124	7c	01111100	¦
125	7d	01111101	}
126	7e	01111110	~
127	7f	01111111	DEL

281

Appendix B

Harvard Graphics Symbols

This appendix lists the contents of the symbol files provided in the Harvard Graphics package. You can access all of these symbols through the Draw/Annotate facility. (At the Main Menu, select the Draw/Annotate option (3) to display the Draw menu. Select the Symbol option (6) to display the Symbol menu. Select the Get option (1) to list all HG symbol files. Highlight the appropriate file and press Enter to display the symbols in that file.)

Figure B-1.   Arrow symbols (ARROWS.SYM)

284

Figure B-2.   Building symbols (BUILDING.SYM)

Figure B-3.   Currency symbols (CURRENCY.SYM)

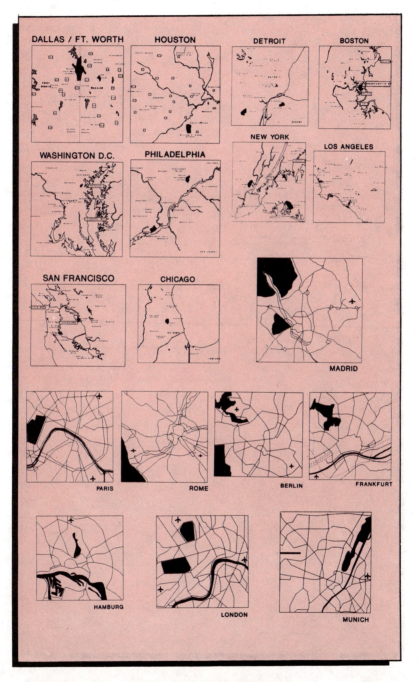

285

Figure B-4.   City maps (CITIES.SYM)

286

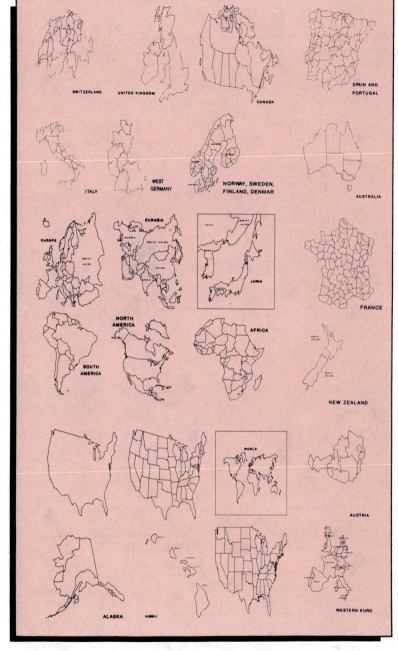

Figure B-5. Country maps (COUNTRY.SYM)

287

Figure B-6. Flowchart symbols (FLOWCHAR.SYM)

Figure B-7. Food and sports (FOODSPRT.SYM)

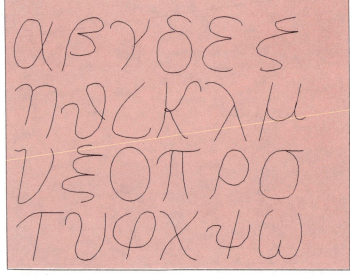

*Figure B-8.   Greek alphabet, lowercase
(GREEKLC.SYM)*

*Figure B-9.   Greek alphabet, uppercase
(GREEKUC.SYM)*

Figure B-10.   People (HUMAN.SYM)

Figure B-11.   Industry symbols (INDUSTRY.SYM)

Figure B-12.   Miscellaneous symbols (MISC.SYM)

Figure B-13.   Office symbols (OFFICE.SYM)

Figure B-14.   Presentation symbols (PRESENT.SYM)

Figure B-15.   Star symbols (STARS.SYM)

292

Figure B-16.   Transportation symbols (TRANSPT.SYM)

INDEX

294

295

296

D

297

298

299

302

303

U–V

W

X

305

Reader Feedback Card

Thank you for purchasing this book from Howard W. Sams & Company's FIRST BOOK series. Our intent with this series is to bring you timely, authoritative information that you can reference quickly and easily. You can help us by taking a minute to complete and return this card. We appreciate your comments and will use the information to better serve your needs.

1. Where did you purchase this book?

☐ Chain bookstore (Walden, B. Dalton)   ☐ Direct mail
☐ Independent bookstore   ☐ Book club
☐ Computer/Software store   ☐ School bookstore
☐ Other _____

2. Why did you choose this book? (Check as many as apply.)

☐ Price   ☐ Appearance of book
☐ Author's reputation   ☐ Howard W. Sam's reputation
☐ Quick and easy treatment of subject   ☐ Only book available on subject

3. How do you use this book? (Check as many as apply.)

☐ As a supplement to the product manual   ☐ As a reference
☐ In place of the product manual   ☐ At home
☐ For self-instruction   ☐ At work

4. Please rate this book in the categories below. G = Good; N = Needs improvement; U = Category is unimportant.

☐ Price   ☐ Appearance
☐ Amount of information   ☐ Accuracy
☐ Examples   ☐ Quick Steps
☐ Inside cover reference   ☐ Second color
☐ Table of contents   ☐ Index
☐ Tips and cautions   ☐ Illustrations
☐ Length of book
☐ How can we improve this book? _____

5. How many computer books do you normally buy in a year?

☐ 1−5   ☐ 5−10   ☐ More than 10
☐ I rarely purchase more than one book on a subject.
☐ I may purchase a beginning and an advanced book on the same subject.
☐ I may purchase several books on particular subjects.
   (such as _____)

6. Have you purchased other Howard W. Sams or Hayden books in the past year? ____
   If yes, how many? _____

7. Would you purchase another book in the FIRST BOOK series? _____

8. What are your primary areas of interest in business software?
- ☐ Word processing (particularly _____)
- ☐ Spreadsheet (particularly _____)
- ☐ Database (particularly _____)
- ☐ Graphics (particularly _____)
- ☐ Personal finance/accounting (particularly _____)
- ☐ Other (please specify _____)

Other comments on this book or the Howard W. Sams book line: _____
_____

Name _____
Company _____
Address _____
City _____ State _____ Zip _____
Daytime telephone number _____
Title of this book _____

Fold here

‖‖‖‖